# POLICING AND VIOLENCE IN INDIA

# POLICING AND VIOLENCE IN INDIA

## COLONIAL ORIGINS AND CONTEMPORARY REALITIES

Edited by

**Deana Heath**

**Jinee Lokaneeta**

SPEAKING TIGER

SPEAKING TIGER BOOKS
125A, Ground Floor, Shahpur Jat
New Delhi – 110049

First published by Speaking Tiger in 2025


ISBN: 978-93-6336-753-1
eISBN: 978-93-6336-903-0

10 9 8 7 6 5 4 3 2 1

Typeset in Minion Pro by SÜRYA, New Delhi
Printed at Chaman Enterprises, New Delhi

*To the survivors of police violence*
*and to all those who have dedicated their lives to challenging it,*
*in the hope of adding to the mounting pressure for change.*

# CONTENTS

# Acknowledgements

This book has been in the making for many years. Its genesis was a series of workshops on policing at the University of Liverpool and Jawaharlal Nehru University in 2016, 2018, and 2019, organised by Deana Heath, Santana Khanikar, along with, for the final one, Jinee Lokaneeta. We thank Santana Khanikar for co-organising the workshops and for her contribution to *Policing and Violence in India*. Her brilliant scholarship, her insights into policing and violence, and her warmth and camaraderie have helped to shape it. She also conducted some interviews for it. We also thank all of the workshop participants, whose insights have informed this book and who have shaped the growing community of scholars and activists working on and concerned about police violence in India.

We would also like to thank our literary agent, Mimi Chaudhury, who reached out to suggest we write this book for a mainstream Indian publisher rather than an academic press, given the scale of public interest in police violence in India following the horrific custodial deaths of Jeyaraj and Bennix in Tamil Nadu in 2020. Thank you, Mimi, for guiding us through the process of developing this book from conception to publication, as well as to Speaking Tiger Books—especially Ravi Singh—for both recognising its urgency and supporting it, especially in light of the challenges of confronting state violence in contemporary India, as well as his invaluable editorial team.

Our thanks go, in addition, to all of the authors and interviewees who collaborated with us on *Policing and Violence in India*, not least for their generosity and patience regarding the length of time it has taken us to get this book to press. We thank Prabhjot Sachdev for transcribing the interviews and Naresh Kumar for translating the interview with Abdul Wahid Shaikh. We are especially grateful to Professor Veena Das, Vrinda Grover, and V Geetha for their willingness to engage with and contribute to *Policing and Violence in India* despite the many demands on their time. Their lifelong work on violence, especially in regard to the state, has informed and inspired all of the contributors to this volume.

*Policing and Violence in India* is, for us, an urgent intervention into a subject that, while shaping many aspects of Indian culture, society and politics, and continuing to have a devastating impact on innumerable Indians, remains a marginal subject in public, political, and academic discourse. This is true despite the tremendous, longstanding efforts of a wide range of human rights activists, lawyers, judges, and others to address and remedy it.

# INTRODUCTION

## Policing and Violence in India

*Jinee Lokaneeta and Deana Heath*

In July 2024, the Delhi High Court ordered that the investigation into the death of twenty-three-year-old Faizan be transferred from the Criminal Investigation Department of Delhi Police to India's premier investigative agency, the Central Bureau of Investigation.[1] Faizan, with four other Muslim youths, was severely beaten by Delhi police in February 2020 following protests against the enactment of the Citizenship Amendment Act, forced to sing the Indian national anthem—a sign of the penetration of Hindu nationalist ideology into the Indian police since the Bharatiya Janata Party (BJP) came to power a decade ago—and illegally detained at the Jyoti Nagar Police Station. He died as a result of the injuries he sustained shortly thereafter.

For Justice Anup Jairam Bhambhani, Faizan's tragic death represented not just a 'gross violation of human rights' but a hate crime, since the police who were responsible for his death were 'motivated and driven by religious bigotry.'[2] The judge detailed how the police tried to cover up their culpability for Faizan's demise and evade justice for it, including by neglecting to seek medical attention for him and failing to identify those responsible for his brutal assault and ultimate death, despite video footage documenting the attack. It was 'very convenient', Bhambhani noted, that according to the police the CCTV cameras at Jyoti Nagar Police Station were not working the night Faizan was detained.[3]

Faizan's tragic death, like those of father and son Jeyaraj and Bennix at the hands of Tamil Nadu Police, also in 2020, demonstrates the chilling routineness of custodial torture and deaths in India—even during a pandemic.[4] Indeed, while according to the National Human Rights Commission (NHRC) five people *per day* died in custody in India between 2010 and 2020, the highest number of custodial deaths occurred in 2020-21, during the height of the Covid-19 pandemic.[5]

The origins of India's system of policing can be traced back to nineteenth-century colonial India.[6] Designed to maintain and secure the British colonial state, rather than to serve the welfare of Indians, this system had a profound impact on the nature of the Indian police.[7] Though armed with tremendous powers—powers that, from the late-nineteenth century onwards, grew in proportion to the perceived threats facing an alien regime of occupation—the subordinate Indian police were considerably underpaid, under-resourced, and undertrained. As a result, they were not only given the authority to enact legal and extra-legal violence in carrying out their duties but forced to rely on these to function.

Following Independence, the post-colonial Indian state, in addition to retaining the undemocratic policing system it had inherited, increased its coercive powers, which ensured that police violence remained ubiquitous, quotidian, and normalised. Such powers are exemplified by extraordinary laws like the 1958 Armed Forces (Special Powers) Act or AFSPA (most recently amended in 2019), which applies to areas deemed ‘disturbed’, and the 1967 Unlawful Activities (Prevention) Act, or UAPA (most recently amended in 2018), under which individuals can be designated as terrorists and detained indefinitely.[8] These laws are routinely targeted at marginalised and minoritised groups, who make up sixty per cent of the undertrial population—those yet to be tried, or sometimes even charged—lodged in Indian jails, in an effort to quell their legitimate protest, dissent, or simply their right to exist.[9] While ostensibly designed to maintain law and order in so-called conflict areas, such laws have fuelled the growth of armed policing units and the militarisation of civilian policing, not to mention the militarisation of social relations.[10] At its root, the militarisation of policing is a form of cultural violence, since it embodies ‘narratives that make… violence appear “normal” or “acceptable” when enacted against particular groups’.[11] This transformation turns ‘ordinary streets into war zones, in which violence is coordinated, calculated, and methodical’.[12]

But police violence in India is enabled as much by ordinary law, or the ‘rule of law’, as it is extraordinary. According to the United Nations, the rule of law ‘is a principle of governance in which all persons, institutions and entities, public and private, including the state itself, are accountable to laws that are publicly promulgated, equally enforced and independently adjudicated, and which are consistent with international human rights norms and standards’.[13] It thus establishes a social contract between a state and its people, in addition to enabling peace and security, the protection of fundamental rights and freedoms, and social and economic progress and development. As the legal scholar Upendra Baxi has emphasised, the rule of law ‘is always and everywhere a terrain of peoples’ struggle incrementally to make power accountable, governance just, and [the] state ethical’.[14]

However, while the Indian constitution enshrines protections against state domination and social injustice, and empowers the state to proactively protect the rights of the marginalised, its promise has been increasingly betrayed by the Hindu-nationalist ethos of its governments since 2014.[15] This is because the operation of the rule of law requires a separation of powers between the executive and judiciary and an inclusive and accountable justice system, which are notably lacking in India despite the efforts of individual justices and courts and a vibrant human rights movement. Such a lack is evident, for example, in India's extremely low conviction rates for police torture and the impunity that sexual, class- and caste-based violence enjoy.[16] Indian law, in many ways, thus facilitates such forms of violence, not least through its laws regarding torture and confessions.[17]

India proclaims itself as a growing economic powerhouse and the world's largest democracy—although it has become, according to a recent report, an 'electoral autocracy'—but its police forces are, as a result of their excessive powers, widely regarded as lawless, violent, ineffective, and severely lacking in accountability.[18] They therefore continue to function as what the report of the 1902 Indian Police Commission described as 'a terror to the people' by using violence as their primary law enforcement tactic.[19] It is the poor, the caste oppressed (or Dalits/Bahujans), Adivasi (indigenous or tribal) or nomadic peoples, women, and religious and sexual minorities who suffer the most from such violence, as well as from police collusion or inaction when it comes to violence committed against them by mobs or other actors. A notable example is the lynching of Muslim men accused of committing 'love jihad'—an Islamophobic conspiracy theory according to which Muslim men seek to convert Hindu women to Islam through seduction, marriage, and kidnapping as part of a demographic 'war' against Hindus. Police violence in India is not, moreover, restricted to any one site. It traverses routine, everyday interactions as well as conflict zones such as Kashmir, central India, and the Northeastern region.[20]

Almost every section of Indian society suffers from such practices, since the Indian police not only fail to promote a peaceful and inclusive society, but often actively undermine such a possibility. In a climate of public alienation and fear, police work, moreover, becomes a vicious cycle of violence and resistance, which negatively impacts the health and well-being of everyone involved, including the police force itself, particularly its subordinate ranks.[21] This, in turn, makes it impossible for the police to cope with the myriad public safety challenges hindering India's development, including armed militancy, terrorism, gender- and caste-based violence, and escalating crime levels.[22]

## Responses to Police Violence

Despite the routineness of police violence in India, particularly torture, the militarised policing of resistance movements, and 'encounters'—in which the police effectively murder criminal suspects—and the fact that it is well-documented, it generates little public or political outrage. In the United States the murder of George Floyd, a Black man, by a police officer in May 2020, just a few months after Faizan's death, brought thousands of people onto the streets in protest against police brutality, in defiance of Covid-19 regulations. This spurred the global spread of the Black Lives Matter movement. But in India, as Sidharth Bhatia, a founder of the prominent Indian news site, *The Wire*, has said, a 'cop mindlessly beating up a hapless man'—or woman—particularly if they are Muslim, Adivasi, Dalit, or from a non-elite caste, 'provokes barely a ripple' of dissent.[23]

As the *New York Times* has put it, despite widespread media coverage of custodial violence, including brutality against religious or social minorities, India has largely 'absorbed case after case of police brutality, torture and extrajudicial killings' with little protest.[24] To be sure, such cases often provoke outrage on social media, but after their moment on X or Facebook, they fade away 'without any national outcry', much less the sort of protests witnessed in the United States.[25]

In India, police violence is often, instead, celebrated, as evidenced by the extrajudicial killing of accused rapists by the police in Hyderabad in November 2019.[26] Politicians, particularly those on the Hindu right, likewise extol the virtues of what they hail as summary justice. In 2017, the strident monk-turned-BJP politician, Yogi Adityanath, upon becoming Chief Minister of Uttar Pradesh, one of India's poorest and most populous states, promised to 'knock...down' criminals.[27] The BJP Chief Minister of Assam, Himanta Biswa Sarma, raised the stakes by praising the virtues of 'shooting down criminals' if they attempted to escape custody.[28] Such attitudes are the product of a range of factors, including caste, class, gender and religious identities, fear of challenging the police, thanks to the impunity they enjoy, and an extremely overburdened and torturously slow judicial system in which conviction rates are low.[29] As a result, not a single police officer has been convicted in cases related to the 500 people who died in police custody, largely due to torture, between 2005 and 2018.[30]

There is, however, a long history of resistance to state repression in India by its strong civil liberty and democratic rights movements. Civil liberty groups first emerged during the course of India's anti-colonial resistance movement. Not long after Independence, they were consolidated during the Emergency (1975-77), a period in which India's democratic institutions were suspended and state violence, including illegal detention and torture, became pervasive.[31] Groups such as the Andhra Pradesh Civil Liberties Committee (APCLC),[32] the Association of Parents of Disappeared Persons (APDP),[33] the Association for the Protection of Democratic Rights (APDR),[34] the Committee for the Protection of Democratic Rights (CPDR),[35] the Naga People's Movement for Human Rights (NPMHR),[36] the People's Union for Civil Liberties (PUCL),[37] and the People's Union for Democratic Rights (PUDR),[38] amongst others, challenged state oppression, including 'encounter killings', extraordinary laws, and the illegal detention and torture of political prisoners associated with social justice movements and those challenging the state's development paradigm. International human rights groups, such as Amnesty International and Human Rights Watch, have supported their Indian counterparts by publishing reports critical of state violence and repression in India.[39] Along with their Indian counterparts, however, the Indian state has attempted to quash them through lawfare, or the use of legal action to hinder and intimidate them—along with other, more forceful, means.[40] In 2020, Amnesty International ceased its operations in India as a result of such pressures.[41]

The Indian state has in the past, however, responded to national and international pressures to protect human rights. In 1993, for example, it passed the Protection of Human Rights Act and established the NHRC, and enshrined the right to life, liberty, equality and dignity of the individual as guaranteed by its constitution and embodied in numerous international human rights covenants.[42] The NHRC has devoted particular attention to torture and deaths in custody and made recommendations for law reform and means to improve the institutional and legislative mechanisms to deal with such violence, not least since the Indian government has failed to ratify the 1984 United Nations Convention Against Torture and Other Cruel, Inhuman or Degrading Treatment or Punishment, which it signed in 1997 but never enacted, or to enact the Prevention of Torture Bill, introduced into the Lok Sabha in 2010 but never made into law.[43]

India's courts have also sought to curb torture and deaths in custody, most notably through the so-called DK Basu judgement, delivered in 1997.[44] There is thus a rich tradition of documenting police and other forms of state violence in India by civil liberty and democratic rights groups, as well as the state.[45] More recently, in 2020, the Indian Supreme Court ordered that every police station in the country be equipped with night-vision CCTV cameras that can record both video and audio, and that the footage they capture be made available to anyone who complains that force was used against them while in custody—since according to former Chief Justice Nuthalapati Ramana, rather than police stations being safe spaces, 'the threat to human rights and bodily integrity…are the highest' in them.[46] In 2023, the court demanded to see evidence of compliance with this order, which applied to all investigative agencies as well.[47] However, such initiatives have done little to change the situation or arouse the collective conscience of the Indian public—or even to promote scholarship and teaching in Indian universities on issues concerning democracy, human rights, and state violence.

Yet resistance to police violence in India has begun to grow. In 2020, for example, the hashtag #JusticeforJayarajandBennix was among the top Twitter topics in India and in the top 30 globally.[48] Movements such as Muslims Lives Matter, Dalit Lives Matter, and Adivasi Lives Matter, inspired by Black Lives Matter, have become more visible.[49] So, too, have the testimonies of those who have survived police and prison violence.[50] The intensification of the Indian government's efforts to stifle freedom of expression and undermine democratic institutions, such as the judiciary and the press, now also elicit more attention to the injustices and violence embedded in every aspect of Indian criminal justice, including the police system.[51] When in 2018 the Maharashtra Police charged sixteen people, including activists, journalists, academics, lawyers, trade unionists, artists, intellectuals, and a Jesuit priest with engaging in anti-government conspiracy, instigating violence, and having links to Maoist groups in the Bhima Koregaon-Elgar Parishad case—despite fabricated forensic evidence—this stimulated increased interest in issues relating to state repression and civil liberties.[52]

As public awareness of state repression grows, Indian cinema's long history of glorifying police violence has, in turn, increasingly come under scrutiny. Not just that, but popular Indian films no longer hesitate in depicting the realities of police brutality, particularly against the poor and marginalised.[53] Most notable are the Tamil films *Visaranai* (dir. Vetrimaaran, 2015), *Karnan* (dir. Mari Selvaraj, 2021), *Jai Bhim* (dir. TJ Gnanavel, 2021), *Writer* (dir. Franklin Jacob, 2021), *Taanakkaran* (dir. Tamizh, 2022), *Santosh* (dir. Sandhya Suri, 2023), and *Viduthalai Part I* (dir. Vetrimaaran, 2023), and Hindi-language OTT shows such as *Paatal Lok* (Amazon, 2020) and *Kohra* (Netflix, 2023).[54] There are positive signs, therefore, the problem of police violence has finally begun to attract public attention in India.

## Why This Book?

The efforts of the Supreme Court, civil and democratic rights movements and groups, human rights lawyers, and many others have brought everyday forms of police violence, such as custodial violence, and more exceptional forms, such as 'encounters' and the militarised policing of resistance movements, into public debate. Yet police violence in India continues unabated.[55] According to the National Human Rights Commission, 2152 people died in judicial custody between 2021 and February 2022 alone.[56]

New penal codes came into force in India on July 1, 2024—the Bharatiya Nyaya Sanhita, the Bharatiya Sakshya Adhiniyam, and the Bharatiya Nagarik Suraksha Sanhita—to replace, respectively, the colonial-era Indian Penal Code (1860), Indian Evidence Act (1872) and Code of Criminal Procedure (1882). But they largely replicate their predecessors, since they give the police even wider powers to make arrests, and force individuals to answer police notices and summons without being informed about the allegations against them. They also transfer crucial judicial functions to the police, undermine the presumption that a person is innocent until proven guilty, and potentially increase the duration the police can hold suspects in custody without pressing charges against them. Among other troubling provisions, the new laws also increase the risk of custodial torture and other forms of police violence.[57] As Tahera Mandviwala, co-chair of the International Bar Association India Working Group, has said, they thus 'curtail civil liberties and violate human rights…provisions'.[58]

How, we should ask, did such a situation come about? What are the origins of police violence in India, and how do we explain its persistence? What part has colonialism played in shaping it, and how does it continue to do so in post-colonial India? How much responsibility should be placed on India's legal, judicial, or political systems and cultures, not to mention political ideologies? To what extent does the new digital infrastructure of policing contribute to police violence? What are the roles and responsibilities of extra-judicial and semi-state actors, such as medical professionals, in shaping the institutional culture of policing?[59] What role does the lack of accountability for senior police officers for the actions of their subordinates play in perpetuating police violence?[60] And to what extent is extrajudicial violence by the Indian police a reflection of hierarchies based on class, caste, gender, religion, and sexual orientation? How important, furthermore, is casteism in our understanding of police violence, considering it serves to criminalise 'different aspects of the lives of oppressed caste communities', as Nikita Sonovane observes?[61] What role, in addition, does the routine dehumanisation of subordinate members of the police play in contributing to the violence they enact, most notably through their dire working conditions? As members of the Delhi Police force declared in a 2019 protest against their mistreatment, they are not regarded as 'humans in uniforms'.[62] In what ways, lastly, has the BJP's assumption of power at the national level and in numerous states exacerbated police violence in India? Some of these questions have garnered considerable public attention, but not others, especially the relationship between the dehumanisation of subordinate police staff and the dehumanisation they, in turn, enact.

A growing body of cutting-edge research by leading scholars of history, anthropology, political science, law, and criminology, as well as legal experts in India as well in the United States of America, the United Kingdom, Canada, and elsewhere explores these themes.[63] Many of the contributors to *Policing and Violence in India* have been at the forefront of such scholarship.[64] But unless their insights are widely disseminated they can do little to shape public discussion on policing and violence in India. The aim of this book is, therefore, to present some of the newest research and insights on policing and violence in India in an engaging, sensitive, and nuanced way. *Policing and Violence in India* hence explores the historical, legal, political, and sociological aspects of the relationship between policing and violence, the everyday nature of police violence, and the connections between 'normal' and 'exceptional' forms of violence. It considers the role of the Indian judicial and political systems in facilitating police violence, while spotlighting some ways in which such violence is being exposed and challenged. This book endeavours to fulfil these goals through forging linkages between academic scholarship and grassroots initiatives that have painstakingly documented and challenged police violence in India.

That so many people now seek to abolish institutions such as prisons, and the police itself, as Michelle Alexander, author of *The New Jim Crow: Mass Incarceration in the Age of Colorblindness*, has observed, is 'a testament to the fact that an enormous amount of work has been done, in academic circles and in grass-root circles', to encourage us to rethink such institutions.[65] Through this book, we hope to encourage similar rethinking in India on the police as an institution and the devastating impact it has had on Indian culture and society, in addition to individual bodies and minds.

## Issues and Themes

*Policing and Violence in India* focuses on five key issues: the continuities and changes in regard to police violence from colonial to post-colonial India; how the law and the state and or semi-state institutions, including the judicial system, the NHRC, and the medical profession, facilitate police violence, particularly against minorities and other historically marginalised peoples; the role of socio-political transformations, including political pressure, in legitimating as well as erasing police violence; civil versus militarised policing and their intersections with martial law; and the often surprising relationships that can emerge between the police and criminal suspects despite—or as a result of—police violence. The nine chapters within the following pages are written by historians, political scientists, anthropologists, legal scholars, and lawyers, and the seven interviews and reflections are by prominent critics of police violence, including a former police officer (Vikash Narain Rai), human rights activists, lawyers, and academics (Shalini Gera, Sanjoy Hazarika, Beatrice Jauregui, Santana Khanikar, Vipul Kumar, and Mangla Verma), and a survivor of police violence and now human rights advocate, Abdul Wahid Shaikh.

The chapters are divided into three sections, 'From the Colonial to the Post-colonial', 'Custodial Violence, Law, and the Courts', and 'Complicating Understandings of Police Violence', which are followed by 'further thoughts' from the noted anthropologist Veena Das, the renowned lawyer and human rights activist Vrinda Grover, and the prominent historian, women's rights activist, and human rights activist, V Geetha.

All chapters in the first section, namely, Deana Heath's 'The Colonial Origins of Police Violence in India', Bhavani Raman's 'Neither at War nor at Peace: Martial Law and Policing in India', and Radha Kumar's 'Everyday Violence: Colonial Past to Post-colonial Present', focus on the nature of colonial policing in India and its legacies, not least the role played by the police since the colonial era in constructing, maintaining, and performing a sovereignty shared between the state and a wide range of competing interest groups. As emblems of state power, deeply rooted in local, social, and political networks, and who, while upholding the law, have been forced to operate beyond it, the Indian police came to play an important role in according the state legitimacy. These chapters, therefore, examine the origins and nature of both everyday and emergency policing, the dynamics through which police violence emerged and is perpetuated, and the role of the Indian police in upholding ordinary as well as extraordinary laws. These chapters also reveal that while the Constitution of newly independent India promised liberty and equality, the persistence of colonial laws—especially The Police Act of 1861, which still governs the police in India over a century and a half later—and continuities in everyday policing practices, such as the location of stations, the composition of police personnel, and police record-keeping practices, have perpetuated the colonial surveillance of communities that are marginal due to their religious, caste, or economic status.

While the first section demonstrates the role of the police in maintaining socio-cultural, economic, and political hierarchies in India in a more pointed way, every contribution to this volume explores these themes. The chapters in the second section—Jinee Lokaneeta's 'Justice in Custody: Doctors as Semi-state Actors', Abhinav Sekhri's 'Confronting the Violence Within: Courts, Police Custody, and Criminal Investigations', and Sharib Ali and Ishita Chakrabarty's 'Hate Crimes as the New "Legitimate": Anti-CAA protests and Policing in Aligarh Muslim University and Jamia Millia Islamia, 2019'—explore how the law and judicial system in India work in conjunction with the police to further marginalise as well as criminalise groups such as Muslims and legitimate police violence, particularly custodial violence and violence enacted in the name of public order policing. They also reveal the role of non-state/semi-state actors like the medical profession and institutions established by the state to protect human rights, including the NHRC, in the perpetration of hate crimes by the Indian police.[66] They do so through focusing on some ways in which the law and legal infrastructure in India, and the courts and bureaucratic apparatuses of the state, facilitate police violence through magistrates, medical professionals, and paperwork.

Such problems reveal the role of socio-political developments, especially political pressure, in legitimating and effectively erasing police violence. These issues are elaborated in the third section of *Policing and Violence in India*, in Pooja Satyogi's 'Perceiving Threats and Policing Concerns: The Annual Conferences of the Director and Inspector Generals of Police in India', Ather Zia's 'Distrusted Force: The Police in India's Counterinsurgency in Kashmir', and Mayur Suresh's 'Policing and Intimacy: Narratives from Terrorism Trials in Delhi'. These chapters demonstrate the Indian state's attitude towards and priorities regarding policing, and how these have shifted over time, and been shaped by political leaders—especially through forging problematic relationships between civil and military authorities, civilian and extraordinary policing, and civil and military law.[67] They also reveal that police violence, despite its historical and ongoing ubiquity, has received little concerted political attention, which signals not only its value to the state in maintaining its power, but one of the many ways in which police violence has been rendered inconsequential or invisible.

These chapters build, in addition, on Bhavani Raman's

insights in chapter two on the colonial origins of the peculiar relationship between civil and military law in India, and civil and military authorities, which transformed the concept of war from an exceptional state to one that could co-exist with peace in the name of public safety, and be enacted through militarised policing. Nowhere is this clearer than in Kashmir, most recently since 2019, after the Indian government revoked its quasi-autonomous status in the Indian union.[68] In the heightened militarisation that followed, for what was already one of the world's most militarised zones, the largely Muslim Jammu and Kashmir Police were sidelined, victimised by their identity in a Hindu majoritarian socio-political system. That the subordinate police can be both victims of state violence—as several contributors to this book intimate with respect to their dire working conditions and the poor treatment they are subjected to—suggests the struggles of the police themselves to retain their humanity. This can lead to surprising acts of intimacy and care, alongside their enactment of violence.

The essays in this book demonstrate some of the ways that police violence in India has and is being conceptualised—as well as challenged, resisted, and redressed. But while the problem of police violence in India is both longstanding and endemic, it is also urgent. Addressing it therefore requires concerted, collective action by, and ongoing conversations with, a range of individuals and interest groups. In the final section of the book, therefore, we think through the problem of police violence with some of those who have worked to address it from within the Indian police, witnessed it as activists and lawyers, closely studied it as scholars, and survived it. Together, these interviews and reflections reveal what is at stake if we fail to address police violence in India—not just for the wellbeing of all Indians, but for its social and economic development and its future as a democratic polity.[69]

*Policing and Violence in India* complicates our understanding of police violence and its origins in numerous ways. Its causes have always been complicated, but as many contributors in this anthology illustrate, they have arguably become less so since 2014, since the violence of civilian and military policing has intensified, especially for communities and groups who fall foul of the Hindu nationalist ideology of the party ruling India. Since then, the boundaries between civilian and military policing—as well as between ordinary and exceptional law—have become increasingly blurred. The contributors also reveal some of the forms of resistance against such violence, from modifying individual behaviour to undertaking collective socio-political movements, litigation, critical investigative reports, and scholarship. The aim of this book is to add to such engaged acts and critically reflective voices.

PART ONE

# From the Colonial to the Post-colonial

## Chapter 1

# The Colonial Origins of Police Violence in India[1]

*Deana Heath*

When, in February 1839, a former bullock *maistry*, or subcontractor, named Mutusamy, a member of the regionally dominant Vellāla caste, had 400 rupees and some jewellery stolen from his money box, he called upon the kotwal of the cantonment of Ootacamund (Udhagamandalam), a Rajput named Koopasing, for help.[2] While the theft was outside of Koopasing's jurisdiction, he was aware that the *maistry* was wealthy and that it would be in his interest to pursue the case. He therefore dispatched some police peons to Kulhutty, the *maistry*'s village, where, with the help of Mutusamy's son and other members of the Vellāla caste, they set about rounding up suspects. These included Chinoo Aucharry, a twenty-year-old lower-caste blacksmith from the Karumān community who had made the lock for Mutusamy's money box, Govindoo, a twenty-year-old coolie of the Reddy caste who lived with Chinoo, and Maroodayee, who had recently pawned two rings to Mutusamy and whose son was accused of acting as a lookout during the robbery.

With Chinoo denying all knowledge of the theft, he was taken to the house of a Vellāla, stripped, beaten, tied, and hung from the roof with stones on his back. Such treatment continued for the next two days, although Chinoo was returned to Koopasing's *choultry* (police station or office) each night. With the stolen goods still not forthcoming, on the third day the police and their accomplices suspended Govindoo and Maroodayee from the roof of the house, along with Chinoo, and subjected them all to torture—which included stripping them, beating them with nettles, lighting a fire below them, smearing their genitals with chilli, and ordering Chinoo and Govindoo to perform oral sex on each other.

When the torturers then threatened to rape Govindoo and emasculate Chinoo, the young blacksmith, pleading the need to urinate, tried to slit his throat with a broken bottle. Chinoo was then taken to the nearest hospital, but Govindoo and Maroodayee were held in police custody for three more days before they were released. None of them were ever formally charged with the theft, and since the police focused all their energies on forcing innocent victims to confess to a crime they had not committed, rather than pursuing other lines of enquiry, the case remained unsolved. Four police peons were later sentenced to five years' hard labour for their acts of torture committed in Kulhutty, but their superior officer, Koopasing, who was clearly complicit in these acts, was never prosecuted—although he was dismissed from the service of the East India Company for investigating a case outside his jurisdiction.

The ordeal of Chinoo, Govindoo, and Maroodayee took place almost 200 years ago. But their experience remains eerily familiar. As Meenakshi Ganguly, South Asia director of Human Rights Watch, has observed, 'it is almost routine that [police] detainees are subject to beating or worse'.[3] According to a report by the National Campaign Against Torture, an average of five people a day died while in judicial custody in India in 2019, many as a result of torture used to extract confessions.[4] Even the types of torture enacted on the bodies of Chinoo, Govindoo, and Maroodayeeur—beating, burning, stripping, suspending victims by the arms or legs, and sexual violence ranging from forced nudity to rape—remain disturbingly routine. Like the three suspects in 1839, the victims of such violence also continue to belong, as the report notes, mostly 'to the poor and marginalised sections' of Indian society, or those who are 'soft targets because of their socio-economic status'.[5] Non-state actors, generally members of the higher or locally dominant castes, likewise often play a role in enacting torture against such people and groups.

In addition, superior police officers enjoy the same immunity from prosecution in contemporary India as Koopasing experienced in the 1830s. As a sub-inspector from Uttar Pradesh confessed to Human Rights Watch, such officers often asked their subordinates 'to do wrong things'.[6] Yet, as noted in the introduction to this book, not a single police officer of any rank has been convicted for their role in the 500 deaths that occurred in police custody in India between 2005 and 2018.[7] Today, such immunity is, in contrast to the Ootacamund case, widely shared across rank and file.

The post-colonial Indian state has largely retained the system of policing it inherited from the British, along with the legal framework, developed in the 1860s, that governed it—the Police Act, the Indian Penal Code (IPC), the Criminal Procedure Code (CrPC) and, a decade later, the Indian Evidence Act (IEA). These were enacted to help the British secure their hold over India following the 1857 Revolt, which threatened to end their rule. Such continuities should therefore come as little surprise. For KS Subramanian, a former officer in the Indian Police Service, India's independence led to 'no structural change in the organisation and functioning of the Indian police' after 1947, barring that they were given more coercive powers.[8] Although voluminous evidence has been produced since the National Police Commission was established in 1977 about human rights violations perpetrated by the Indian police, and innumerable recommendations have been made and Supreme Court guidelines issued to reform them, none of these have, furthermore, ever been implemented. Indeed, though Prime Minister Narendra Modi has attempted, since 2014, to rid India of what he terms its 'colonial mindset' through various projects of renaming, redesigning, and rebranding Indian places and institutions, the Indian police have been exempt from such a process.[9]

Little wonder that, of the 12,000 police officers interviewed for a 2019 report on the status of policing in India, over eighty per cent maintained that it was justifiable to beat up individuals who they believed were criminals to extract confessions from them.[10]

## The Nature of Colonial Policing

But while the Indian police undoubtedly are, as the journalist Praveen Swami has said, 'the children of their colonial predecessors', the nature of colonial policing in India (and other former colonies) has received relatively little attention.[11] Some studies have been done on the establishment and development of colonial policing in India, as well as on the role of the police in the maintenance and demise of British rule in the subcontinent. But questions remain about the nature of the system that such 'children' inherited. What, for example, were the dynamics or rationales of the policing system in colonial India? What role did policing play as an attribute of state power, and why was its functioning heavily reliant on extra-legal violence? Moreover, what drove Indian police recruits to become what scholars of policing in Brazil call 'violence workers', and exactly on whose behalf were they enacting violence?[12]

To answer such questions, this chapter will first examine the role of violence in the operation of colonial states. Since such states needed to keep colonised peoples in a permanent state of fear and, it was hoped, quiescence, violence was central not just to their formation but their functioning. It will then go on to explore the system of policing that the post-colonial Indian state inherited, as well as its role in exercising British control over India not least in making the Indian police, as the 1902 Indian Police Commission report put it, 'a terror to the people'.[13] Turning next to the colonial judicial system, the chapter will consider how it worked, in particular its reliance on racial discrimination, on untrained judges who were given excessive powers, and standards of evidence in which Indian testimony was discounted and confessions secured through dubious means. It will also analyse the lack of separation of powers between the different branches of the colonial state, and the considerable powers of official discretion the police were given to uphold the law and act extra-judicially to sustain such a system. The chapter will, lastly, explore the role of police training and working conditions, as well as the punitive powers the police were given, in enabling police violence in colonial India—particularly the role of poor supervision, divided loyalties, caste, and clannishness in creating an in-group dynamic in which violence was normalised.

## Policing and Colonial Violence

Since colonisers were alien occupiers who governed by force rather than consent, and consequently lived in constant fear of the fragility of their rule, colonial regimes were inherently violent. But such violence was also a product of the conviction of the colonisers that colonised peoples were 'backward' and 'irrational', if not outright barbaric, and therefore could only be governed through violence.[14] I am not suggesting that colonies were places in which violence proliferated unchecked. Colonial states enacted reams of legislation to curb forms of violence that they regarded as a threat to their rule, such as those that threatened social stability. Nor were colonial states necessarily more violent than the regimes they superseded. But they undoubtedly spent far more money on preserving their rule than their pre-colonial predecessors. By the late-nineteenth century, the British spent no less than a third of their annual budget in India on maintaining their security forces.[15] The violence they carried out was also based on a rationale different from that of their antecedents, namely that of 'civilising' the colonised, or making them, as Talal Asad has argued, 'fully human'.[16]

As a result, types of violence ranging from land taxes that induced wide scale impoverishment or the use of famines as a means of social and economic transformation, to whipping, torture, and judicial murder—which the British resorted to a great deal more than their forebears—were regarded as disciplinary and, ironically, even humanitarian, if properly administered and legitimated. It was such dynamics, for the Cameroonian historian and political theorist Achille Mbembe, that transformed colonies into 'terror formations'.[17]

The police were central to the construction of such terror

formations. By the late -nineteenth century, the Indian police had developed the reputation of being 'an engine of oppression of the most exquisite and pernicious kind', and a 'terror to young and old…alike'.[18] Such a reputation had, however, been a long time in the making. Since the introduction of the Cornwallis Code in 1793, through which the British began to usurp and transform the pre-colonial criminal justice system, British magistrates, judges, colonial officials, and most of the Indian public, were aware of the violent and predatory nature of the Indian police.[19]

In the first half of the nineteenth century, for example, criminal courts in colonial India drew the attention of magistrates to the issue of police torture numerous times, although largely because it threatened to 'disgrace the established system of judicial procedure' rather than because of its effect on Indian bodies, and legislation was enacted penalising police violence.[20] While, furthermore, the system of policing that the British developed after the 1857 Revolt has long been regarded as representing a distinct break from the one that preceded it, little changed in reality. Some new posts were created, various ranks were renamed, Indians were removed from positions of administrative responsibility, and the police became subject to greater (European) supervision.[21] But as ex-district magistrate Robert Carstairs declared, not just its staff, but 'much of its old spirit, and many of its methods, forbidden though they might be, remained'.[22]

This is because such changes were designed to ensure that the British retained their 'occupation of the country', as the report of the first pan-Indian police commission frankly confessed in 1860.[23] This priority was clear in the provisions of the Police Act of 1861, which was applied to all provinces in British India apart from Bombay and Madras. In contrast to the system of civil policing as it developed in England from 1829, which focused on the duty of the police towards the public, the foremost duties of the police in India, according to the Act, were to obey orders and collect and transmit intelligence. The police were to be aided in this by the IPC and the CrPC, both enacted in 1862, which prioritised maintaining public order and protecting the state over the well-being of the public.[24] Though ostensibly a civil police, the Indian police also retained many para-military elements, from weapons training and armed units to drills, a highly regimented and hierarchical structure, and an officer cadre dominated, until late in the nineteenth century, by former British military men.[25]

## Violence and the Judicial System

But while such provisions helped transform India into 'the policeman's kingdom', it was the colonial judicial system that enabled this transformation to take place.[26] The British claimed to govern India through the rule of law, rather than the consent of the Indian populace—a claim that was used to justify and provide moral legitimacy for their occupation of India. In reality, however, the colonial judicial system was an alien and despotic one manned by untrained judges, since the British believed that 'common sense' was the only qualification required for administering law in India. It was also a racially discriminatory one and, like India's system of colonial policing, it was more concerned with preserving the colonial state than the welfare of its Indian subjects.[27]As the renegade colonial judge John Bruce Norton fumed, since their subjects were, for the British, 'only "niggers"', then provided a certain number of cases were dealt with each month it did not matter what the outcome of these were.[28]

What made British justice in India particularly pernicious was the lack of separation of powers between the judiciary, administration, and police. Not only did provincial governments intervene in legal cases they disagreed with and remove judges who met with their disfavour, but district magistrates (referred to as deputy commissioners in some provinces) were vested with what the *Calcutta Review* regarded as 'the powers of a whole Bench of Magistracy', along with wide-ranging executive powers.[29] They were also required to supervise the police while acting as a judicial restraint upon them. Such a lack of separation of powers ensured that the Indian police were given extensive discretion in how they applied colonial law, including the power to supersede it. Nowhere is this clearer than in their reliance on confessions as judicial evidence.

Beginning in the late-eighteenth century, the British introduced new methods of crime investigation and legal process, which included granting police officers the authority to record confessions and use them as evidence. They quickly began exercising these powers to extort confessions, which colonial magistrates and judges had few qualms about accepting. This was true even in the considerable number of cases—in one province as high as seventy per cent—in which confessions were the *only* form of evidence used to secure convictions.[30] This reliance on confessions helps explain why inducing them was not made an offence until the enactment of the IPC.

The CrPC, also enacted in 1862, barred the police from recording confessions, but an amendment in 1869 made information given by an accused, 'whether it amounts to a confession of admission of guilt or not', admissible as evidence.[31] Confessions to the police, provided they were recorded in the presence of a magistrate, were also made admissible. Such confessions were widely acknowledged as being 'as little to be trusted as those made before the police, being generally made through their agency', yet the power to record confessions was never taken away from magistrates.[32]

It was not until the IEA came into force in 1872 that confessions were deemed 'irrelevant' as evidence if they 'appeared' to have been induced.[33] There were, however, a number of ways in which such a provision was undermined, as Abhinav Sekhri also discusses in his contribution to this book. Confessions were, for example, still admissible as evidence if the 'impression' that they had been induced was 'removed'. This, as an amendment to the CrPC clarified in 1898, simply required a written statement from a magistrate that they believed a confession was voluntary.[34] The IEA also authorised the use of confessions even when acquired through deceit, or when the accused was inebriated, or not informed that they were not obliged to make a confession, or told that their evidence could be used against them.

Since it was, furthermore, legally possible for a magistrate to send a suspect into police custody for up to fifteen days, and nothing prevented the police from detaining accused persons for weeks or months before presenting them before a criminal court (despite the prohibition since 1816 against holding such individuals for more than forty-eight hours without a warrant, and from 1872 for no more than twenty-four hours), the legal safeguards against police torture, as the eminent jurist Syed Ameer Ali once scoffed, were 'more or less illusory'.[35] The British, however, never sought to combat police torture by making confessions illegal as a form of evidence in colonial India because they relied on the extra-legal violence the police employed to secure them to maintain colonial sovereignty.

The colonial judicial system exacerbated police violence

in other ways, such as evidentiary norms born of the British conviction that Indians were pathological liars, whose evidence could not be trusted. As Norman Chevers put it in his pioneering manual of medical jurisprudence, published in 1856, deceit was particularly 'inherent in the character of the lower class of natives'.[36] Such a lack of faith in Indian testimony led, in turn, to a belief in medical evidence as the definitive source of truth, particularly, from the 1870s, following the passage of the Coroner's Act and the IEA. This was despite the often poor knowledge of medical experts, their difficulties in obtaining reliable evidence—due to problems ranging from a climate in which bodies decomposed quickly to the weak investigatory skills of the Indian police—and their often questionable methods and morally-inflected views. As the medico-legal expert Major Cox noted seventy years after the publication of Chevers' text, 'medical legal work' in India was not, as a result, 'well done'.[37]

Weak evidentiary norms ensured, furthermore, that complaints against the extra-judicial violence carried out by the Indian police were mostly declared false, or failed. When it became impossible, however, to ignore police violence, as when it resulted in death or scandal, it was largely dealt with through commissions of inquiry, which avoided judicial scrutiny. But since the lack of separation of powers in colonial India ensured, as the reformist Member of Parliament Frederic Mackarness noted in 1909, that 'the decision as to whether a prosecution shall take place depend[ed] on the same men who conduct[ed] inquiries in the first instance', such commissions generally resulted in the exoneration of the perpetrators.[38] They also, therefore—along with the entire criminal justice system in colonial India—spawned a virtual culture of impunity for police violence.

## Police Deprivation and Excess

A number of other factors enabled police violence, including poor training, underfunding, and terrible working conditions, particularly for the lower ranks. To begin with training, none at all was provided for the village police, and constables were taught little more than the basics of reading and writing until provincial training schools were set up in the late-nineteenth century. Such schools provided little training, however, in the duties recruits had to perform, particularly regarding the prevention and detection of crime. It is because of this that the police largely investigated cases (after the payment of a bribe) by rounding up so-called bad characters, and sometimes entire villages, and keeping them in informal custody until they determined who the culprits were.[39]

The training of superior officers, who could be recruited as young as eighteen, was equally deficient. Like their subordinates, they were expected to learn on the job, or glean its essentials from 'the school of experience'.[40] Such a dismal lack of training sent a clear message to police recruits that the colonial regime cared little for *how* they carried out their jobs, but virtually *ensured* that they used violence since they lacked the requisite skills not to.[41]

Endemic underfunding further forced the colonial Indian police to resort to violence due to the paucity of their numbers. So, too, did their appalling pay and working conditions, particularly for the lower ranks. For the village police, the pay was often so poor that they were kept, as the Lieutenant-Governor of Bengal, Frederick Halliday, remarked in 1856, in 'a permanent state of starvation'.[42] This, in turn, forced the police to rely for their survival on what Anastasia Piliavsky calls 'plunder-policing' (plundering those who refuse to patronise them).[43]

Constables fared little better, since for much of the colonial era they were paid less than unskilled labour but expected to work for as many as seventeen hours a day, in often appalling conditions, with little prospect of promotion. As a result, in some years, provincial police forces could lose as much as half their constabulary to desertion and resignation. Yet despite their obvious disaffection, even low-ranking police were armed with extensive punitive powers, ranging from the surveillance of 'habitual' offenders, to vagrants, 'suspected persons', and so-called criminal tribes, through acts such as the CrPC and the 1871 Criminal Tribes Act.

They even engaged in the armed occupation of allegedly 'unsettled' areas. During such campaigns, referred to by the British as 'punitive policing', the police often unleashed a reign of terror of robbery, rape, and general mayhem.[44] Yet such powers continued to expand from the late-nineteenth century, fuelled by a surge of new legislation designed to suppress the growing Indian nationalist movement.[45]

## Dehumanisation and Power

Poor training, dire working conditions, and poverty are some of the ways in which the subordinate police were dehumanised in colonial India. But they were also given extensive powers to resist such dehumanisation. Forced to choose between predation and starvation, the subordinate police, unsurprisingly, chose the former. Apart from generating a group dynamic in which violence was normalised, an array of factors, including poor supervision, divided loyalties, and caste dynamics, aided this process.

Poor supervision, to begin with, was partly a product of underfunding, and partly geography. A district superintendent of police, for example, could be responsible for supervising almost 1,000 policemen at over two dozen police stations and twenty outposts spread across a district of over 5,000 square miles.[46] While stations, and sometimes outposts, were headed by police officers ranked no higher than head constable, communication between stations was poor, and they could be completely cut off during the monsoon. Superior officers also spent more time carrying out inspections and dealing with paperwork than in supervising subordinates.

In-group dynamics were furthered—as Chinoo's case reveals—by the loyalty of the police being divided between the colonial state and other competing interest groups. Since it was a way of securing local influence, an aspirant chaukidar could be willing to pay his local zamindar up to five months' salary to become a village policeman.[47] Such patronage, in turn, enabled local elites to co-opt state power, for their own benefit and that of their fellow caste members. This one of the many ways in which caste was woven into the dynamics of policing in colonial India.

Though local elites, superior officers and colonial officials largely favoured recruitment to the police from the higher castes (or from so-called 'martial' castes), the low pay often made this difficult to achieve in the lower ranks.[48] As the identity of a lower-caste man was shaped by those higher in the caste and class hierarchy, the subordinate police were under particularly strong pressure to conform to group dynamics.[49] But caste also served to undermine a sense of individual responsibility for police violence, by alleviating feelings of personal guilt, and even empowered perpetrators to feel self-righteous about enacting what they saw as justice.[50] It contributed, in addition, to what has been referred to as the 'clannish feeling that pervade[d] the force'.[51] This was exacerbated by how hierarchy was demonstrated in the police, such as through officers being accompanied by a posse of subordinates wherever they went.

But caste not only played a role in normalising violence, it also shaped the form such violence took. As David Canter contends, 'different ways of assaulting the body carry implications for different ways of relating to the person whose body it is'.[52] That police in colonial India resorted frequently to sexual violence, for example, to enact their power is because it is a potent means of asserting authority over individuals from different caste, ethnic, or religious groups by humiliating them and undermining their identity.[53] For Mutusamy, the bullock *maistry* who Chinoo was accused of robbing, it could therefore be used, as he saw it, to 'cut the genealogical root…' of the caste of the man he believed had stolen from him.[54]

## Conclusion

The Indian police were valued by the colonial state and local elites as violence workers who furthered their respective desires. These were not, however, always mutual, since the police were part of the colonial regime in India, as state agents, but positioned outside of it, as native subjects.[55] As a result, they were, as the *Calcutta Review* protested in 1860, often unfairly 'vilified and abused till the whole vocabulary of vituperation has been expended.'[56]

Indeed, the inadequate system of criminal justice in colonial India generated a situation in which members of the Indian public used the police for their own ends, such as by pressuring them to 'give a sound thrashing' to errant neighbours or relatives.[57] But for those who were poor and marginal, contact with the police was to be averted at all costs. This, as Norman Chevers put it, went to the extent of 'the concealment of crime by those'—including victims—who were 'unwilling to incur the trouble or risk of a police investigation', since attracting the attention of the police posed the risk of *more* violence, theft, and exploitation.[58]

Although for the British such predation was a sign of the incomplete humanity of their Indian subjects, rather than being a by-product of the needs of a regime of conquest, as the *Ananda Bazar Patrika* rebutted, the Indian police were guided by the will of their superiors', who were 'mostly Englishmen.'[59] It was the British, in other words, who were ultimately to blame for the violent system of policing they developed in India, not those they employed to serve in it.

CHAPTER 2

# NEITHER AT WAR NOR AT PEACE

## Martial Law and Policing in India

*Bhavani Raman*

Military laws and courts, which are distinct from criminal legal systems, are overseen by military authorities and govern the conduct of soldiers, in addition to punishing those deemed enemies of the state. During political emergencies, however, they can be invoked to try civilians if martial law is declared and ordinary laws are suspended.[1] Post-colonial India has not experienced periods of martial law, even during the draconian national Emergency, in the 1970s, during which the fundamental right to protection from illegal detention was undermined.[2] Nor has the Indian state used military courts to try civilians, in contrast, for example, to Israel, which established military courts after it occupied the West Bank and Gaza in 1967, and now routinely uses them to try Palestinians.[3] Nonetheless, in India, the mechanisms of policing resistance against the state have historically drawn on martial law. Therefore, exploring the colonial-era relationship between martial law and policing offers new insights into how martial law became a foundational tool of modern governance in India.[4]

To make sense of such a dynamic requires examining not the Indian police but the history of military law, since the armed services in India are regularly tasked with internal security duties, such as to help quell rebellions and riots, not least in areas the Indian government classifies as 'disturbed' under the Armed Forces Special Powers Act (AFSPA).[5] Since it was introduced in 1958 to suppress Naga nationalists, the AFSPA has been implemented numerous times elsewhere. It has been in force in Jammu and Kashmir since 1990, and has also been implemented in parts of Nagaland, Assam, Arunachal Pradesh, Meghalaya, Tripura, and Manipur.[6]

In addition to giving policing powers to the Indian army, under the overall control of civilian authorities, the AFSPA empowers army officers to fire upon and even kill anyone contravening the law, make arrests without a warrant, and conduct stop and search operations.[7] Through placing constraints on judicial checks that protect human rights, it also protects military officers from criminal prosecution for such tasks. In effect, it legitimises internal occupation by the armed forces and enables the Indian government 'to impose what can be justifiably called martial law' without suspending the law, the Constitution, or *habeas corpus* (protection against illegal confinement).[8] Areas in which AFSPA is enacted are thus rendered into places of conflict where protections under the law are not in place, nor suspended—places where, in other words, neither war nor peace prevail.

The AFSPA is not, however, a recent innovation in India's history. As a result of its colonisation by Britain, India was an early site in which policing and military powers were interwoven. The East India Company, after conquering Bengal in the mid-eighteenth century, conquered much of the Indian subcontinent. It then passed martial law regulations that created military courts in each of its presidencies—Bengal, Madras, and Bombay. Such regulations did not suspend the law or close criminal courts. Instead, they empowered governors and governors-general to constitute military courts even when criminal courts continued to function.

This interlocking of military and criminal courts made it possible for a colonial government to deploy violence in a flexible but targeted manner against particular social groups or classes of people in the name of public safety and the rule of law. It meant that the law was underpinned by violence.

## Defining Wartime and Martial Law

To tease out the implications of the application of military powers to civilian populations and how they operated in practice requires going back to the early-nineteenth century—specifically to 1804, when Richard Wellesley, the Governor-General of India, passed martial law regulations to try offences against the state.[9] This decision played a key role in transforming martial law from a royal prerogative and tool of interstate wartime governance into a form of executive power that could be used to punish those who resisted the British throughout their empire.[10]

But how did a trading company acquire the power to enact military law? The English Crown first delegated the power to declare martial law during war or invasion to the East India Company in 1624.[11] In 1683, Charles II's Fifth Royal Charter gave further powers to the Company to make war or peace with rulers in the 'East Indies' and to enact martial law to protect itself from foreign invasion or rebellion.[12] It was not until the nineteenth century, however, that such powers became foundational to the Company state in India as a means of combatting the problems posed by its limited jurisdiction over the Indian subcontinent.

The reasons for such limitations on the Company's legal authority in India were twofold. Firstly, while the Company governed India as an agent of British colonialism, and as a result was given the power to sign treaties or make war, it could not prosecute individuals for treason—since this was, by British convention, the sole prerogative of the British sovereign.[13] It lacked such a right, moreover, under Mughal law, since in addition to being subject to British sovereignty the Company was also subject to Mughal sovereignty. It was accorded the right to govern, collect taxes, and establish courts of justice by the Mughal emperor—and such courts, which administered Islamic law, did not recognise treason against the Company.[14]

The problem for the Company, however, was that there was no clear definition as to what constituted martial law or its applicability, although English legal scholars had long tried to limit its operation to moments of exception or emergency—most notably, to wartime.[15] This had become part of English legal traditions by the early-seventeenth century when, in the face of protests against Charles I's imposition of martial law in England to compel his subjects to house, feed, and clothe his soldiers, Parliament issued the Petition of Right, which guaranteed protection from arbitrary state violence, including the right to habeas corpus.[16] For the renowned jurist Sir Edmund Coke, martial law could not operate during peacetime.[17] But although Coke restricted martial law to use in wartime, it continued to thrive beyond this because of the emergence of new conceptions of wartime and peacetime.[18] In colonies such as British Jamaica, for example, governors repeatedly closed the courts to create a legal state of war in order to build fortifications and make militia duty mandatory for their free subjects.[19]

As notions of war became more elastic, martial law was, in turn, adapted during the eighteenth century to suit the needs of colonial governance, in contexts ranging from North America to Asia.[20] While Britain itself largely resisted such transformations, thanks to the Petition of Right, it did witness the passage of the 1714 Riot Act, which authorised civil authorities to call for military aid to suppress riots and rebellions in the name of public safety.[21]

By the nineteenth century British understandings of wartime and peacetime continued to evolve to meet the needs of British, and wider European, colonial expansion. This is because war, rather than being fought solely between sovereigns, was increasingly being fought between European armies and non-state entities, such as nationalists, republicans, autonomous polities, and what were called irregulars (namely, combatants who did not belong to a regular, or state army) in different parts of the world. The act of 'civilising', or colonising, had inevitably, therefore, led armies to develop violent forms of policing to quell those resistant to such developments.[22]

To return to India, the increasingly elastic understanding of wartime underpinned the East India Company's use of martial law to punish rebels even before it began to incorporate martial law into its regulations in 1804.[23] For example, in South India, after forcing unequal treaties on the kingdoms of Arcot and Mysore in the aftermath of the Third (1790-1792) and Fourth (1798-1799) Anglo-Mysore Wars, the Company began to pursue the region's autonomous warrior chiefs (*palayakarar*) who resisted its authority.[24] But in light of the jurisdictional conflicts in which the Company was enmeshed, it was unclear whether such chieftains were obligated to be loyal to it.

The Company, therefore, resorted to the violence of martial law to eliminate such resistance instead of signing a treaty with the *palayakarar*, as it had with Mysore and Arcot, through the use of summary court-martials and hanging those found guilty of rebellion or treason.[25] The Company justified such acts by arguing that the warrior chieftains were plunderers who could not be relied on to be treaty partners, and that it was acting to bring peace and good government to South India. It was through such means that martial law was transformed from a royal prerogative and delegated power to a technique of colonial policing—and colonial governance—that could co-exist with criminal law. The court-martial, as a result, became a tool for Company officials to calibrate violence over life and death, or to define who is killable, as a foundation of modern law.

## Waging War for Good Government

It was, however, in the Bengal Presidency, not Madras, that martial law was first legally codified in India. It was spurred by a letter from John Ryley, a local magistrate, to the Governor-General, Marquess Richard Wellesley. Ryley was a Company magistrate in Etawah, on the banks of the river Yamuna in the north Indian plains. He wrote to Wellesley to complain that the local commanding officer, Major Bowie, had usurped his civil powers as a magistrate by declaring martial law in his district and suspending the local law courts.[26] What concerned the magistrate was that 'the authority which Major Bowie ha[d] declared to be vested in himself could not possibly be exercised by the military power of martial law'.[27]

Ryley sent his complaint at a time of considerable challenges for the Company in Etawah, a region it had occupied only recently, during the second Anglo-Maratha War (1803-05), because Etawah's landlords were refusing to pay their annual revenue demands to it.[28] It was for this reason that Bowie had been instructed to consider the area under martial law and to 'make such prompt examples of severity' against local landlords as necessary 'without reference to the civil power'.[29]

Bowie had thus used the temporary authority of martial law to override Ryley's civilian government and enforce 'capital or corporal punishment on any person or persons found guilty of acts of rebellion against the state', which he did by announcing that those who refused to pay revenue to the Company would be dispossessed of their lands without recourse to legal means of redress and would 'suffer death and total ruin'.[30] For Ryley, the issue at stake was not the severity of such an act but that such a military government was not legal, according to British norms, even when enacted in an overseas colony.[31]

Wellesley responded that he supported the imposition of martial law, but that Major Bowie had misconstrued his military powers under martial law by completely suspending civil power in Etawah. This Wellesley could not condone, since it would lead to 'evil consequences' by compromising the Company's ability to forge relationships with local elites that would advance British power in India.[32] He thus ordered that, from then onwards, only civilian authorities, namely magistrates, could proclaim martial law—not military officers. This would, in turn, preserve the power of civil authorities to punish rebels through courts of law, and thus maintain the Company's credibility as a good governor in India.[33] For Wellesley, maintaining the law thus required periodically suspending, not usurping it.

It was such concerns that led to the enactment of Bengal Regulation 10 of 1804, which gave the Governor-General power 'to provide for the immediate Punishment of Certain Offenses against the State by the Sentence of Courts Martial'.[34] These included the power to declare martial law in times of inter-state war or internal rebellion, as well as to wholly or partially suspend ordinary criminal courts and try rebels by courts-martial, through which they could be sentenced to death. The regulation gave the Governor-General the power, *at any time*, to try such individuals by either ordinary courts or military courts, or to pardon those convicted of crimes against the state. It thus served to blur the boundaries between enemies and rebels, and war and policing, and interlocked martial law with criminal law.

The Bengal regulation was not, however, the first time that martial law was codified in the British empire, since Regulation 10 closely resembled an earlier, Irish Act, the 1799 Suppression of Rebellion Act.[35] This was enacted by the Irish Parliament in response to the filing of a *habeas corpus* petition in the Court of King's Bench, in Dublin, on behalf of Wolfe Tone, who had been captured, court-martialled, and sentenced to death when trying to liberate Ireland with the help of the French military during the 1798 Irish insurrection against British rule.[36] The petition questioned the legality of the court-martial on the grounds that, as Tone was not a soldier of the Crown he could not be tried by a military court, and that martial law could not prevail while the king's courts were open.[37]

While the court was sympathetic to the view that martial law and civil law were incompatible, and that the power of execution could only rest with civil courts, the Irish Parliament was not. The Suppression of Rebellion Act therefore empowered the Lord Lieutenant of Ireland (the governor) to punish rebels or those believed to be rebels by martial law courts and sentence them to death, even if the King's courts were open. It also denied the right to *habeas corpus*.[38] As in India and England, the Irish Act therefore reframed martial law as a tool of public safety.[39]

In removing protections granted by British jurisprudence—particularly by granting military courts the power of execution, which had previously been restricted to civil courts—the statute also created a new category of subjects: namely, those for whom protection from military violence and illegal arrest could be withdrawn. It therefore fashioned a new relationship between law, violence, and public safety—one that would travel to other colonial contexts, including India.

Bengal Regulation 10 of 1804 went one step further, however, than the Irish law, which gave the Lord Lieutenant the power to punish rebels during a specific rebellion without undermining the royal prerogative to exercise martial law. It did so by framing specific rebellions as part of a wider war between the Company and princely, or 'native', powers.[40] Furthermore, it created the court-martial as a permanent option for trying rebels accused of state offences. In doing so, it interlocked criminal law with military law and restricted the power to impose martial law to civilian authorities, rather than the army.

Instead of being seen as the opposite of peace, wartime had therefore become conceptualised as being *pro tempore*—'for the time being'—to target any group perceived as a threat to the state by civilian authorities. If martial law was declared, any person caught with arms and charged with rebellion—whether or not they were formally the Company's subjects, whether or not the courts were open—could be severely punished, either by death or by incarceration in the Company's penal colonies, and only the governor-general had the power to grant a reprieve. Capital punishment was to be carried out, moreover, in an exemplary fashion, specifically in a public space, where it would be visible to spectators. The Bengal law therefore enabled the Company to retool martial law to assert its authority over life and death, in a context where its claim to sovereignty was, at best, contingent and highly fragile.

Another aspect of the Company's martial law regulations worth noting is that, for the interweaving of military law and criminal law to work, it was vital to maintain the integrity of the court-martial's procedures. Sometimes, this meant that governors who tried to interfere in the decisions of military courts were censured, which undermined the very executive authority the regulation was intended to strengthen. An example from southern India illustrates this problem.

## Neither War nor Peace in Wayanad, Malabar

In December 1806, Pallur Emman Nayar, a Malabar aristocrat declared a rebel by the British East India Company, was captured and arrested in the forests of Wayanad.[41] Nayar had participated in the 1799-1805 Malabar Rebellion, led by Pazhassi Raja, which challenged East India Company authority after the Company defeated the ruler of Mysore, Tipu Sultan, and conquered the kingdom in the Fourth Anglo-Mysore War. Yet while Nayar was captured well after the end of the war and the rebellion, the Governor of Madras, Lord William Cavendish-Bentinck, deemed him too dangerous to be tried by a criminal court and ordered that he be tried, instead, by a military one.

Although a martial law statute had not yet been enacted in Madras at the time of Nayar's arrest, the Company had nonetheless been regularly imposing martial law in Malabar, as it had in the rest of South India, to repress autonomous warrior chiefdoms.[42] In contrast, however, to Etawah, in Malabar, civil and military operations were closely coordinated. The local Company magistrate was also involved in determining when, why, and how martial law would be declared, and court-martials were held even when the ordinary courts of law were functioning.

The consequence was that peacetime and wartime had become completely blurred. In one notable instance, Malabar magistrate Thomas Warden persuaded the local commanding army officer to try individuals before a military court who were merely 'suspected of being acquainted with the entrance of any rebel or party of rebels into the district' or of 'having furnished them with arms, ammunition, or provisions'. Their guilt, moreover, was to be determined 'without any [due] process'.[43] In Malabar, therefore, military courts tried *suspected* rebels, not just those who openly resisted Company rule.

As a result, it was Thomas Warden who impressed upon Governor Cavendish-Bentinck the urgency of trying Nayar by 'the summary process of a court-martial, in the same manner as other proscribed rebels were lately tried and executed', even though he had not been caught in arms.[44] But during his court-martial, Nayar sought a pardon by making a fervent plea that he had been compelled to revolt against the Company against his will. It had not been his intention, he declared, 'to oppose the British Government', and his offences were, as a result, 'involuntary ones'. He therefore entreated the court to intercede with the Governor of Madras to pardon him and promised that, if granted, his future life would be lived 'in atonement for [his] former offences'.[45] In response, the military court spared Nayar's life and sentenced him to lifelong transportation to the Company's penal colony in Penang (now in Malaysia).

Such a sentence, however, plunged the Madras Government into crisis, since the ruling undermined the governor's authority to punish acts of rebellion. For the governor, since Nayar had 'been found guilty of the most flagrant violation that can be committed of the laws of civil society, it was the unquestionable duty of the court to have pronounced a sentence adequate to the offence'—namely death—as well as to have left it to *his* judgement to determine whether or not to grant Nayar mercy by saving him from execution.[46] But the military court refused to revise its sentence to one of death.[47] In the face of this struggle over whether a military court or civilian executive had the ultimate right to decide who should live and who die, Governor Cavendish-Bentinck was forced to accept the military court's verdict. Nayar was sent to Penang, where he died a decade later.

But in sparing his life, the military court undermined the governor's sovereign power to decide whether a rebel died or lived out the rest of his life in prison. To ensure such a situation would not arise again, martial law was enshrined on the statute books in Madras in 1808 by a regulation modelled on Bengal Regulation 10.[48] A newly expansive understanding of war had thus made possible the proliferation of martial law—on the purported grounds of public safety—as the basis of executive authority. Instead of being merely a wartime measure, martial law therefore became the foundation of modern government and its legal system in India.

## Conclusion

This chapter has dwelt on some of the seeming paradoxes of martial law. As a controversial royal prerogative, martial law migrated, over the eighteenth and early-nineteenth centuries, from its use in wartime to serve as a tool of colonial policing. Its temporality also became open-ended, as represented by the term *pro tempore*. Martial law, consequently, could be used indefinitely as a policing measure, and evade judicial review, without suspending the law, habeas corpus, or closing the courts.

The record of martial law across the British empire illustrates, furthermore, how colonial interests blurred the boundaries between war and rebellion, and state security and policing—in addition to the tools left at the disposal of the post-colonial Indian state to police resistance or rebellion, not least the power to enact laws without judicial review. The AFSPA is a result of this global imperial history, a continuation of colonialism through militarised policing. As such, it illustrates that the power to 'make' law, rather than be accountable to it, is not simply a colonial legacy but part of the ongoing history of colonialism.

## Chapter 3

# EVERYDAY VIOLENCE

## Colonial Past to Post-colonial Present

*Radha Kumar*

Few would dispute that there has long been caste inequality in the Indian countryside, but explaining its persistence is a harder task. Individuals and institutions, past traditions and present practices, economic structures, religious beliefs, and political machinations—all of these have been variously held responsible for the persistence of caste inequality. This chapter focuses on one institution, the state police, to explain its role in maintaining caste hierarchies in one part of India, namely the southern Tamil region, over the course of the twentieth century. It argues that in both colonial and post-colonial India, police violence, manifested on the beat and in preventive arrests, played a crucial role in subduing the resistance of the lower castes to caste inequality.

Consider Chatram Kudiyiruppu, a small village near Thazhaiyoothu, itself barely a town in Tirunelveli district in southern Tamil Nadu. The town's principal claim to fame is a cement factory, established by India Cements in 1949. The company's website notes that when it established the plant,

Thazhaiyoothu was 'an almost unmapped tiny hamlet'.[1] And yet, not only this tiny hamlet, but even Chatram Kudiyiruppu village (which had not yet made its way on to Google Maps at the time of writing), were on the radar of the state government's police force from the early twentieth century onwards. Under British colonial rule, the government of the Madras Presidency had a police station in Thazhaiyoothu, and its officers maintained detailed files on each village under its jurisdiction—including Chatram Kudiyiruppu. In 1947, following Indian independence, the Madras (from 1969, Tamil Nadu) government took over these files from its colonial predecessors, and added to their contents over the ensuing decades.[2]

What was in these files, and why did police forces in the Madras Presidency (and later Tamil Nadu state) care enough to maintain records on nondescript villages in the Tamil countryside? The short answer is that these records enabled the state's coercive maintenance of everyday order, in the face of minor and major challenges to existing social hierarchies. In the colonial era, a new economic formation had transformed the Indian countryside: agrarian and forest commodities were harvested in unprecedented quantities for export, while manufactured products from Great Britain flooded the Indian market. Some Indian subjects, including landlords and traders, benefited from this new global economic exchange, but the vast majority, who toiled for low wages or were simply excluded from the logic of market exchange, did not.

Agrarian and factory labourers' continued participation in the colonial economy was therefore dependent on the underlying threat of force, embodied in the form of the Indian police. That said, the police was a poorly funded institution in the Madras Presidency, with scarcely enough resources to monitor labourers scattered across the vast countryside. To overcome this numerical disadvantage, the police largely directed their energies to policing the lower castes and classes. Consequently, from the early decades of the twentieth century onwards, even insignificant police stations in Madras Presidency maintained detailed records of the caste and class demographics of villages in their jurisdiction.

Since the colonial police force was manned by Indians, except at the highest ranks, police records were maintained by Indian colonial subjects, who used this knowledge to guide their everyday surveillance and investigation work. In the southern districts of Madurai, Tirunelveli, and Ramnathapuram, police inspectors and constables were typically drawn from the higher and middle castes, including Brahmins, Pillais, Naidus, and Raos. Importantly, Dalits were severely underrepresented in the provincial police, comprising less than three per cent of the force in the 1930s.[3] Additionally, well into the 1960s, the Madras police force was entirely male. Such skewed demographics, added to police underfunding, ensured that gender, class, and caste hierarchies in Madras were enacted and reaffirmed through everyday policing practices in the Tamil countryside, including through the police beat and crime investigation.

Because discrimination based on class, caste, and gender was so baked into the routine practices of the Indian police, it did not magically disappear with Independence in 1947. Admittedly, the economic and social priorities of the independent state were different from those of its colonial predecessor. For instance, India in the 1950s and '60s prioritised food self-sufficiency and import substitution, not global trade. At the provincial level, the strength of Periyar EV Ramaswamy's Self-Respect Movement against caste-Hinduism and patriarchy, which began in the 1920s, also ensured that the government paid attention to matters of caste equality. Certain priorities within the Madras police therefore shifted in line with these broader policy changes, resulting in some measure of police protection for women and Dalits from outright upper-caste oppression.

On the other hand, the ruling Congress party very quickly set limits to the caste and class radicalism it would support, such as by putting down struggles for workers' rights by the Communist Party of India with brute force. Moreover, Dalit voices were rarely included in administration at any level, village or state, until the end of the twentieth century. Accordingly, maintaining the social order endured as a state priority after independence, and the police, as a result, continued to classify and regulate subjects based on their caste and class.

These included using extra force against certain castes which, under colonial law, were deemed 'criminal', which undermined attempts by the lower castes to be treated as equal in public spaces, and stationing additional personnel in villages where labourers demanded higher shares of the produce during harvests. In each of these cases, drawing upon records from select police stations in colonial and post-colonial India, this chapter will show how the colonial police contributed to maintaining social hierarchies in the twentieth-century Tamil countryside, and how the policing of such groups survived the transition to independence, some modifications notwithstanding. It will conclude by considering the continued menace of police violence against the marginalised—Dalit women in particular—in present-day Tamil Nadu.

Together, these descriptions provide a stark indictment of the popular notion that caste violence occurs when the state, in the form of its law and its police, are absent.[4] Instead, this chapter argues, the police have been essential to the endurance of caste inequality in the colonial and post-colonial Tamil countryside, and police violence has become embedded in its social fabric.

## Caste and Power in the Tamil Countryside

Caste inequality has been a longstanding reality in the Tamil countryside. Chola inscriptions and Bhakti poetry from a millennium ago tell of social distinctions that enabled the extraction of labour from men and women of the lower castes. Skipping forward to the early-nineteenth century, when the British established control in the southern Madras Presidency, they witnessed slave-like agrarian servitude among Dalits. Although this was the era of global anti-slavery movements, the importance of cheap Dalit labour for land revenue meant that neither the East India Company nor, from 1858, the British Crown, intervened to abolish the system.[5]

Consequently, well into the early-twentieth century, agrarian relations in the Tamil countryside continued to be marked by inequality between upper-caste landowners (often belonging to the Brahmin and Vellalar castes) and lower-caste (Pallar and Paraiyar) landless labourers. In addition to Dalits, there were other occupational caste groups that also held low status in local communities. These included Nadar, once called Shanar, who were derided for their hereditary occupation of making palm liquor, which was taboo according to Brahminical teetotalling norms.

The persistence of caste inequality does not mean that lower-caste communities did not fight for equality, dignity, or at least better living conditions. They did, often. Some organised to acquire education, move to towns, and change occupations.[6] Others emigrated to the tea plantations of Sri Lanka (then Ceylon) to escape the caste restrictions of their villages. Yet others opted out of Hinduism by converting to Christianity or Islam, both of which proclaimed the theoretical equality of all persons.

Yet even as they reaped the stray benefits of these acts of courageous resistance, they also faced hostile reactions from their neighbours for challenging the status quo. For example, through the late-nineteenth and early-twentieth centuries, Nadar attempts to reinvent their caste status were resented by Maravar, who stood just above them in local caste rankings. Likewise, upper-caste communities continued to deny Dalits who had converted to Christianity or Islam access to certain village streets and spaces, by claiming that they would pollute them.

It is perhaps no surprise that those immediately and directly impacted by challenges to social hierarchies opposed them. What is noteworthy is the extent to which the state, via its police force, participated in this project of maintaining caste hierarchies. To explore this, I will draw upon journals from select police stations in the Tamil countryside to reveal the ways in which police power intersected with caste power at the village level.

## 'Criminal' Castes and the Police

Manur is a small village, approximately twenty kilometres from Tirunelveli town, which was the capital of Tirunelveli district in British India. Its police station, originally built in 1867 at a cost of Rs 540, has undergone numerous repairs over the past century and a half.[7] Inevitably, it must have lost some of its records, too. But some remain, dating from the early

1930s. One of these is the Marava Sheet: a four-page printed form containing eleven questions, the answers to which the police filled out by hand.

The form reflects a longstanding, but mistaken, British colonial belief that Indians could be classified and understood by their caste identities, so that an Indian belonging to a certain caste would necessarily behave in accordance with its dictates.[8] According to British administrators, this *community* identity sharply distinguished colonised Indians from colonising, enlightened Europeans, whose actions reflected their *individual* will and reason. Thus, colonial administrative and ethnographic records routinely described the entire membership of specific castes as thrifty, sly, honest, respectable, or, as we will see, criminal.

By the late-nineteenth century, castes regarded as inherently criminal by the colonial government were subject to extrajudicial policing through a draconian legislation called the Criminal Tribes Act (CTA), 1870. Those who fell under the remit of the CTA could be convicted of certain crimes with far less evidence than was the legal norm, and their movements were severely restricted even when they had committed no crime. The CTA was extended to Madras Presidency in 1911, and Maravar were brought under its ambit soon after.

The reason the British perceived the Maravar as being inherently 'criminal' was their participation in a precolonial policing system called *kaval*, which skirted the line between pillage and protection. In some cases, villagers paid *kavalgar* (policemen) for their security from thieves. In others, villagers paid the policemen fees to be exempted from theft by the *kavalgar* themselves.

Condemning the practice as pure extortion, Madras administrators committed themselves to eradicating it for well over a century, albeit in vain. The Marava Sheet, which the police filled out for each village in their jurisdiction, was part of this futile state initiative. Through it, senior police officers sought to collect information on the prevalence of *kaval* in each village within the region and based on their findings, allotted personnel and resources to tackle it.

In reality, the form did no more than strengthen the stereotype that Maravar were criminal, which rendered them vulnerable to further police intervention. Consider one of its questions: 'What form does Marava oppression take? Does it arise from *Kaval*?' The question takes Marava oppression for granted, without attempting to ascertain whether it occurred or not. The assumption of Marava criminality informed not only the printed questions that came from police headquarters in Madras city, but also the handwritten and typewritten answers filled in by inspectors for each village across Tirunelveli district. Police responses were logically inconsistent within each form and revealed no clear pattern about the practice of *kaval* across the region.

For instance, a form from one village declared that 'there [was] no oppression by Maravas', but that the (high-caste) village munsif [magistrate], Rangasubbaraya Iyer, was 'afraid of the Marava' and that someone would, therefore, 'come out boldly to depose against the Maravas'.[9] The village of Mavadi, on the other hand, apparently had no *kaval* system according to one of the responses on the form, but another response, on the same form, noted that the 'Maravars will commit any type of crime if *kaval* is refused'.[10] Despite these inconsistencies, police administrators used such data to divert resources to policing Maravar in the region, by placing additional police stations and scheduling more frequent beats near villages where Maravar lived. Police harassment was thus woven into the everyday lives of these communities.

The CTA was repealed in 1947, but its impact on criminalised communities did not end then, for multiple reasons. Firstly, many who had been classified as 'criminal tribes', while now denotified, were reclassified as 'habitual offenders' under the Habitual Offenders Act, enacted the following year, which kept them just as firmly under the thumb of the police. By 1952, of the 5,268 persons who had been registered province-wide under the Act, as many as 4,097 (almost seventy-eight per cent) belonged to denotified tribes.[11] Even those members of former 'criminal tribes' who were not reclassified as 'habitual offenders' continued to be policed as 'denotified members', a pejorative term that lives on, three-quarters of a century after independence and the repeal of the CTA. Several recent Tamil films, notably *Paruthiveeran* (dir. Ameer Sultan, 2007) and *Jai Bhim* (dir. TJ Gnanavel, 2021), have poignantly explored these ties between denotified tribes and state authority.

A second reason for the lasting legacy of the CTA is the location of police stations. Under colonial rule, police stations were not evenly distributed across the landscape. Administrators took into account various factors, such as population density and demographics, to concentrate stations in areas deemed more deserving of security. Accordingly, European settlements received extra police presence, but so did regions in which the so-called criminal tribes dominated. Unlike the colonial government, which put a lot of time and money into determining and fine-tuning the location of stations, the post-colonial government invested its resources in building better housing for police personnel, around half of whom lived in houses without electricity, running water, or adequate sewage facilities at the time of Independence. The outcome of this shift in priority was that the colonial geography of policing endured well past 1947. As a result, denotified communities continued to be policed harshly in independent India.

A third and final reason for the enduring legacy of the CTA is that the notion that certain castes were inherently criminal was not restricted to British administrators. Indians, including policemen, appropriated it over the course of time. Individual beliefs could not be revoked with the repeal of an act. Consequently, even after 1947, the police institution as a whole, as much as individual policemen, was guided in its practice by the notion that certain castes tended to criminality. As late as 1964, for example, the Madras Police Research Centre conducted a study of criminality among a denotified caste, the Valayar of Madurai, 'with an exhaustive report to serve as a guide to the investigating staff in handling Velaya [sic] crimes'.[12]

## Caste Dignity

Apart from monitoring those directly criminalised by state law, colonial policemen also kept an eye on lower-caste resistance to caste norms, especially those pertaining to the ordering of rural space. Admittedly, this was in part a product of personal biases because, as previously noted, there were few Dalits in the police. But policing caste resistance was not just a function of individual bias; it also stemmed from state policy. In the years after the widespread Revolt of 1857 against East India Company rule, the British colonial government tried to walk the line between two contradictory positions: respecting caste hierarchies on the one hand, and treating all castes equally under the law, on the other.

The outcome was a century of legal ambiguity and popular discord. For instance, if a lower-caste community demanded the right to take processions through a street in their village or town that had previously been reserved for the higher castes, the rule of equality before the law dictated concession to the lower-caste community's demand. However, Queen Victoria's Proclamation of 1858 had promised non-intervention in Indian customs. So, if the higher-caste community could prove its exclusive 'customary' right to that street, the law was bound to recognise that right.

In the resultant impasse, police priorities lay in maintaining 'order', which translated to preserving the status quo—and with it, typically the rights of the higher-caste community. This situation occurred innumerable times in the colonial Madras Presidency, especially following religious conversions. This is because when a lower-caste community in a village converted *en masse* to Islam or Christianity, as a means of resisting its position in the Hindu caste hierarchy, it typically sought to inscribe its new status in the village spatially, by seeking access to sites earlier denied to it. If other castes opposed this, the situation led to the police intervening as the arbiters of public order.

Let us return to our villages in Tirunelveli to see how such events often unfolded. Kurichikulam, according to police records, was a small village with a total of '20 Muslim, 20 Pillai, 6 Marava, 100 Palla, 2 Barber, and 2 Dhobi' households, as of May 1943.[13] The Muslims of this village were Labbai, an old community that had descended from intermarriage between Arab traders and local Tamils, according to the famed colonial ethnographer Edgar Thurston.[14] In the view of the local police inspector, Natarajan, the Labbai of Kurichikulam were 'mostly barbarous and of rude character'.[15] He held, moreover, that:

> The character of these Muslims in general was bad and they have got illicit intimacy with the harijan girls and in course of time convert them to Muslims and even instigate

> the Navamuslims to do things annoying the Hindu harijans. They have been warned by the [police] official during 1948 and then they were quiet. Now there is information that the Muslims of Kurichy Kulam have instigated the Navamuslims of Seedaikurichi to conduct prayers in the prohibited areas and to give trouble to the Christians. They have been warned [sic].[16]

We can see from this note that the inspector held the Labbai in low esteem because they threatened a social order premised on certain caste and gender norms in multiple ways. First, Labbai men had relationships with Dalit women. Second, they encouraged Dalits to convert to Islam, thereby challenging their position as outcasts in Hindu society. The converts were known as Navamuslims, or 'New Muslims', which differentiated them from their erstwhile Dalit peers (the 'Hindu Harijans' Natarajan refers to) as well as from the Labbai themselves, who did not trace their ancestry to Dalit status. Third, the Labbai supported the Navamuslims in their efforts to challenge local spatial hierarchies. All of these were thorns in the flesh of the local police.

These tense interactions—between the Labbai, Hindu and Muslim Dalits, Christians, and the police, in various permutations—were a long time in the making and involved three neighbouring villages, Kurichikulam, Therkupatty/Therkukulam, and Seethaikurichi. According to local police records from the 1930s, there was 'ill-feeling between some Mussalmans and Pallars of Therkupatty', and when one group did not allow the other to drive manure carts through its neighbourhood, 'there was small rioting'.[17] The handwritten notes for the next decade are frustratingly impossible to decipher.[18] But in this period, the Pallar must have converted to Islam, for a note from May 1946 refers to 'the Therkupatti Islamic conversion and the consequent troubles'.

By converting to a religion that did not officially recognise caste, the erstwhile Pallar sought to escape their subordinate caste status in the village. One expression of this subordination in Tamil villages was that the Dalit settlement (the *ceri*) was separated by a kilometre or so from the caste settlement (the *ur*), or main village. Dalit access to the *ur* was inevitably resisted by the upper castes, as is evident in the clashes over manure carts in the early 1930s mentioned above. Inevitably, the metaphoric doors to the *ur* did not automatically open when a Dalit community converted to Islam or Christianity: they had to be pried open.

Accordingly, there was an increase in local conflict after the Therkupatti conversion. Aware of these happenings, the local police inspector assigned a temporary daily beat to the village, even though regular village beats had been abolished in India in 1902 for being impractical and ineffective. Thereafter, constables were only assigned to beats to tackle particular perceived dangers. By identifying Therkupatti village after a Dalit conversion as a dangerous place and time, the colonial state and its police were, in effect, deploying resources to preserve the status quo.

Not that the converts buckled under police pressure. In December 1946, when one of the recent Navamuslim converts of Therkupatti lost a child, the community wanted to bury the body in a plot which, it claimed, 'had been purchased for the construction of a mosque and use as burial ground'.[19] The Hindus of the village objected to this, however, 'and prepared themselves for a fight'. The Navamuslims managed to bury the child in their chosen location, but did not gain outright access to the space, which remained in contestation for a few more years. During this period, the Dalits of the adjoining hamlet, Seethaikurichi, also converted to Islam and joined the struggle for *ur* space. By 1948, the Therkupatti Navamuslims, with the help of the Kurichikulam Labbai, had managed to construct their mosque.

The construction of a mosque in a small village may appear insignificant in the annals of this era, when India won independence from colonial rule. But the transfer of power from the British to the nationalist Congress government did not automatically translate to dignity of life for India's lower castes—they still needed to fight for it, including in confrontations with the police. Despite some immediate transformations in the police force after 1947, its attitude towards Dalit rights took time to change. Although Indians began to occupy the most senior ranks of the police force (previously largely limited to Europeans), there was not as much change at the level of the constabulary, where Dalits remained under-represented for several decades. Accordingly, the Madras police from the 1950s continued to express concern about the construction of the Therkupatti Navamuslims' mosque, by directing the local constabulary to watch over events and warning the Navamuslims against any further attempt at construction.[20]

Piecing together these snippets from different police files, the story that emerges is of caste solidarity across villages and through decades towards subverting existing caste hierarchies. Contrary to nineteenth-century colonial stereotypes, the Indian village was not an isolated socio-political unit. In addition, in contrast to enduring upper-caste nostalgia for a once-harmonious caste order that rested on patronage, vertical caste relations were often tense.[21] Caste resistance was, furthermore, mounted against both caste *and* state power.

The notes also shed light on multiple tools wielded by the police against caste resistance: in particular, the inspector repeatedly states that the Dalits were 'warned'. Warned about what precisely? 'Warning' might be a police euphemism for physical coercion. But the police had legal means to handle subject-citizens like Dalit resistors who ostensibly threatened public order. These options included extra police beats and preventive arrests, both of which were frequently used by the colonial and post-colonial police to curb popular resistance.

Despite such efforts on the part of the police, the Dalits of Therkupatti and Seethaikurichi achieved significant milestones in the 1930s and '40s. After converting to Islam and building a mosque in the *ur* near the church (which also annoyed village Christians, who had most likely made a similar social and spatial journey in the preceding half-century but did not look kindly upon others joining their ranks), they resumed attempts to build another mosque and a burial ground, this time near the village's Hindu temples. This was a strike to the heart of caste power, and the police reacted decisively by warning them to 'select some other site far away from the Hindu temples'.[22] They also threatened them with legal action through Section 107 of the 1898 Criminal Procedure Code if they did not.

This legal provision enabled a magistrate, when informed that someone was *likely* to breach the peace or 'do any wrongful act', to detain them for up to over a year. In effect, it gave wide latitude to the police to preventively arrest anyone who, in their view, threatened the peace. Presumably, these drastic measures worked, as the following updates reveal:

Aug. 1954. 'There is no trouble now.'
Feb. 1955. 'There is no trouble now.'
Dec. 1955. 'There is nothing important to note.'
Dec. 1956: 'There is nothing particular important in this village.'

It would be a mistake to read these entries simply as dull, or as denoting a lack of activity in the Tamil countryside. Instead, they point to the successful use of police force in suppressing caste-related protests. 'No trouble' and 'nothing important' in police vocabulary translate as the effective and violent working of the state from the perspective of the subordinated.[23] In contrast to their earlier victories, by the 1950s, the promise of independence notwithstanding, the Navamuslims of the region had been thwarted by the police in their efforts to achieve social and spatial equality with caste Hindus.

## Caste and Class

As subordinated members of a caste- and class-based society, lower-caste communities struggled not only for equal access to public space, but also for higher wages. Both the colonial and post-colonial states were hostile towards class struggle, since they saw it as disruptive of economic stability, especially when it occurred during critical moments in the agrarian calendar, like the harvest season. Labour conflicts, like those over caste, unfolded over several decades, with multiple caste communities and the police entering the fray.

For instance, in 1938, the Pallar (Dalit) labourers of Chatram Kudiyiruppu village struck work, demanding a higher share of the harvest. The landlords refused, citing inadequate profits. 'Fortunately for the landlords', as the local police inspector noted in his records, the village Maravar stepped in to supply the labour.[24] At this point, the Pallar, fearing the loss of their meagre livelihoods, 'compromised their differences with the landlords' and returned to work in the fields. The restoration of order notwithstanding, the local police decided to deploy additional men to the village during the harvest season in the ensuing years.

Two points stand out in this otherwise low-key sequence of events. One, the class fight had subsided for the moment, but at the cost of intensifying caste tensions between two labouring caste communities—the Maravar and the Pallar. Two, the local agrarian labour supply was maintained at a low cost over several years not only because of the competition between Maravar and Pallar, but also because of a potentially violent police presence. The innocuous vocabulary of 'compromise' to which the inspector alludes, in other words, cannot be accepted at face value. Far from a voluntary compromise between two somewhat equal parties, the return of Pallar labourers to the fields resulted from a lack of options and a watchful police authority.

Following independence and through the late 1940s and early '50s, however, the Communist Party of India joined forces with agrarian labourers in Madras State to agitate for better wages. One among the many sites of protest was Chatram Kudiyiruppu village, where, in 1954, the Maravar and Pallar communities united, rather than competing against each other, to challenge the local Brahmin landholders. Wishfully describing the 1954 unrest as coming out of nowhere, the police inspector recalled that the Dalits and Maravar of the region had worked for Brahmin landlords 'for a long time', thereby erasing the region's history of caste and class struggle.[25]

As in 1938, the police intervened once again to put down the protest. Peasant dissatisfaction was real, though, and thanks to the fact that India had become a democratic republic with universal adult franchise in 1950, members of the lower castes were gradually able to access state power. In 1958, a Dalit Member of Parliament from the locality, RS Arumugam, resuscitated the struggle of the workers for better wages. In a superb euphemism, the police noted that the struggle had 'received due attention' from them.[26] It thereafter disappeared from police records and, presumably, from their concerns. The police had triumphed once again over the struggles of Dalit labour.

## Conclusion

This chapter has shone light on the history of one region, spanning no more than a few hundred square kilometres, in the southern state of Tamil Nadu. The purpose of this microhistory is not to assert the uniqueness of this region, but rather to reveal the dense human and institutional ties that went into maintaining caste inequalities in it over the course of several decades. Marginalised communities faced everyday hardships from dominant members of society, who relied on police authority to maintain their power. Conversely, the police did not function in isolation from the rest of society. They worked hand-in-hand with local stakeholders when exercising power over marginalised groups. Thus, the social positions of Dalit agrarian labourers were shaped not just by Brahmin landholders but also by the local police, who used the power of the law to maintain class and caste inequalities.

Likewise, when lower-caste communities converted to Christianity or Islam to escape their subordinated status within Hinduism, their struggles for equality were opposed not just by their upper-caste neighbours, but also by the police. These police interventions were justified by a colonial law that prioritised social and economic stability over lower-caste rights.

In 1950, the Republic of India made a constitutional promise to end untouchability and improve the lot of its poor. However, the laws specific to policing, namely the 1860 Indian

Penal Code, the 1861 Indian Police Act, and the 1898 Code of Criminal Procedure (first enacted in 1862) were adopted almost verbatim by the Republic, resulting in considerable continuity in policing. Institutional continuity in the form of station distribution, personnel, and record-keeping practices further contributed to the persistence of police surveillance of lower caste/class communities. In this socio-political context, which persisted throughout the latter half of the twentieth century, a new language of rights clashed with an old structure of power.[27] Upper-caste, upper-class stakeholders routinely put down Dalit struggles, sometimes with a spectacular show of violence, as in the infamous Keezhvenmani massacre of 1968, in which 44 Dalit agrarian labourers were burnt to death in a hut.[28]

In 1993, the Indian Parliament enacted a constitutional amendment to strengthen institutions of local self-governance in its villages. In a significant attempt at correcting historical injustices in political representation, the amendment required that a third of village officialdom comprise women and members of the Scheduled Castes and Tribes (Dalits and Adivasis). In the years since, the representation of Dalit women in Tamil Nadu's village bodies has increased. But Dalit women routinely face discrimination from upper-caste villagers in the performance of their tasks.[29] Unsurprisingly, the police are entangled in these politics.

Returning to our villages in southern Tamil Nadu, Krishnaveni, a thirty-year-old Dalit (Arunthathiyar) woman, was elected head of the Thazhaiyoothu village council in 2006. She achieved much in her tenure, including the construction of a public toilet for women, a library and roads, as well as the provision of drinking water to the village.[30] Many of these projects were financed by supportive members of the public, since the government often blocked the flow of money to her. While she had support from some villagers, she also met with much casteist and sexist harassment in the form of emotional and physical violence. Her detractors tried to bully her not to enter her workplace, taunted her to clean the sewers herself, and threatened her with murder and rape were she to carry on with her job. In 2011, such threats were carried out when Krishnaveni was brutally attacked on her way home from work and had to be hospitalised.[31]

What did the police do to help Krishnaveni during these years? In short, nothing. More disturbingly, they actively enabled her persecution through their position as gatekeepers to the criminal courts. In other words, they selectively pursued criminal complaints registered with them in a way that disadvantaged Krishnaveni. Over several years, Krishnaveni filed twenty-two police complaints against those who harassed her; the police did not investigate even one of them. Conversely, they accepted as valid several false complaints of embezzlement filed against Krishnaveni by those who were trying to get her convicted in a criminal case. Even the case regarding her attempted murder of 2011 remains pending in court. The accused came out on bail within a few days of their arrest, and Krishnaveni often encounters them on the streets—a visible and daily reminder of the inequalities of a patriarchal caste society which is backed by the violence of state policing.

## Further Thoughts

*Veena Das*

The three papers on colonial policing in this section on *Policing and Violence in India* lay out the background against which we can see the administrative and legal apparatus through which policing was instituted in India in the different territories controlled during the early and late period of British colonialism. This is not to suggest that techniques of policing were not already instituted in India by the Mughal Empire and by other regional polities but what seems unique is the volume of documentation produced under the auspices of the East India Company and the British Raj.[1] These documents provide the authors the opportunity to inquire into the continuities between colonial policing and the spectre of police violence in post-Independence India.

In what follows, I highlight the concepts that emerge through which police violence is made visible and intelligible in the archive. An important cue to the shape that the arguments take in this part is provided by Deana Heath in her opening chapter, 'The Colonial Origins of Police Violence in India'. Heath argues that since the postcolonial state inherited its administrative and legal apparatus from the colonial state, many of the pathologies of policing in contemporary India could be traced to this colonial origin. Heath is echoing a widely held view shared by journalists, politicians, and many human rights organisations that resort to origins rather than genealogical investigations to account for contemporary police violence. However, despite this claim of continuity and its rhetorical force, what I found more exciting in this section on historical background is attention given to the details of the organisation of colonial policing and the way the heterogeneity in the archives offers not only actual histories of policing but also *possible* histories in the sense of different potentials that were not actualised. In other words, the fact that one kind of reform was instituted while another was rejected, for instance, was not because the force of history went only in one direction but because of multiple accidents and contingencies. Since ideas and practices that were defeated or disappeared left some traces we can retrieve other possible paths not taken.[2] From my perspective what is at stake is not the generalities—e.g. the characterisation of colonial policing as violent, which, when stated in such broad terms leaves little room for argumentation—but to ask what new questions are generated about how we understand the relation between law and governance, and the fraught questions about the forms and techniques of violence that come to be embedded within the fabric of the social. How are ruptures, seemingly minor, such as whether a case comes under the jurisdiction of a civil court or a military court, or modifications made in the questions on survey forms used in police stations for collecting data on areas under their jurisdiction, to be located in the archive and evaluated? I found that taken together, the papers all raise questions that are highly relevant for understanding violence both within and outside the law but cannot be simply contained under the well-known binaries of founding violence and maintaining violence, or boundaries between times of war and times of peace.

I would like to propose two specific issues relating to (a) theories of jurisdiction as performing the labour of law and its transgressions; (b) investigation into the question of how documents produced as part of the state apparatus are different from other kinds of texts (the ontology of documents and documentation). In the process of considering these issues, I also take a sideways glance at issues of sovereignty, law, and bureaucratic form.

## Jurisdiction and the Labour of Law and Governance

Scholars of early colonial history in India have provided prolific evidence of the way in which warfare conditioned the practices and ideologies of the East India Company and was crucial for the resources that it could command.[3] Douglas Peers cites a rueful note by an observer in 1844 who wrote that 'It will, we think, be found that our century of dominion in the East has been one of unintermitted [sic] warfare, or something very like it.'[4] But, as the prolific archive of letters and petitions to the British Parliament by functionaries of the Company and the controversies that were generated around actions of officials testify, there was also great apprehension around proper boundaries between civil administration and the power wielded by the army that could become a threat to civil authorities, and a palpable anxiety around the difficulties of deciphering the actions of subject populations. Yet, how did the attempt to mark out the jurisdiction between civil and military authorities, or the attempts to make sharp distinctions between the rational use of force by a properly instituted constabulary and forms of policing attributed to traditional modes of control through excessive violence, repeatedly fail in the assessments made by the British themselves as demonstrated in various commissions of inquiry and police commission reports? How do we take into account the different kinds of contracts the colonial administration made with tribal chieftains or strongmen who controlled frontier regions where it would have been too costly for the British to maintain order on trade routes?[5] The story of coercion here is entangled with the story of affordances that were provided and made use of for good or ill by those who constituted conceptually the 'outside' of sovereign power.

In an ideal division of jurisdiction between the military and policing, the army is used for waging war against external enemies and policing is for controlling crime within a territory inside the polity.[6] In the related division between civil courts and military tribunals, the former deal with ordinary crimes and the latter with acts that threaten the sovereignty of the state usually through special legal provisions. This neat division of jurisdiction is hard to find in the complex picture of the East India Company, in which there were overlapping sovereignties exercised by Mughal rulers, the various princely states and the areas controlled by the East India Company. Bhavani Raman's chapter, 'Neither at War nor at Peace: Martial Law and Policing in India', shows the legal mechanisms through which military courts came to establish jurisdiction over matters relating to policing when the crime was classified as rebellion against Company rule or refusal of loyalty to the Company after it had established its authority either through conquest or coerced treaties. Raman argues that further modifications of these legal provisions through which the jurisdiction of the military courts expanded are found in contemporary laws that allow the state to suspend civil or criminal law in certain areas by declaring them as disturbed and putting them temporarily under army control.

Such legal provisions also enable the army to be called in for assisting in establishing order during riots, or to aid civil authorities during natural disasters. Here, the first sense of jurisdiction is the labour it performs in creating zones of exclusion to isolate areas in which civil law can be suspended even in the absence of war. This provision can sometimes aid in states of emergency to rescue people during, say, floods or earthquakes. Its dark side, however, is the violence that can be committed with impunity by invoking laws such as the Armed Forces Special Powers Act (AFSPA, 1958), which many contributions in this book refer to, that gives the Indian Armed Forces special powers to maintain public order in areas designated as 'disturbed'.

The second sense in which questions of jurisdiction arise in the chapters in this section of *Policing and Violence in India* is the internal organisation of policing, particularly for the purpose of the surveillance of populations defined as dangerous because, though they might not have committed any crime, they are defined as those *likely* to do so either due to habit or custom. The legal provisions under the Criminal Tribes Act, 1871, which Raman discusses in her chapter, were an important instant of disciplinary mechanisms under which the local police could gather systematic information on members of so-called 'criminal' tribes by obliging them to live in restricted areas and making it compulsory for them to report on their actions and movements to the police.

In a different version than that of the 'dangerous individual' made famous by Michele Foucault, in the Indian case it was the science of criminology and colonial ethnography (and not psychiatry) which was called upon to justify restrictions upon the movement of whole groups on mere suspicion that they were likely to commit crimes rather than any evidence of crimes having been actually committed by them.[7] Some scholars have called this mode of policing an instance of the panopticon model of surveillance.[8] Radha Kumar's chapter, 'Everyday Violence: Colonial Past to Post-colonial Present', makes significant contributions to our understanding of how jurisdiction comes to apply to the practices of policing in everyday life to approximate if not replicate this model of surveillance. Set in small villages in the Madras Presidency, Kumar's chapter asks a very interesting question: why do police forces in the Madras Presidency care to maintain records on nondescript villages in the Tamil countryside? Her short answer is that these records enabled the state's coercive maintenance of everyday order in the face of minor and major challenges to existing social hierarchies. Kumar rightly points to the turbulences created by the upheavals in rural economies both because of changes in terms of trade and the extremely coercive practices of revenue extraction, as demonstrated by the report on torture in colonial Madras.[9] However, the heterogeneity of the police archives and the fixing of jurisdiction in territorial terms at the lower levels of the police hierarchies also determines which kinds of police documents will be found and where these will be found.

This mode of classification by placing certain groups as 'crime-prone' and hence in need of being put under strict surveillance carries methodological implications for the notion of the archive.[10] But here is a stunning insight from Kumar. She writes:

> …the police was a poorly funded institution in the Madras Presidency, with scarcely enough resources to monitor labourers scattered across the vast countryside. To overcome this numerical disadvantage, the police largely directed their energies to policing the lower castes and classes. Consequently,

> from the early decades of the twentieth century onwards, even insignificant police *stations* in Madras Presidency maintained detailed records of the caste and class demographics of villages in their jurisdiction. (Emphasis added)

In fact, the very location of police stations shows that due to scarce resources police stations came to be located in areas where Europeans lived in order to provide them with enhanced security or in areas which were seen to be crime-prone because of the clustering, there, of lower castes or tribes who were defined as 'dangerous' either because they were part of traditional arrangements of thieving and pillage or because they challenged the presumed sovereignty of the Company. By making private policing and the marketing of private arrangements for security punishable, the Company was trying to establish its monopoly over policing and the use of violence. We have enough evidence of its repeated failures to do so in many frontier regions, or in mountainous areas where policing tasks were contracted out. However, jurisdiction in these cases was established through the territorialisation of space, and the distribution of authority *within* civil policing.

The third sense of jurisdiction, which is derived from its etymological meaning as the speech of law, has often been interpreted in legal scholarship as asking: how does law speak to itself?[11] Posing the question of jurisdiction in this way identifies the specific features of legal language such as the prolific use of the passive voice, the long sentences and overlapping phrases, and the division between the language through which facts are presented versus decisions conveyed. Citations of precedents play one kind of role in lower courts and another kind in appeal courts evoking jurisdictional authority through different framing sentences: the imperative voice appears only in the court's final decision, or the *ratio decidendi*, part of the judgement. The site on which much of the discussion of jurisdiction in relation to language has taken place is that of courtroom talk. The papers in this section, however, look at other kinds of documents, such as police commission reports, police orders, records maintained in police stations about fights, small thefts, visits by strangers to the village, and other details that Kumar's paper gives. These accounts could be further supplemented by culling data from police diaries, or archives of chargesheets (known in India as first information reports) to see how questions of jurisdiction come up in everyday police work. It is not within my scope, here, to give anything more than certain suggestive directions on how differently the linguistic apparatus works at different levels of documentation. The prose of legal judgements, for instance, is different from the prose in village level records, district level records, or in documents which have moved further up to the directors of the East India Company or even the British Parliament.

In her chapter, Heath often juxtaposes a citation from a colonial report with a similar-sounding statement from a contemporary journalist or a human rights organisation. For example, she writes early in the chapter that, 'The ordeal of Chinoo, Govindoo, and Maroodayee took place almost 200 years ago. But their experience remains eerily familiar. As Meenakshi Ganguly, South Asia director of Human Rights Watch, has observed, "it is almost routine that [police] detainees are subject to beating or worse".' I would argue that as a narrative strategy such a juxtaposition pays much less attention to the differences and finer grains of experience and generates a common sense understanding of a particular way of speaking about law and policing. The broad brush with which police violence is rendered with its air of familiarity absolves journalists and other public intellectuals (including human rights workers) of the responsibility to get close to that register in the documents that we might just pass by because it seems familiar. Yet, a closer attention to its details of say, punctuation, or stylistic turns might reveal that it is not so easily reducible to an assumption of similarity or by acts of aggregation. Difficulties of interpretation that are often obscured by the ironing out of variations through aggregation come at the cost of losing sight of contingency. I understand the disquiet many may feel as I emphasise the need to defamiliarise ourselves with categories that have become too familiar, because those involved in finding solutions to the haunting issues of violence against vulnerable groups may feel that this makes issues more complex in the short run. However, acknowledging that we do not always act on the basis of full understanding might help us escape the moralism and rigidity that sometimes comes at great costs.[12] I take the help of a couple of examples to show what might be gained through a distrust in these aggregations.

Heath writes that by the nineteenth century the police had acquired the reputation of exercising indiscriminate violence and that British magistrates and judges, not to mention other colonial officials and the bulk of the Indian public, had been well aware of the violent and predatory nature of the Indian police since the British began, with the introduction of the Cornwallis Code in 1793, to 'usurp and gradually transform pre-colonial systems of criminal justice'. There is a somewhat uncanny resemblance in Heath's language and the language of the various police commission reports in India, in that they speak of a 'system' of precolonial policing and the imperative to stamp out the so-called traditional methods of policing that were said to result in terrorising the population. Yet, as

Kumar's paper shows, there was no 'system' as there were enormous variations in such practices as the kaval practice in the Madras Presidency, in which different villages reported different arrangements with the members of the Maravar caste. In some cases, as Kumar reports, villagers paid *kavalgar* (reputed for their physical prowess) for their security from thieves. In others, villagers paid these 'policemen' fees to be exempted from theft by the kavalgar themselves, and in still others, villagers reported that there was no such practice in their village. It was when these village-level records were aggregated at the higher levels of administration to prepare consolidated reports that a 'system' emerged as a documentary artefact made comparable to other 'systems' such as 'dacoity' and 'thugee' in police commission reports.

Even as regards the Cornwallis Code, which Heath sees as part of the 'terror formation' in the colonies after Achille Mbembe's usage, others have noted a much more fluid situation.[13] DH Kolff, for instance, finds different methods used by British civil servants when having to cope with the dilemmas of administering a code that in no way addressed the day-to-day challenges they found themselves confronted with. For example, in the upper Doab area, Kolff describes raging controversies over issues like the use of police spies and informers, and negotiations with entrenched groups such as the Gujjars, who were in great demand to serve as chowkidars, horsemen and *piyadahs*, as well as being able to hire themselves out in the military labour market in the region.[14] The military labour market was, of course, complex, and members of the Rajput clans could negotiate several positions among the armies of princely states and the East India Company.[15] In some districts in the Upper Doab, the conflicts between the judiciary and police led to the downfall of the district magistrates; in others, the rigidity of the Cornwallis Code was completely ignored, and much more cooperative solutions were found to settle depopulated villages and initiate ambitious programs of public works. The point is not that police violence was not a matter of great concern but a frozen picture of police violence that simply transports concepts like 'violence workers' from the contemporary experience of Brazil to early period of the Company rule does not do justice to the rich archive of not only documents that have now received attention such as revenue records and police orders, but also the records that did not circulate very much. Among these, Kolff identifies the proceedings of the local courts—the nitty-gritty of the colonial dealings with the Indians on the ground which remained mostly untranslated and unread beyond the level of the provincial courts of circuit and appeal.[16] While it is possible to simply aggregate all these findings into the generic notion of 'police violence', the impulse of all three papers here is to pay attention to changes in technique, and to the small tools of knowledge demonstrated in these documents.

As we move to the brief discussion of documents as objects and documentation as method in the next section, I hope that the concept of jurisdiction that I have culled here to bring the three papers within a single framework that is both less broad than that of colonial or police violence but also closer to concerns articulated in various police commission reports, debates in Parliament, petitions and letters submitted to the Board of Directors of the East India Company, as well as many court proceedings, might help to bring the image of law better in focus. The move does not so much circumvent the issue of violence as attend to its modalities so that it does not become a thing-like object with sharp boundaries, but one which is discerned through its traces in the colonial records themselves. Such a move allows some interesting questions to emerge, such as, why is the law applied in some cases but not others; why pay such attention to the quotidian details as who visited the village which we find in the police records even for insignificant villages with small populations; and how should we think of modes of articulation between emergent capitalist forms with their scale and complexity and tribal chieftains with whom legal contracts were being signed? In other words, the attention to jurisdiction opens up a range of issues that move up and down different scales and are particularly helpful for thinking of emergent phenomenon that are not yet settled as routine practices in policing. Even though 'jurisdiction' outside of its role as legal technology might be less explicitly singled out in these chapters, I found it very useful as a lens with which to read the issues of war, violence, surveillance, coercion, and contract in the colonial records. The question of what are documents still remains and I briefly address this question in the next section.

## Documents and Documentality

The study of documents and documentality has emerged as a major field of study in its own right in the last three decades. The three papers help us in understanding the specificities of colonial policing contained in these documents, but also show how the very acts of recording and documenting are knitted into the project of governance itself. For many scholars writing in the Weberian tradition the requirements of documentation in the conduct of government are related to the normativity embodied in the ideas of impersonality, objectivity, and transparency as the basis of legitimacy of bureaucratic authority. In this view the mediation of paper and the inscribing of signatures allows the authority of the sovereign to be present through delegation. However, this very importance placed on the signature also enables forgeries, and other means of usurping authority through simulation, or production of false documents. As I have argued earlier, the forms of illegibility, partial belonging, and disorder that seem to inhabit the margins of the state constitute its necessary condition.[17] But even more decisive for this argument is Bodhisattva Kar's demonstration of the manipulation by the tribal subjects on the North-Eastern Hill areas in relation to the fate of identity documents. Kar gives a telling example from an observation in the Annual Report on Frontier Tribes for 1914–15, on how proofs of identity issued to tribal chiefs in order for them to claim *posa*, or allowances paid to them by the East India Company, could enter a market in certificates (known as *hāth-chithās*, or handwritten notes of sums owed that bore the signature of an official) despite an elaborate system of verification.[18] As he says, 'Set up as proofs of inalienable identities, the *hāth-chithās* entered that exact domain of circulation from which they had been designed to keep off. They could now be bought and sold in the incalculable market of the hills', in addition to being 'stolen and pocketed by the runaway "slaves" on their way to…British territory'.[19] According to Kar, then, 'The markers of fixed identities began to travel in the bazaar of mobile values, rearticulating, contorting and confounding the logic of lineage'.[20] The point is that a document stored in an archive has, by definition, been elsewhere and it is only by tracing how documents were used that we can understand how they became social objects.[21]

Seen in this light, it is a fascinating question to ask what was at stake in the kinds of records that were produced that include not only Police Commission Reports that had weighty consequences for reorganising the police force, but also the kind of quotidian writing done in police stations in small villages, that Kumar demonstrates? If documents are representations of what come to count as facts, Kumar shows that interpreting an entry in the file needs attention to the linguistic apparatus used. For instance, she reproduces the entries made in the police dossier on an unfolding communal conflict in the 1950s:

> Aug. 1954. 'There is no trouble now.'
> Feb. 1955. 'There is no trouble now.'
> Dec. 1955. 'There is nothing important to note.'
> Dec. 1956: 'There is nothing particular important in this village.'

Kumar deciphers the phrases 'no trouble now' or 'nothing important to note' in these sentences to mean that in police vocabulary they encode the success of the police in quelling the disputes between higher caste Hindus and newly converted Muslims from lower castes in favour of the upper castes by the use of violence or threats of preventive arrests against the Muslims. She also notes that piecing together snippets from different police files reveals that the Dalits in Therkupatti and Seethaikurichi (the villages involved in these disputes) had achieved significant milestones in the 1930s and 1940s in challenging the existing caste order. This interpretation of how the threat of violence might have been deployed is very helpful, but given that these files provided the opportunity to show in more detail what the 'police vocabulary' was and how it changed over the years, I hope attention to language can show us what kind of expressions were used in files from different periods, and how the relevance of such facts as myths and customs of people in the area under the jurisdiction of a police station be established. In fact, Kumar's other writings show how broadening what counts as instance of police writing, even when it is excluded from the formal record, might show the relation between different genres of writing (scientific, bureaucratic, literary) in this period.[22] The presence of what Peter Becker and William Clarke have defined as 'little tools of knowledge'—graphs, images, surveys, questionnaires, reports, tables, and dossiers maintained on everyday events—in police documents invites more research into how these tools migrated into police documents, and whether, in turn, these became incorporated in other kinds of textual productions.[23]

Let me suggest two further directions in which it would be helpful to get historians to bring their expertise to bear on the scholarship on documents and documentality. The first is 'police writing' that seems to have no immediate or direct relevance for the daily tasks that policemen performed but was nevertheless produced for use by the police; and the second is the material artefacts such as places of storage, tools of writing, quality of paper and so on that was necessitated by changes in the media through which knowledge was produced and stored.

As an example of the first point, let us take a book composed by Fredrick S Mullaly in 1892, entitled, *Notes on Criminal Classes of the Madras Presidency*.[24] In the Preface, the author, himself a police officer, states that the notes were compiled and published on the suggestion of Colonel Porteous, Inspector General of Police, and the author hoped it would be of some value to police officers as they dealt with members of these 'criminal classes'.[25] Yet the book not only has extensive observations on the modes for stealing, whether members of a particular group use disguises or not, their patterns of marriage, divorce, and deities they worship, but also gives the genealogical charts that establish royal connections between the Maravars and the regional kingdoms. In its narrative construction there is a recognition that the 'lawlessness' of the Maravars could be narrated within a different narrative frame—that of local chieftains who once ruled over the area and took to plunder and pillage as they lost power because their royal patrons were defeated. I do not have the space to elaborate on the question of this mode of narration compared with genealogical charts of succession of chieftains, or the organisation of topics that came under the rubric of 'bureaucratic writing', but it surely troubles the idea that the ontology of a document is contained within its material form.[26] There is a seed of the thought here on the precarity of power, but it remains a puzzle as to how such thoughts were expected to help policemen dealing with everyday violence for whom the notes were supposedly written.

On the second point on material artefacts, I offer just one observation. We get a fleeting glimpse in Kumar's paper on the files being stored in the police station's almirahs. We don't get much of a description of the interior of the police stations which Kumar visited, which in fact can have an important bearing on the archival material being retrieved. The seemingly insignificant things that might be hanging on a wall or stacked on top of an almirah may tell a counter story to the official picture of the police. In my recent book, *Slum Acts*, I describe one such artefact, drawing from Abdul Wahid Shaikh's book, *Begunah Qaidi* and my own work in slum areas in Delhi where the poor have a different relation to police stations than the relation of English-speaking, middle-class citizens. This is simply the *patta*, or the leather belt, hanging in some police stations which is often used to beat up suspects, especially those who are poor and lack the resources to protest against such treatment. The grim humour underlying what circulates as coded language is evident in the inscriptions of Hindi film titles written on these belts that reveal the underlife of law and its complicity with violence. Phrases such as *Andha Kanun* (blind law), or *Meri Awaz Suno* (hear my voice), make the sensory experience of the police station a different kind of event for the poor, or for a terror suspect, than for a well-endowed person with social capital. We do not, however, have much knowledge about the diversity of these practices.

I suspect that it might be very difficult to find traces of these of objects in the archival record. But it is also possible that some traces of the artefacts might emerge if we are as mindful about details that seem insignificant at first sight, such as the table placed in people's courts that separated the judge from the litigants made famous by Foucault, or filing cabinets designed for the vertical storing of files rather than their horizontal placement in almirahs.[27] Again, it is the detail that seems insignificant that can be brought to bear on the varieties of reference that open up.

Perhaps we can let Foucault's table have the last word on the perspective provided through the pursuit of a detail or if these details have disappeared from one genre of writing we might try to trace them in another. Speaking of the arrangement of furniture in a court as undermining the aim of courts to deliver justice, he wrote:

> What is this arrangement? A table, and behind this table, which distances them from the two litigants, the 'third party', that is, the judges. Their position indicates firstly that they are neutral with respect to each litigant, and secondly this implies that their decision is not already arrived at in advance, that it will be made after an aural investigation of the two parties, on the basis of a certain conception of truth and a certain number of ideas concerning what is just and unjust, and thirdly that they have

> the authority to enforce their decision. This is ultimately the meaning of this simple arrangement. Now this idea that there can be people who are neutral in relation to the two parties, that they can make judgments about them on the basis of ideas of justice which have absolute validity, and that their decisions must be acted upon, I believe that all this is far removed from and quite foreign to the very idea of popular justice.

I leave this discussion at this point and turn to another powerful methodological point in Bhavani Raman's paper, *viz.* her use of the 'case' as method to identify and elaborate on her point about the trial of a civilian by a military court. There are some fine studies of the court martials of enlisted officers and sepoys in the military courts of the East India Company that argue that the actual cases of trials showed military law to be more flexible, less prescriptive, and less predictable than what might otherwise appear if one read only the Mutiny Act, or the Articles of War.[28] For instance, officer John Thompson was charged for conduct unbecoming the character of an officer and a gentleman in having embezzled monies entrusted to him for the payment of the men of the 6th Company under his charge in 1831.[29] Such cases were more focused on issues of honour and dishonour, whereas the case of Pallur Emman Nayar, discussed by Raman, was different because he was charged with treason and tried in a military court. As Raman explains, according to British law, a civilian had to have been caught 'in arms' in order to be tried by military court when the local criminal court was *not* sitting, and martial law had been proclaimed. None of this, however, was the case. Not only had martial law not been proclaimed in Malabar when Nayar was caught, but martial law had not yet been enshrined in Madras as a regulation, as it had been in Bengal a few years earlier. Unlike the cases of court-martial discussed by GJ Bryant, or the case of Thompson cited above, the question here was not of honour and dishonour, of behaving in a way that was not gentlemanly, but of sedition against the Company state.[30]

Yet, methodologically, we can see a similarity in that the case shows much greater unpredictability and flexibility because it brings out the moment in the life of the law when it is being applied to a particular individual charged with a crime. Nayar was not punished with the death penalty, as the Governor had hoped, but was banished to a penal colony in Penang. Raman seems somewhat surprised at this outcome, but given the conflicts and tensions between the civil authorities and the army, between the royalist officers and the Company officers in the armed forces and also the bitterness between the civil police and the army over jurisdictional issues, there was probably much more contingency, and uncertainty, than is admitted in teleological or linear accounts of merchants to rulers, narrative plots.[31]

This brings us to the question of war. Raman writes that the issues of jurisdiction raised by the trial of Nayar in a military court without the formal declaration of war was part of the global experimentation with martial law that was beginning to remake the legal definition of war itself. But the rapid ascent from a case to a general theory of war may need a more careful elaboration. Raman speaks of *states* targeting a threat to their sovereignty. Yet, the assumption that the Company State in this period had already taken the form of the nation-state, not to speak of the overlapping sovereignty between the Mughals and the East India Company, requires a larger diet of examples (as Wittgenstein would say implying that examples nourish the description) of the conflicts over jurisdiction since Nayar's case at least hints at the difficulties of assuming that what is inside and what is outside were already settled.[32]

Many theoretical, philosophical, and strategic reflections have been veering toward thinking of war through a *family* of related terms, rather than a rigid definitional structure. There is the thin line of difference between small wars and imperial policing in Charles W Gwynn's *Imperial Policing*, as well as other writings on this period.[33] There are also the kind of reversals of Carl von Clausewitz's famous formulation on war being a continuity of politics by other means, or the proliferation of wars waged by so-called non-state actors in theories of 'new wars'.[34] This literature vastly complicates any settled notion of war and its jurisdiction. Nevertheless, Raman opens up the interesting question of the shifting relation between legal definitions of law and their relation to the history of crime and punishment in India.

I conclude by saying that the chapters in Part I made me rethink seriously how an anthropology of violence might benefit enormously from taking this period of Indian history to ask how the methods of archival research, and the relation between archive and documentation, inform or challenge its own certainties. For this education I received and that I have shared here I am very grateful.

# PART TWO

# Custodial Violence, Law, and the Courts

CHAPTER 4

# JUSTICE IN CUSTODY

## Doctors as Semi-state Actors

*Jinee Lokaneeta*

While the Black Lives Matter movement, since 2013, has drawn attention to the killings of unarmed Black Americans by the police in the United States, it was not until 2020, following the murder of forty-six-year-old George Floyd and twenty-six-year-old Breonna Taylor, that protests erupted not only across the US but globally.[1] That same year, Indian newspapers exposed the horrific custodial deaths of P Jeyaraj, aged sixty-two, and his thirty-two-year-old son, J Bennix, who were tortured to death in Tuticorin jail, Tamil Nadu.[2]

As with the deaths of Floyd and Taylor in the US, the deaths of Jeyaraj and Bennix generated unprecedented outrage and protests in India, despite the fact that custodial torture—often leading to death—is routine in India, and that they died amid strict mobility restrictions imposed by the Indian government during the Covid-19 pandemic.[3] Their death also provoked public debates on India's need for anti-torture legislation, and, for the first time, detailed critiques of Bollywood films that glorify police violence.[4]

But as in the case of the numerous reports published in recent decades by the Law Commission of India and human rights organisations, the critiques focused solely on the role of the police in carrying out and facilitating custodial torture. The role of other actors, such as physicians, in enabling such violence was largely overlooked.[5] Medical doctors must adhere to a code of occupational ethics, the Hippocratic Oath, which obliges them to protect patients. They are also bound by international law which prohibits them from engaging 'actively or passively…in acts which constitute participation in, complicity in, incitement to or attempts to commit torture or other cruel, inhuman or degrading treatment or punishment'. Yet doctors routinely fail to adhere to such directives.[6]

Focusing on the Jeyaraj and Bennix custodial torture and death, this chapter will explore how medical professionals fail in their ethical duty to protect those in police custody in India, particularly during the pretrial phase, in which the detained are particularly vulnerable. It will also dissect the reasons for this, including police pressure and the lack of procedural accountability in regard to their role in the criminal justice process—in addition to considering how doctors can play a more proactive role in ensuring justice for victims of custodial violence.

## The Custodial Deaths of Jeyaraj and Bennix

Jeyaraj and Bennix lived in a small town in Sathankulam, Tamil Nadu, where they owned a shop that sold mobile phones. They were arrested on June 19, 2020, ostensibly for violating pandemic protocols—their shop was open after curfew.[7] Jeyaraj was the first to be arrested at 7:30 p.m., by a group of policemen who included an inspector and a sub-inspector, K Balakrishnan. When Jeyaraj's son, Bennix, went to the Sathankulam police station to find out why his father had been arrested, he saw Balakrishnan beating him.[8] A scuffle ensued between the police and Bennix, and he was arrested. The police thereafter began to torture him—reportedly to 'teach him a lesson on how to behave with police'—and his father, an assault that lasted seven hours.[9]

The torture of the two men included sexual assault. According to the Central Bureau of Investigation (CBI), which took over the case, they were stripped down to their underwear, made to lower themselves onto a wooden table, and their hands and legs were restrained by police officers. They were then 'subjected to...severe beatings with [a] *lathi* [a wooden stick] on [their] buttocks', backs, and other parts of their bodies. Although Jeyaraj informed the police that he was diabetic and had high blood pressure, and would not be able to survive the injuries being inflicted on him, the police continued to torture him until 3:00 a.m.[10] The police then filed a First Information Report (FIR), in which Jeyaraj and Bennix were charged with lockdown violations and for an altercation with the police at Kamarajar Chowk, Sathankulam.[11] The CBI later confirmed that these charges were false.[12]

Article 22 (2) of the Indian Constitution and Section 167 of the Criminal Procedure Code (CrPC) say that an arrested person must be brought before a magistrate within twenty-four hours, a process known as 'first production'. Section 54 of the CrPC requires a medical check-up of the arrestee before this. These provisions are designed to ensure the legality of arrests, diminish the risk of custodial violence, and provide evidence of such violence should it have occurred.

Accordingly, the morning after their ordeal, Jeyaraj and Bennix were taken to the Sathankulam Government Hospital for an examination. The chargesheet in their case noted that the two had severe injuries on their buttocks and backs and blood was oozing from their wounds when they were brought to the hospital. Dr N Vinila, who examined them, filled out a medico-legal certificate that reportedly declared them fit for remand, and recommended their return to police or judicial custody. They were then taken to the local magistrate, who remanded them to a Kovilpatti sub-jail, where individuals in custody, undertrial prisoners, and those sentenced to imprisonment for a month or less, are confined. This was at 2:30 p.m. on June 20.

Upon their arrival, Jeyaraj and Bennix were examined by the Chief Head Warder, Alagarsami, and Warder Sr Marimuthu, who documented their injuries in a 'Proforma for Health Screening of Prisoners on Admission to Jail'. The sub-jail's admission register, signed by the jail superintendent, recorded their names and those of the police officers who accompanied them, PC Muthuraja and PCS Chelladurai, both of whom have been accused of causing their deaths.[13] That the police officers who allegedly tortured Jeyaraj and Bennix were willing to sign a document testifying to their injuries suggests that custodial torture is so routine that they were confident of being able to escape accountability for it.

Two days later, on June 22, the jail doctor, Dr Venkatesh, was called when Bennix reported being in severe pain. The Jail Superintendent found evidence of blood oozing from the buttock wounds of both father and son. After dressing their wounds, the doctor gave them medication and requested follow-up tests the next day. But first Bennix and then Jeyaraj had to be taken to a government hospital in Kovilpatti—in autorickshaws, not ambulances—that evening, Bennix as a result of severe breathing difficulties and Jeyaraj a high fever.

Bennix then underwent an electrocardiogram and was

referred to the Thoothukudi Medical College Hospital for further tests, but he died before he could be taken there. His father died the following morning. According to the CBI, these tragedies were a result of the custodial torture they had been subjected to, which was 'sufficient in the ordinary course of nature to cause their death[s]'.[14] It also recorded that, in failing to identify their injuries before they were presented before a magistrate, Dr Vinila denied father and son the medical treatment that may have saved their lives.[15]

## Medical Professionals and the Rule of Law

To make sense of how the medical checks, designed to protect suspects from custodial violence, failed to do so requires understanding their history. There are two main moments when medical examinations are done in the pretrial phase of an Indian criminal case: before the accused is first brought before a magistrate, and when they are sent to judicial custody. In the first instance, such examinations are a product of the 1996 Supreme Court ruling in *DK Basu* v *State of West Bengal*, a case involving custodial deaths. To help prevent these, the court recommended that arrestees 'should be subjected to [a] medical examination by [a] trained doctor every 48 hours' during custodial detention.[16] From 2009, when the DK Basu guidelines were codified into the CrPC, an accused no longer had to request a medical examination; it was done before the police presented them before a magistrate.[17] Therefore, between 1996 and 2009, doctors got a greater role in protecting the accused from apparent custodial violence.

Where do magistrates, another actor in the pre-trial phase of an Indian criminal case, fit in this process? The role of the magistrate during the 'first production' hearing is to inquire into the reasons for the detention of the accused, to check the arrest memo to ensure that they have not been detained illegally, and to confirm that they have not been subjected to custodial violence. The magistrate is expected not only to examine the accused's medico-legal certificate but ask questions regarding their well-being.

The magistrate then remands the accused into police custody (for up to fifteen days, for the police to carry out further enquiries relevant to the investigation) or judicial custody (for up to sixty or ninety days, depending on the offence). Magistrates thus have an important role, alongside doctors, in protecting the accused from custodial violence, and ensuring their well-being if they are subjected to it. This is true even for those accused of crimes under extraordinary laws such as the 2002 Prevention of Terrorism Act, which undermined the safeguards designed to protect against custodial violence.[18] This Act permitted the police to detain those accused of terrorist offences indefinitely, and even though it was repealed in 2004, there are still suspects incarcerated under it.

Take, for example, the 2006 Mumbai bomb blast case, in which 189 people were killed and over 800 injured in bombings of local trains. These safeguards technically existed at the time, but Abdul Wahid Shaikh, one of those falsely accused of the crime, was detained for nine years and severely tortured. He wrote a book about his experiences (see Shaikh's interview in this volume), recording how magistrates, just like doctors, often fail to perform their legal responsibility of ensuring that those in police custody have not been subjected to violence, with some even enabling it by merely checking, at the first production, that the police have provided the necessary paperwork and not questioning its validity, or even asking the accused about their well-being.[19]

This is what happened to Jeyaraj and Bennix. Jeyaraj's daughter told the CBI that when her father and brother were taken to the court, they were surrounded by police officers, which prevented them from speaking freely about the torture to which they had been subject. The presiding magistrate, moreover, remained on the second floor of the courthouse while they were with the police, and so was unable to assess their well-being.[20]

The experiences of Shaikh, Jeyaraj, and Bennix reveal that magistrates, when it comes to custodial violence, play a merely bureaucratic role—one designed to uphold the appearance of rights for those accused of crimes rather than protecting those rights.[21] For Jeyaraj and Bennix, the due process of law therefore served only to create a paper trail—from a false FIR to a flawed medical certificate, and a magisterial order that remanded them to custody—based purely on bureaucratic formalities.

## The Failure of Medical Professionals to Protect the Accused

The case of Jeyaraj and Bennix illustrates the lengths the Indian police go to present themselves as efficient and complying with the rule of law through meticulously documenting their procedures. It also illustrates how the police use the sinews of bureaucracy to erase the illegal violence they commit, and how doctors and magistrates facilitate this.[22]

Yet the role of doctors as facilitators of police violence has largely been overlooked in India. In the case of Jeyaraj and Bennix, the medico-legal certificate produced by the doctor who examined them failed to mention the serious injuries on their bodies.[23] The witness statements in the chargesheet on their case indicate that they were bleeding so severely due to the torture they had endured that it saturated their clothing. They had to change their *lungis* (loincloths) and shirts several times during custody, including before they were taken to the hospital, during their medical examinations, and before they were taken to the magistrate's court.[24] Relatives and friends brought them dark-coloured clothes to help conceal the extent of their bleeding. Relatives witnessed that Jeyaraj and Bennix were limping, and that their hands were so swollen that they could not eat the food brought for them.[25] Why, then, did Dr Vinila declare them to be fit for remand?

The answer can perhaps be found in a statement made to the CBI by a Sathankulam Government Hospital worker, P Natarajan, who witnessed blood oozing from the buttocks of Jeyaraj and Bennix but said nothing about it to Dr Vinila. This is because, he said, it was routine for the Sathankulam police to bring 'accused persons in such condition to hospital for examination'. Hence it was not considered worth commenting on.[26] According to an enquiry conducted by medical experts into their deaths, Dr Vinila failed to conduct a proper examination of Jeyaraj and Bennix, or to note all of their injuries, and simply passed off some of their serious injuries as 'abrasions'.[27]

Moreover, another witness, a nurse, informed the CBI that when she did tell Dr Vinila that Jeyaraj and Bennix had exhibited very high blood pressure, the doctor recommended medication for both and rechecking their blood pressure. After their third test, their blood pressure had declined.[28] Throughout their medical examination, there was clear evidence that the father and son were seriously injured, but the medical professionals responsible for their care simply managed their symptoms. This suggests that not only were signs of torture the norm for suspects brought to the hospital by the Sathankulam police, but they decided not to treat or raise concerns about it. Instead, they stabilised their condition so that they could be produced before a magistrate and successfully remanded into custody.[29]

What about the medical professionals who note the injuries on the accused during the mandatory inspection before being admitted to jail? Why did they not act upon the evidence of torture of Jeyaraj and Bennix during this stage? According to M Shankar, the Kovilpatti sub-jail superintendent, when Bennix was examined, 'blood stains on both sides of [his] buttocks, [and] swellings in both ankles' and a foot were found, while Jeyaraj had 'blood stains on both sides of [his] buttocks', in addition to high blood pressure.[30]

The Jail Superintendent claimed that when informed by jail officials about these injuries, he asked the accused whether they needed medical treatment, but they told him that they had medication and were not in pain. Like the medical professionals at Sathankulam Government Hospital, the jail officials at Kovilpatti sub-jail treated clear evidence of custodial violence upon inmates as routine, and as not worth raising an alarm about or investigating further. It appears that the National Human Rights Commission's guidelines about the conduct of medical examinations when an accused is admitted to jail—including that they be conducted by medical professionals—were ignored. That Jeyaraj and Bennix were conveyed to a hospital by autorickshaw when they fell seriously ill indicates the cavalier attitude towards the well-being of inmates of Kovilpatti Jail.

When asked by the CBI investigators why Jeyaraj and Bennix were admitted to the sub-jail despite evidence of injuries on their bodies, Jail Superintendent Shankar responded that since the police brought their 'fit for remand' medico-legal certificates, they could be admitted with injuries, provided these were recorded in the jail's admission register.[31] When asked why he did not have them hospitalised on learning of their injuries, Shankar said that 'about fifty per cent' of those brought to the subj-jail had similar injuries. Rather than taking them to hospital, a doctor would visit them 'as and when required'.[32] The treatment meted out to Jeyaraj and Bennix was thus standard procedure.

These exchanges reveal that routine violence renders custodial police torture banal, which leads all those in a position of power over individuals in custody to fail to protect their rights—the medical professionals at the Kovilpatti Government Hospital as much as the magistrates and jail officials. It is unsurprising, then, for demands to be made for doctors to be held accountable for facilitating police torture—especially since there is evidence that some Indian doctors support custodial violence.[33] Doctors, indeed, are also pressured to conform to police accounts of the injuries of detainees. Dr Vinila, for example, initially claimed that the Sathankulam police maintained that father and son had merely 'suffered scratches' as a result of falling 'on the ground'. Later, she said she was 'acting under police pressure when providing the fitness certificate'.[34]

According to the activist and scholar of medical ethics, Amar Jesani, 'normally when doctor-patient interaction takes place, the patient is in fetters and a police person is guarding the detainee'.[35] This suggests that doctors lack independent access to those in police custody, which undermines their ability to make independent assessments of such individuals' state of health, regardless of their attitude towards custodial violence. Also, as the medical inquiry on the case revealed, there is a lack of standard operating procedures in Indian hospitals for responding to evidence of custodial violence.[36] Even the medical examination used to produce medico-legal certificates lacks a standard format through which custodial violence can be adequately documented. Such procedural failures thus place the burden of responding to custodial torture onto individual doctors to address to the best of their abilities.

## Conclusion

Is it possible, then, for medical professionals to play a more independent role in protecting the rights of Indian citizens from custodial violence? Sameena Mulla, in *The Violence of Care*, a fascinating ethnography of the role of forensic nurses in rape cases in Baltimore, Maryland, in the United States, offers some insights into this question. According to Mulla, despite the desire of such nurses to care for rape victims, the institutional context in which they work shapes their professional practice to conform more to the needs of the US legal system than those of their patients.[37] This is because, in their desire to collect evidence to be used at trial, they enact what Mulla terms a 'violence of care' that subjects rape survivors to further violence rather than alleviating their suffering.

'This violence is born not from the intentions of individual forensic nurses who consciously set out to alienate the victim-patient with whom they are working', Mulla explains, 'but rather from the particular institutional, professional, and historical location of forensic sexual assault intervention'.[38] In other words, the forensic needs of the US legal system require nurses to focus their energies on gathering evidence, which leads them to commit unintentional violence towards rape victims in the form of indifference towards them, or disbelief in their stories. What needs to change, Mulla suggests, is that the role of forensic nurses with regard to such victims shifts from being largely that of gathering legal evidence to providing care for them.

In my book *The Truth Machines*, I examine Indian forensic psychologists who, like nurses and clinical psychologists, see themselves as providing therapeutic care to victims of custodial violence when they tend, instead, to play a role in the extraction of confessions from suspects by the police.[39] They try, however, to dissociate themselves from such violence by ensuring, for example, that the police are not present during their enquiries, which indicates that they endeavour to adhere to medical ethics in such cases.[40]

It is the strict ethical guidelines to which doctors are subject that makes it necessary, I would argue, to regard them as being distinct from other actors involved in custodial violence. The World Medical Association, for example, requires that doctors refrain from sharing patients' medical information with the police and remain independent from them in assessing the physical health of patients, in addition to refraining from participating in torture.[41] The United Nations' 'Manual on Effective Investigation and Documentation of Torture and Other Cruel, Inhuman or Degrading Treatment or Punishment', commonly known as the Istanbul Protocol, furthermore, sets out specific guidelines for doctors on how to document and carry out effective medical and legal investigations into allegations of torture and other forms of ill-treatment.[42] The ethical guidelines doctors are required to follow thus oblige them to document any cases of torture that they encounter rather than facilitate them.[43]

In the case of India, human rights groups such as the Commonwealth Human Rights Initiative and the Centre for

Enquiry into Health and Allied Themes have added to such international efforts by issuing guidelines for doctors to follow during medical examinations of suspects in custody (alongside the guidelines for autopsies) on the grounds that 'India does not have guidelines for a standardised medical examination for those detained in police custody or in prison'.[44] These place the burden on doctors to generate forensic evidence on custodial violence in addition to providing medical care, and urge them to recognise the courage of torture victims in 'disclos[ing] details of torture against those in power', particularly against the police.[45] To assist doctors in this, the guidelines include a detailed list of torture techniques, how to identify these, and their potential health consequences.

If these guidelines are formally adopted by the Indian state, this would require doctors to fulfil their ethical responsibilities independent of police pressure by filling out medico-legal forms that explicitly address torture, with a failure to do so implying 'complicity in dealing with torture cases'.[46] While such measures will not solve the problem of custodial violence or provide justice to the family of Jeyaraj and Bennix, they would undoubtedly help to diminish the risks of such deaths—and with it, to challenge the impunity of the Indian police to commit torture and other forms of ill-treatment.

## Chapter 5

# CONFRONTING THE VIOLENCE WITHIN

## Courts, Police Custody, and Criminal Investigations[1]

*Abhinav Sekhri*

The violence meted out at the hands of police officers across India is as cruel as it is banal. Even as the Indian police are becoming more tech-savvy and are using ever-more sophisticated technologies to solve crimes, the heart of the everyday investigative enterprise in police stations in India still involves custodial interrogation to get confessions, often through the use of force—through techniques ranging from beatings that are designed to leave no visible marks on the body to the use of weapons that leave clear traces of their use, which can result in death.[2] While, moreover, the Supreme Court is often regarded as a source of redress against such violence, since it does at times hold the police accountable for it, the Court in fact serves, in many ways, to enable it.[3]

Beginning with an overview of the ways in which Indian law facilitates custodial violence, this chapter will then examine the role of the Supreme Court in regulating police investigations in India, particularly through anticipatory bail (through which bail can be granted to an individual in apprehension of their arrest) and the utilisation of custodial interrogations as an investigatory tool—although as the chapter will demonstrate, rather than undermining their use, the Court instead not only endorses them, but sanctions the use of force to extract confessions. Because the Supreme Court establishes the legal precedents that lower courts in India follow, this serves to ensure that custodial violence remains a cornerstone of the entire Indian policing and judicial systems.

## The Legal Landscape

In December 2023, the three statutes that dominated criminal law in India for nearly 150 years—namely the Indian Penal Code of 1860 (IPC), the Indian Evidence Act of 1872 (IEA), and the Criminal Procedure Code of 1973 (CrPC)—were repealed by Parliament and replaced by the Bharatiya Nyaya Sanhita (BNS), the Bharatiya Sakshya Adhiniyam (BSA), and the Bharatiya Nagarik Suraksha Sanhita (BNSS), respectively, which were enacted on July 1, 2024.[4] Since the new law codes, which largely replicate their predecessors, contain few—albeit key—changes to the scheme of investigating and prosecuting crime in India, this makes it possible to use existing legal precedent both to make sense of how the legal system in India works and how it serves to uphold custodial violence.

An investigation into crime in India most often begins with someone reporting an incident to the police, either orally or in writing, who then record it. This triggers the investigatory process, the purpose of which is to gather evidence that can be used in a trial; it culminates in the filing of a First Information Report (FIR), or 'chargesheet', before a court.[5] This is a dossier which contains the investigating officer's recommendation as to whether a case should be prosecuted (or not), and all the relevant material gathered during an investigation. This recommendation is not binding upon a judge, but in my experience as a lawyer, it is rather uncommon for judges to disagree with the police when they recommend prosecution.[6]

The CrPC details the investigatory powers of the police and the terms of their use, which include, for instance, the power of search and seizure (namely to search for and seize items relevant to an investigation), the power to summon individuals for questioning or to produce materials pertinent to an investigation, and, of course, the power to arrest those suspected of committing an offence.[7] It gives the police, moreover, a wide berth in exercising these powers. For instance, in the case of search and seizure, the CrPC allows the police to dispense with the usual process of obtaining a search warrant from a judge if they deem the search urgent.[8] It also permits the police to arrest anyone suspected of committing a cognisable crime (a crime for which an arrest can be made without a warrant) against whom 'credible information' is received.[9]

These are very broad and subjective powers that can be easily abused—not least since the CrPC does not explicitly require the police to offer reasons for their decision-making during an investigation. In the case of search and seizure, for example, the police are not required to disclose the grounds upon which they regard a search as being so urgent that they must dispense with obtaining a warrant to carry it out.

As opposed to the ability of the police to interfere with property through search and seizure, their ability to interfere with an individual's *person* through arrest is relatively better legally safeguarded. Article 22 of the Indian Constitution, for example, in addition to the CrPC, confers a right upon a person who is arrested to be informed of the grounds of their arrest and to engage lawyers of their choice to defend them. It also imposes a limit of twenty-four hours in which an individual can be held in police custody without being charged with an offence, which can only be extended by a magistrate.[10]

While the Constitution does not enshrine bail as a right, the CrPC classifies offences into two kinds: those in respect of which individuals have a right to bail, and those in which bail is entirely left to the discretion of a court. In addition to the ability to seek bail *after* an arrest, the CrPC also provides for anticipatory bail.[11] Although the key investigative purpose behind an arrest is for the arrested person to be used as a source of evidence, article 20(3) of the Constitution prohibits compelling such a person to be a witness against themselves. This right is somewhat modified, however, by the CrPC, which while it does not permit the police to demand the *active* cooperation of those who are accused of crimes in witnessing against themselves, permits the police to demand their *passive* cooperation by, for instance, using their bodies as a source for clues through obtaining bodily or handwriting samples.[12]

When it comes to active cooperation with investigations, furthermore, the constitutional right against compelled self-incrimination is, arguably, magnified in section 162 of the CrPC, which renders the statements made by *any person* to the police, including confessions, inadmissible as evidence.[13] As Deana Heath also discusses in her chapter in this volume, the protection this prohibition provides against the attempt of the police to extort confessions is, however, undermined by section 27 of the IEA, according to which, if a confession by an individual in police custody leads to the discovery of facts relevant to an investigation, then the part of their confession which led to such a discovery is rendered admissible as evidence.[14]

If, therefore, an accused person, during custodial interrogation, confesses that, 'I killed D using a knife, which I hid in the well behind my house, and I can take you there to recover it' and the police then do this, the IEA makes those parts of their confession that 'relate distinctly' to the discoveries made by the police admissible as evidence which can be used against them in court.[15] Furthermore, if the fact discovered by the police was that a knife was used to commit murder, instead of that a knife was hidden away at a spot known to the accused, entirely different parts of the confession become usable as evidence for the prosecution.

The law thus gives the police an incentive to downplay their knowledge about a case to make it appear as though more facts were discovered through confessions in order to render more parts of them admissible as evidence—and with it, a motive to elicit confessions, if need be by force.

## The Role of the Supreme Court in Regulating Police Investigations

How, then, do Indian courts respond to such custodial violence? To begin to make sense of this, it is important to note that the judiciary regulates the rights and duties which govern the exercise of investigative powers by police officers, since whether the police want to search for property or arrest someone, a magistrate from a local district or *taluka* court—the first-instance, or lowest level of courts in the Indian judicial system—must decide whether such requests are in accordance with Indian law.[16] The decisions of such magistrates thus play an important role in facilitating custodial violence.[17]

But since first-instance courts are necessarily bound by the decisions of the superior courts in India, namely the High Courts and Supreme Court, to understand the role of Indian courts in enabling custodial violence requires examining the role of the Supreme Court in interpreting the legal rules governing both anticipatory bail and investigative questioning, or 'interrogation', as it is commonly known.

## Anticipatory Bail

Beginning in 1949, criminal lawyers in India began to plead that their clients were being targeted by malicious criminal cases filed by powerful and influential opponents, who had the local police in their pockets and used them to engineer arrests. What the lawyers sought was bail *in anticipation* of such an illegal arrest, on the grounds that allowing the person to suffer an arrest in such a case would be a travesty of justice.[18]

Such a form of bail was eventually codified in section 438 of the 1973 CrPC, as a result of legislative acceptance both of the fact that the law was being used for such purposes and that the police undertook illegal arrests even in cases in which there were no allegations of malicious prosecution.[19] Section 438, as a result, did not make it a mandatory requirement for those seeking anticipatory bail to allege malicious motives for their arrest—all that it required was for a claimant to show that they harboured a *reasonable apprehension of arrest* for an offence for which bail was not available as a matter of right.

This was a revolutionary development in Indian law, since while police investigatory procedure involved making an arrest and then seeking custody, during which the arrested person remained either in a police lockup or in jail until a court could be convinced that there were grounds for bail, section

438 undermined the power of the police to arrest and seek custody and thus inverted the power dynamic between the police and those they earmarked as suspects. It also created a scenario in which courts could dominate the investigative process by deciding the necessity and legality of every arrest in which a litigant was resourceful enough to file a plea for anticipatory bail.

As a result, there were, not surprisingly, misgivings about this legal development. The State of Uttar Pradesh, for example, removed the clause from operation within its borders in 1976 (UP Act XVI of 1976), and that same year an amendment was passed in the Rajya Sabha to remove anticipatory bail from the CrPC (although following the dissolution of Parliament after the 1975-1977 Emergency it was never enacted).[20] Aware that liberally granting anticipatory bail neuters the effective investigation of crime by taking away the key investigative tools of arrest and custodial interrogation, India's High Courts also sought to limit the power to grant it. The Punjab and Haryana High Court, for example, issued guidelines in 1978 to the effect that individuals accused of certain classes of offences involving the public interest, such as corruption, national security, and so on, should never be granted anticipatory bail.[21]

Different opinions in the High Courts about how to interpret the law on anticipatory bail set the stage, furthermore, for an intervention by the Supreme Court, which delivered its first verdict on the issue in 1980.[22] It clarified that no classes of crimes could be excluded from the scope of anticipatory bail as the text of the law contained no such restrictions. At the same time, it recognised the serious interference an order of anticipatory bail brought to police investigations and declared that the solution to this was the exercise of judicial discretion, or entrusting courts to balance requests for anticipatory bail with the needs of investigations in determining whether to grant such bail.

In the 1980s, the Indian Parliament, as well as state legislatures, also began to enact laws that denied the right to anticipatory bail for offences such as terrorism and caste-based violence, on the grounds that the interest of the state in such offences was too serious to be left to judicial discretion.[23] Such efforts to limit an individual's right to anticipatory bail reveal that custodial investigations were viewed as being too important for the successful investigation of crime to undermine. In order for courts to grant it, an accused person essentially had to demonstrate that the allegations against them were malicious in nature.[24] But since the state could not be accused of malicious intent when it came to allegations involving offences affecting the public interest, anticipatory bail largely ceased to be granted in such situations, which undermined its initial potential to curb unnecessary arrests and reduce the reliance of the police upon interrogations to conduct investigations.

This was aided by the Supreme Court assertively donning the avatar of public-interest and anti-corruption crusader beginning in the late 1980s, particularly in cases involving politicians.[25] While dealing with such a case in 1998, for example, the Court acknowledged that custodial detention ensured the effective interrogation of suspects, which was of considerable advantage to the police in carrying out their investigations.[26] When it came, moreover, to concerns about the use of 'third degree methods' by the police to extract confessions as a rationale for anticipatory bail, the Court essentially dismissed such reasoning by declaring that it could be 'advanced by all accused in all criminal cases'.[27]

In other words, the fact that any accused person could

request anticipatory bail on the basis that they would be subject to custodial violence nullified *anyone's* right to request bail on such grounds when it came to public interest cases. Although the Supreme Court has occasionally, over the past two decades, sung the praises of anticipatory bail for its emancipatory potential, in cases involving allegations that affect the public interest Indian courts largely heed its wariness of such a form of bail and rarely deprive the police of their prerogative to interrogate an accused by granting it—which essentially accords the police the power to enact custodial violence with impunity.[28]

## Interrogations

Such impunity is the product of a key set of assumptions by Indian courts about the custodial setting, in which interactions between the police and accused occur. In stating that claims about the police using 'third degree methods' during custodial interrogations ought not to be taken seriously, as anyone can make them, the Supreme Court essentially suggested that the majority of custodial interactions are not coercive. This assumption contrasts notably with countries such as the United States where, since the seminal case of *Miranda* v *Arizona,* in 1966, the legal assumption has been that interrogations are essentially coercive and that accused persons have the right not to incriminate themselves in them.[29]

Indeed, just five years before *Miranda,* the Indian Supreme Court passed judgement on a case that could be termed India's 'anti-Miranda', namely *State of Bombay* v *Kathi Kalu Oghad.*[30] The origin of this case can be traced to 1955, to the small district of Gohilwad, in what was then the state of Bombay. In Sessions Case No. 7 of that year, one Kathi Kalu Oghad and an accomplice were charged with murder.[31] A key source of evidence of Oghad's guilt was a chit (a note recording a sum he owed) recovered during the police investigation. To prove that he had written it, while he was in their custody the police made Oghad copy its contents several times, and then sent these copies for forensic handwriting analysis. According to the analysis, Oghad had written the chit. But to prevent this crucial piece of evidence being used against his client, Oghad's lawyer sought to exclude it from his trial by invoking article 20(3) of the Indian Constitution on the ground that such evidence had been obtained through coercion, which violated Oghad's fundamental right against compelled self-incrimination.[32]

The court conducting the trial did not find any clear evidence of compulsion in the form of marks of violence on his body, and nor did Oghad claim that the evidence had been obtained through coercion. But as Oghad had been in police custody for ten days, during which he made the copies, the court considered that 'the element of compulsion was implicit' in such a setting and barred the copies from being used as evidence, since admitting them would be contrary to his right against self-incrimination.[33] Even after excluding this particular evidence, however, the court held that there was enough evidence to convict Oghad and his accomplice of murder and sentenced them to life in prison.[34] Oghad then filed an appeal against his conviction before the Rajkot Bench of the Bombay High Court, which not only affirmed the trial court's observations that the handwriting evidence was constitutionally barred, but found that the remaining evidence was insufficient to establish his guilt.[35]

The Bombay Government challenged this verdict before the Supreme Court in 1957, arguing that the lower courts had wrongly determined that police custody was innately coercive.

An eleven-judge bench on August 4, 1961, determined, in two separate opinions, that the right against self-incrimination had been wrongly interpreted by the lower courts in two crucial respects. Eight judges held that since the main concern with evidence obtained through coercion was its potential unreliability, the right against compelled self-incrimination could not be extended to fingerprints or handwriting samples since these would remain the same no matter what circumstances they were obtained under.[36] Excluding such evidence would also, the judges pronounced, hinder the efficiency of police investigations in 'bringing criminals to justice', which was surely not the intention of the framers of the Indian constitution.[37]

All eleven justices, furthermore, concurred that 'the mere fact of being in police custody' when a person made any statement would not automatically 'lend itself to the inference that the accused was compelled to make the statement'.[38] The simple fact of custody, in other words, did not amount to compulsion. According to the Court, police interrogations could not be conceived of as a form of compulsion, since they took the form of 'mere questioning'.[39] The justices went further, arguing that compulsion could not be conceived of as mental duress, as in an accused being compelled to self-incriminate because of being in a state of fear or anxiety, but had to take the form of a 'physical objective act' akin to duress.[40]

They also placed the onus of proof of evidence having been obtained through such a narrow definition of compulsion on the accused, by arguing that to exclude evidence from a trial necessitated *the accused* demonstrating that they had been compelled to give it, and thus incriminate themselves. Only if the accused could *prove* that they had been compelled to give evidence by the police, in other words, would they be entitled to invoke the constitutional guarantee to exclude it as evidence.[41]

There are a number of disturbing aspects of this judgement. It ignored voluminous evidence as to the nature of custodial interrogations in India, which include both mental and physical duress. A contemporary observer, for example, made clear that because there were no legal limits on the length of time a police interrogation could take, an accused person could be questioned for days until they demonstrated clear 'signs of exhaustion' and confessed to whatever the police wanted them to, or paid bribes to bring an end to such abuse.[42]

Such interrogations were also reliant on 'third degree methods' in order to make suspects confess, all of which left investigations in a state of 'utter bankruptcy'—of being devoid, in other words, of any validity.[43] In short, the kinds of violence experienced by accused individuals in the Indian custodial setting involved various forms of duress, most of which it was impossible for them to prove—particularly when they left no visible bodily marks of violence. Presumably, this is why the Gohilwad Sessions Judge and the Bombay High Court felt that a degree of compulsion was 'implied' when Oghad was asked to give handwriting samples during his ten-day remand in police custody.

To sum up, the fundamental right against compelled self-incrimination in the Indian Constitution offered the Supreme Court a chance, in Oghad's case, to enable the Constitution to challenge the investigatory practices that the post-colonial Indian police had inherited from their colonial predecessors. It elected, instead, to ensure that the Indian judicial system would continue to uphold such practices. It chose, in other words, to undermine the emancipatory potential the Constitution offered to protect Indian citizens from custodial violence at the hands of the police.

## Conclusion

In 2019, in the case of *GS Mani & Anr* v *Union of Indian & Ors*, the Supreme Court entertained petitions seeking an independent inquiry into the deaths of accused persons who had been taken into the custody of police officials in Hyderabad during the course of a sexual offence investigation.[44] The Court then appointed a committee to investigate such deaths, which filed a damning report calling for the prosecution of the police officials concerned in them. The case attracted considerable attention in the Indian press, adding to the existing set of interventions by the Supreme Court in custodial violence cases which paint the Court in a largely favourable light.

But as this chapter has demonstrated, while the Court has, on the one hand, endeavoured to put a stop to custodial violence in India, it has also essentially endorsed such violence as being an invaluable tool for conducting effective police investigations. Since such endorsement has encouraged courts lower down the judicial ladder to do the same, the Indian judicial system thus perpetuates the very brutality that the Supreme Court has become so renowned for ostensibly seeking to stop.

There are few signs, moreover, that such a situation will change, since in July 2023, the Supreme Court sought to re-evaluate the longstanding legal limitation on custodial detention to fifteen days after an arrest by suggesting that such detention may be extended beyond this period on the basis of the purportedly invaluable role of custodial interrogations for the Indian police—a change that has been included in the law that will replace the CrPC.[45] Such a change in the law, rather than putting an end to custodial violence, will therefore accord it even greater impunity.

Tackling police violence, therefore, requires confronting the mundane elements of coercion that are inherent in how police investigations are both conducted and endorsed by the judicial system, not simply by intervening when police violence leads to fatalities. Without confronting the complicity of the Indian judicial system in police violence, in other words, courts will fail in whatever efforts they undertake to make the custodial setting a fairer and less violent one.

CHAPTER 6

# HATE CRIMES AS THE NEW 'LEGITIMATE'

## Anti-CAA Protests and Policing in Aligarh Muslim University and Jamia Millia Islamia, 2019

*Sharib Ali and Ishita Chakrabarty*

In India, police forces have been complicit in communal violence by allowing Hindu mobs, or vigilante gangs, to target Muslims or other minorities and, in some cases, have even joined mobs in carrying out such violence.[1] This chapter will explore one such incident, in which the Indian police targeted Muslim students at Aligarh Muslim University (AMU) and Jamia Millia Islamia (JMI) during protests against the Indian government's enactment of the Citizenship Amendment Act (CAA), which denied Muslim emigrants who had fled religious persecution in Afghanistan, Bangladesh, and Pakistan, in contrast to those from other religious groups, eligibility for Indian citizenship. Drawing upon student testimonies collected as part of three fact-finding reports, this chapter will focus, in particular, on police violence against students on one fateful night—December 15, 2019—which precipitated first a three-month sit-in, largely by Muslim women, at Shaheen Bagh in Delhi, and the larger nationwide anti-CAA movement.[2]

Did the police, we ask, have the right to enter university campuses, as they did at AMU and JMI? Is it legally permissible, furthermore, under the terms of 'reasonable force' and controlling 'law and order', for the police to treat students like enemies and subject them to brutal and targeted violence?[3] How should the various violations the police committed be understood, as well as accounted for? Our aim in asking such questions is to show that the actions of the police on December 15 were intended to subjugate and decapacitate democratic voices through acts that would, at least, legally qualify as 'cruel, inhuman and degrading treatment' but were also anti-Muslim hate crimes.

They cannot be isolated, in other words, from the wider context in which they have taken place since the right-wing Hindu nationalist Bharatiya Janata Party (BJP) came to power in India in 2014, in which Muslims have been rendered, at best, second-class citizens, and at worst as a scourge to be eradicated from the Indian body politic.[4] AMU and JMI have been at the forefront of such assaults on Indian Muslims, as evident in the treatment they have been subjected to by the BJP government, which has sought to eradicate their legal status as 'minority institutions', under which fifty per cent of their places must be reserved for Muslim students.[5]

We aim to demonstrate, in addition, that in the aftermath of the violence on December 15, not only was there no accountability for police violence against Muslim students, but that such violence was inscribed as legitimate by the National Human Rights Commission (NHRC), whose remit is to investigate human rights violations, including when carried out by public servants. While the recommendations of the NHRC have, since its founding in 1993, led to successful criminal prosecutions that have served a beacon of hope for victims of human rights abuses, in failing to protect the rights of minority student protestors, the NHRC not only undermined the human rights of such students, but its decades-long commitment to human rights.[6]

## The Anti-CAA Movement

The 2019 anti-CAA movement was a unique constitutional moment in Indian history; one in which vast numbers of people, regardless of their identity or political orientation, protested to uphold the rights enshrined in the Indian Constitution relating to religion, equality, protection from discrimination, and non-violent resistance.[7] Compared to other recent protest movements, such as, in 2016, the Jat reservation agitation (in which Jats demanded their inclusion in the Other Backward Class, or OBC category, in order to become eligible for affirmative action benefits), and protests by Dalits over attacks against them by right-wing Hindu groups, the anti-CAA protests were also surprisingly peaceful.[8]

As Ranabir Samaddar has put it, they were marked by an 'insurgent constitutionalism', a silent defiance against the unequal status to which Muslims had been consigned in Indian law.[9] This is evident in the form that protests took, namely the blooming of many 'Shaheen Baghs', or sit-ins, across the country. There were also candle-light vigils and human chains, along with the invocation of ideals from anti-caste icons such as BR Ambedkar and Savitribai Phule, and advocates of Hindu-Muslim unity such as Maulana Azad and Mohandas Gandhi. In essence, the protests—in which more than 10 million people came onto India's streets—were therefore a celebration of the democratic spirit of resistance.[10]

However, the response of the Indian state to these peaceful protests was brutal and repressive. Troops were deployed around major sites of protest, and telecom services were suspended in pockets of Delhi, Uttar Pradesh, Karnataka, Assam, and West Bengal, for varying periods of time.[11] District level authorities also imposed section 144 of the Criminal Procedure Code (CrPC), which authorises a magistrate to prohibit the assemblage of four or more people in any given area, to prevent public gatherings. The police used violence, moreover, to suppress anti-CAA protests. At least thirty-one protesters, for example, were killed by the Indian police, and more than 1,100 severely injured. More than 8,000 people were also preventively detained and another 3,000 arrested under different charges related to attempts to murder and riot.[12]

While the anti-CAA protests, furthermore, were not confined to Muslims, Muslims were nonetheless depicted as being solely responsible for them—as being, in other words, a disgruntled minority who resented the CAA's ostensibly noble intention to offer refuge to Hindus and other religious minorities from countries that were predominantly Muslim. This rhetoric also allowed the state to target Muslims as a homogenous community who were opposed to those who 'naturally' belonged in India—namely Hindus.[13] Muslims, as a result, bore the brunt of the police violence, surveillance, intimidation, and criminalisation of anti-CAA protests.[14] Indeed, such policing tactics were deployed in Muslim neighbourhoods in Delhi, Uttar Pradesh, and Assam even before the protests began through preventive policing.[15]

## The AMU and JMI Protests and Police Violence

The most prominent example of this is the surrounding, by the police, of the AMU and JMI campuses before protests really erupted. To make sense of why these campuses were targeted for preventive policing requires understanding their role in the symbolic association between place, national identity, and minorities in the Indian state and its democratic framework.[16] As principal sites of higher education of and by Muslims, the history of the two universities is intricately tied to the Indian independence movement, state-making (and Partition), and the conceptions of plurality and secularism in the Indian constitution.

While AMU's founding in 1875, for example, was rooted in an effort to provide a modern education to Indian Muslims to enable them to meet some of the challenges posed by British colonial rule, it was also a key centre of Muslim political life. JMI, on the other hand, was founded in 1920, during one of the first mass movements against British rule, the 1920-22 Non-Cooperation movement, and it sought to cultivate progressive educational spaces as an essential element of the Indian freedom struggle. Its aim was 'to give meaning and content to freedom once it had been achieved' and 'to resist marginalisation and [assert] the right to belong'.[17] The two universities therefore represented not just an effort to provide world-class education for Indian Muslims, but ideas of both Muslimness and the nation, in particular of the Indian nation as being made up of a plurality of identities (*tehzeeb,* or way of life). Both universities have thus come to represent the lives of the Muslim minority in India.

In recent decades, shifts in the idea of what India is and represents, including about secularism, have also become inscribed onto the two universities. With Muslims being perceived of as threats to the nation, both AMU and JMI have been targeted as breeding grounds for anti-nationals, and their funding restricted, alongside attempts, as already noted, to strip them of their minority status. However, despite this, the two universities are still formidable cultural forces, since they educate almost 40,000 students a year and have a long history of participation in and influence over national politics. It is in this context that the policing of the two universities in regard to the CAA needs to be seen.

## The Tense Build-up to 15 December

The 2019 Citizenship Amendment Bill was cleared by the Union Cabinet for introduction to the Lok Sabha on December 4th. Over the next five days, protests against it began in the Northeast, particularly in Assam, over fears that the CAA could legitimise the presence of what were seen as Bengali 'illegal immigrants'.[18] In AMU and JMI, while groups of fifty to one hundred students had gathered to discuss the bill, no protests had yet taken place. Yet according to students, by December 9th police and paramilitary forces had been stationed outside the AMU university gates, while at JMI the presence of the police in and around the university had visibly increased. Barricades had also been placed around the arterial roads leading to the campus, and the police began conducting stop-and-checks of students and frisking them. At both institutions the police were also visibly carrying arms, while some were also dressed in riot gear.

It was not until December 10th, however, that around 4,000 students participated in a protest march within the AMU campus. When the march reached the university gates, the police asked the students not to leave the campus, a request with which they complied. That night, however, AMU students learned that the Aligarh police had pre-emptively registered a First Information Report, or chargesheet, against twenty-one student leaders and 500 unnamed others for rioting and other offences.[19]

In response, the next day the AMU Students' Union called for a hunger strike to protest against both the Bill and the police action against students. Over the next two days also students boycotted classes and organised community kitchens to distribute food to residents in neighbouring areas who were supporting the students in their protests, and prominent activists such as Yogendra Yadav, Dr Kafeel Khan, Fawaz Shaheen, and Mashkoor Usmani came to address them.[20]

On December 12th, when the Bill became law, more than 10,000 students at AMU organised a march to the District Magistrate's (DM) office to submit a memorandum, to be submitted to the Indian Chief Justice, regarding the illegality and unconstitutionality of the CAA.[21] However, the police stationed outside the campus prevented the students from leaving it, and the Aligarh Superintendent of Police agreed to receive the memorandum on behalf of the DM.

Similar protests took place the next day in JMI, in Delhi, when more than 4,000 students started a march to Parliament. This was stopped outside the university premises, however, by the police, who charged at the students without any warning or provocation, then detained fifty of them overnight. While the students were allowed to leave in the morning, after being warned about participating in future protests, such acts against peacefully protesting students sparked a fresh round of protests, with gate number seven, which opens onto the arterial road connecting the Muslim suburbs of Okhla Jamia to Delhi, becoming a key protest site.[22]

By December 15th, police strength was heightened at JMI in anticipation of two calls for protest—one led by students and the other by locality members. On the evening of that day, when the two protests met and became one large body, the police started violently attacking protesters, who then fled. The police then invaded the campus and continued their attack on students. No intimation was made to the university administration that such an attack would take place, or warning notices issued to students.[23] A similar situation unfolded in AMU a few hours later, after students marched in protest from the library to the main gate after hearing reports of the police violence in JMI.

## The Attack

For over three and half hours, the police entered libraries, reading rooms, mosques, and hostels at JMI and AMU, attacking students with *lathis* (wooden sticks), tear gas, rubber bullets and even live ammunition. They also groped female students and tore off their hijabs, and broke CCTV cameras to erase evidence of the violence they had enacted. Elements of this were captured, however, on students' mobile phones, including the use of live ammunition and attempts to break CCTV cameras.

As a result of this treatment, the attacks left at least 400 students between nineteen and twenty-four years of age, half of whom were women, injured. Sixty-three JMI students were admitted to hospital, twenty with serious injuries. Sixty students were likewise rushed to the hospital from AMU, three with life-threatening injuries–although the police had initially prevented ambulances carrying injured students from leaving the campuses and detained some injured students without providing them with medical aid.

## Verbal Abuse and Humiliation

Student testimonies given to the investigation into police violence at AMU and JMI carried out by the National Human Rights Commission, as well as fact-finding efforts by civil society groups, reveal how physical assaults by police officials were accompanied by the ritual humiliation of students, such as through parading them with their hands up, and calling them names and ridiculing their religious identities. This included labelling students '*jihadis*', '*katuas*' (a derogatory term for circumcised Muslim men), '*aantankwadis*' (terrorists), and '*Jinnah ke pille*' (dog of the founder of Pakistan, Mohammad Ali Jinnah)—and telling them, '*Mulla jao Pakistan*' (meaning Mulla—a common derogatory term used for Muslims—go to Pakistan).

Women wearing head scarves were particularly targeted for abuse, as were Kashmiri students, with policemen shouting abuses such as '*Kashmir chahiye? Hum tumhe azadi denge*' (Want Kashmir? We will give you freedom). Prime Minister Narendra Modi's name was often invoked as part of this ill-treatment, through threats such as '*Bharat mein rehna hai to Modi kehna hai*' (if you want to stay in India, do what Modi says). Such abuse was often accompanied, moreover, by a denigration of Islam. In addition to specifically targeting mosques at JMI and AMU, in which the police desecrated the Koran and beat up imams and congregants, some students were made to chant '*Jai Shri Ram*' (hail Lord Ram)—a Hindu invocation that has come to be widely used to threaten and intimidate Muslims.[24]

## Detention

Over one hundred students were detained overnight without being charged with any offence or told why they were being held, and their relatives were not advised of their detention, in contravention of Supreme Court guidelines for the arrest and detention of individuals.[25] Lawyers and journalists were also denied access to them. The students were made, in addition, to sit on cold floors, without food, water, or medical attention. AMU students also reported that they were beaten throughout the journey from the university to the police station, packed into small trucks and later into small cells, and in one case at least, made to strip before being beaten with leather belts.

That same night, the Delhi Minorities Commission (DMC), a statutory body entrusted with the protection and promotion of minorities in the territory, which has quasi-judicial powers, issued a directive to the police station heads where fifty students had been detained overnight to immediately release them. They were, however, not released until the next day, and after being charged with rioting and arson.[26]

## Police Action and Law

The police were widely denigrated for attacking, abusing, and humiliating students, and for vandalising institutions it was their role to protect.[27] They maintained, however, that they were merely exercising the discretionary powers of arrest and use of force accorded to them by the colonial-era Indian Penal Code, and the CrPC. These still govern policing in India to maintain 'public order' and 'tranquillity', particularly sections 129 and 144 of the CrPC, which give the police wide-ranging powers to disperse 'unlawful assemblies'.[28]

The powers of the police have, however, been checked by regulations and conduct guidelines, as well as by judicial verdicts, including their right to intervene on university campuses.[29] Since universities are 'bastions of academic engagement and precursors to developing the intellectual climate and spirit of free enquiry', as the report of the 1964-66 Education Commission Report put it, the police are bound by a duty of care to them.[30] Although the Indian police have wide powers to arrest without a warrant in areas outside their territorial jurisdiction, they can largely only intervene on a university campus at the request of university authorities or, in the case of criminal investigations, upon prior authorisation by or intimation to university authorities.[31]

In some cases, however, which have been regarded as 'law and order situations' that cannot be protected by the right to 'assemble peacefully and without arms' under article 19 (1) (b) of the Indian Constitution, India's higher courts have directed or allowed the police jurisdiction within universities in relation to 'indiscipline' that hinders administrative operations, such as sit-ins, electoral-related violence by students, and the selling and consumption of drugs.[32] They have also not looked favourably on student protests carried beyond campuses, and even asked university authorities to shoulder the responsibility for such protests.[33]

To separate warranted cases of police intervention on university campuses from those that are unwarranted the courts have, however, sought to clarify what constitutes a 'law and order' problem, and when the violation of a law requires a law-enforcement reaction such as arrests or use of force.[34] These have come to include everything from undermining public tranquillity and orderliness to acts that endanger public safety or national security concerns, including, in the latter case, riots, rebellions and insurrections.[35] The higher courts have also critiqued police interventions on campuses as a 'sordid development' that threatens to undermine the academic atmosphere and autonomy of educational institutions.[36]

According to India's higher courts, therefore, police interventions on university campuses should only be undertaken in exceptional and narrowly understood circumstances—specifically, threats to life and property.[37] To justify their actions on December 15th, police officials therefore claimed that they were responding to 'unlawful assemblies' at AMU and JMI.[38] Relying on section 144 of the CrPC to defend their actions also enabled the police to charge students with executing a common plan for committing an unlawful act, namely protesting, or preventing the execution of a law (in this case, the CAA) and using criminal force.

In reality however, the protests were anything but an 'unlawful' assembly.[39] The right to protest peacefully is not only enshrined in Indian law, it is also a critical element of the exercise of fundamental rights and of a healthy democracy.[40] Since the protests at JMI and AMU were legitimate and the students were unarmed, did not undertake any acts of vandalism, and did not threaten life or property, in acting as they did on December 15 the police thus blatantly disregarded the authority of university officials, their own policies, and the law.

## Cruel, Inhuman and Degrading Treatment and the Lost Discussion on Hate Crimes

Indian courts have limited the use of force by the police to 'dispersing' people who are unlawfully assembled with 'as little[force] as possible', and directed that the police be disciplined or even prosecuted for failing to do so.[41] This includes prosecution for torture, which is how aspects of the violence committed by the police against students at AMU and JNI on December 15th, 2019 could be legally considered. Although India lacks legislation that defines coercive practices by the police as torture, it is a party to the 1966 International Covenant on Civil and Political Rights (ICCPR), which enshrines freedom from cruel, inhuman, or degrading treatment or punishment as a human right and prohibits any exceptions to this, including during emergencies.[42]

Not only have most of the protections enshrined in the ICCPR been incorporated into Indian law, but the Supreme Court has also long upheld the validity of international law in India as long as it does not contravene municipal or domestic law.[43] Since what is considered cruel, inhuman, or degrading treatment can vary according to the nature of the act committed and the age, sex, or state of health of a person, even legally sanctioned use of force by the police could therefore be categorised as such, including as torture (such as, in the events of December 15th, the targeted nature of police violence, the infliction of serious injuries, and the failure to provide medical assistance)—although Indian police officers are rarely prosecuted for this.[44]

In 2017, following the Arab Spring—a series of anti-government protests, uprisings, and rebellions throughout much of the Arab world—and subsequent state repression, the United Nations General Assembly passed a resolution noting that what could be deemed torture encompassed not only cruel, inhuman, or degrading treatment or punishment perpetrated by police forces against those within their custody but outside it as well, especially when used against people who were unarmed or defenceless and when it resulted in grievous injuries and deaths.[45] In other words, such violence could constitute extra-custodial torture.

Other international guidelines on the use of force by the police, in regard to its proportionality relative to the offence, its necessity, and the use of lethal weapons—such as the United Nations' Code of Conduct for Law Enforcement Officials, enacted in 1979, and the 1990 Basic Principles on the Use of Force and Firearms by Law Enforcement Officials—have come to represent what is called customary international law, namely rules and practices so widespread and authoritative that they have been accepted as international norms.[46] It is against these guidelines that the conduct of the police in India should be measured, and which they violated in their treatment of AMU and JNI students on the night of December 15th, 2019.[47]

This exercise of state power on predominantly Muslim university campuses was intended to quell resistance against the CAA. However, as the physical abuse to which students were subject demonstrates, it was also motivated by hatred, prejudice, and contempt.[48] This is evident, furthermore, in the verbal abuse the police subjected students to. It is for such reasons that, we argue, the assault by the Indian police on students at AMU and JMI legally qualifies not only as cruel, inhuman, or degrading treatment but as a hate crime (namely a crime designed to degrade and insult).[49]

While international law on cruel, inhuman, or degrading treatment and punishment technically encompasses hate crimes, it does not single out identity as a motivator in driving the choice of victims or what, exactly, is done to them. Yet hate crimes can be used to proceed legally against states for violations of their obligations to guarantee freedom from cruel, inhuman, or degrading treatment and punishment for their citizens, particularly where the state is complicit in their perpetration.[50]

Indian law does not, however, specifically penalise hate crimes, and only minimally addresses hate speech.[51] In 2018, for example, the Law Commission of India, which carries out research on law and makes recommendations to the government in response to concerns raised by the Supreme and High Courts and the Department of Legal Affairs, proposed the addition of a section to the IPC (153C) prohibiting incitement to hatred. This would penalise the use of '"gravely threatening" words, signs and visible representation' on the grounds of religion, race, caste or community, sex, gender identity, sexual orientation, place of birth, residence, language, disability, or tribe 'within the hearing or sight of a person'. It would make, in addition, the intention of causing fear or alarm or advocating hatred that incites violence punishable by imprisonment for up to two years or a fine of up to Rs. 5,000, or both.[52]

This proposal has yet, however, to become law, and while the onus is on courts to investigate the motives behind acts of violence and sentence accordingly, neither Indian courts nor the National Human Rights Commission have endeavoured to scrutinise, in regard to the events of 15 December, 2019, whether ant-Muslim hatred was institutionalised in the Indian police or what the motivations of the police were in targeting specific student anti-CAA protesters.[53]

What we describe as hate crimes were part, moreover, of a longer process of legal violence against JNI and AMU students who participated in anti-CAA protests. A total of 165 students—the entirety of the student leadership across organising committees, support groups, and individually active students—were named by the police as suspects for offences ranging from rioting and assaulting police officers to attempted murder and terrorism-related crimes, with an additional 2,500 unnamed.[54] This mass charging of students therefore effectively cast the entire student body at both universities as criminal suspects, and rendered them subject to ongoing surveillance and police investigations. Such a situation was exacerbated by the media treatment of AMU and JNI students, since news channels like Aaj Tak portrayed the named students as masterminds of what they labelled the 'student attack' on the police.[55]

The identities of many students were also compromised by the media (although such a situation was exacerbated by the police, who released photos of sixty-nine JNI students under suspicion for rioting and other forms of violence).[56] Since some AMU students who were not on campus during the anti-CAA protests but were known to the university administration for their activism were summoned by the police in regard to the protests, the AMU administration may, furthermore, have divulged their identities to the police. A female student who was called before the AMU administration and advised that she would face adverse consequences if she participated in any further protests was also interrogated twice by the police in her home; the police also carried out an inquiry in her neighbourhood about her political associations and activities. When AMU students, in addition, undertook a protest against their vice-chancellor, Prof Tariq Mansoor, for participating in the continued police harassment of students by the police, they were arrested.[57]

## NHRC: Declaring Police Violence 'Reasonable'

In the immediate aftermath of the events of December 15th, several petitions were filed in courts and with the NHRC, seeking an inquiry into allegations of police violence, specifically into the excessive use of force by the police, including custodial torture, as well as the role of religious discrimination in this and the police denial of medical aid to and detention of students. The Allahabad High court, in response, directed the NHRC to undertake such an inquiry.

Yet despite video footage and testamentary evidence of police violence on the night of the 15th being widely available, the NHRC—whose remit is to protect human rights in India—only cursorily identified some police actions as 'excessive' and 'unprofessional' (namely, damage to vehicles and the caning of students who were not part of the protests). This amounts to individualising the actions of the police rather than viewing them systematically, and trivialising the damage inflicted by them.

The NHRC also characterised the protests as illegal, and essentially blamed the students for the violence enacted by the police.[58] It failed, furthermore, to afford adequate opportunities to students to record their depositions and confined its recommendations to monetary compensation to injured students on 'humanitarian grounds', rather than legal proceedings being taken against the police, and was selective in its application of legal principles to the raised issues.[59] In the case of JMI, for which the evidence regarding police violence was the strongest, it offered a summary judgement without putting student depositions on record or disclosing the evidence it relied upon to draw its conclusions.

In the case of AMU, the NHRC denied entire bodies of evidence. In one incident, for example, which is well substantiated by CCTV footage, empty tear gas shells and medical reports, the police entered a hostel well beyond the site of the protests, broke windowpanes to throw tear gas shells inside, and then dragged out asphyxiated students and beat them. As a result, many students lost consciousness, and several, along with the hostel guard, were grievously hurt. The NHRC, however, found that two asphyxiated students were not the original occupants of the room they were found in, and were therefore 'members of the violent mob' that, it argued, took refuge in the hostel.[60] It also claimed that the forensic report on this incident found that the window was broken from within rather than from outside, and that due to the 'non-availability of material evidence' the charges against the police remained 'neither proved nor disproved'.[61]

The NHRC employed a similar logic in regard to custodial violence against students, by concluding that since the Senior Superintendent of Police, Aligarh, had informed it that CCTV footage of such violence was not available, the allegations could not be verified.[62] Such logic goes against existing NHRC and court practices in regard to the burden of proof for custodial violence which, since evidence such as CCTV footage is rarely available, has shifted to using medical evidence of bodily injuries as constituting sufficient proof. Both the Supreme Court and the NHRC have also, however, recommended that CCTV cameras be installed in all places in which the police and civilians can come into contact, particularly places of custody. The NHRC has, in addition, recommended the installation of CCTVs that can record both audio and visual images, and that footage be preserved for at least eighteen months.[63]

Yet when it came to violence enacted by students, such as their attack of a gate at AMU (for which there was CCTV footage), it carried out a full investigation. The NHRC also focused its attention on the events of December 15th, without placing them in the broader context of what preceded or followed them. In doing so, it essentially reframed the issue it was investigating as one relating to the legitimacy of the protests, instead of the legality of police violence.

The two campuses, according to the NHRC, using rhetoric that undermined the agency of students, had also been infiltrated by outside 'political leaders', and it conflated the student protests with protests in largely Muslim localities near the two universities as constituting one large 'violent' mob and 'unlawful assembly' consisting of 'anti-social lumpen elements'.[64] Since the university administrations could not 'contain' the situation they found themselves in, for the NHRC the police were therefore legally justified in their use of section 144 of the IPC to enter both campuses and bring the situations there under control.[65]

In order to deter future protests, the NHRC also recommended that the police develop 'robust intelligence gathering systems'.[66] In legitimating the actions of the Indian police in regard to the anti-CAA protests at AMU and JMI, the NHRC thus justified what we have argued were hate crimes by the police as being 'well justified and reasonable for restoring law and order'—and in the process set dangerous new legal standards for policing minorities in India.

## Conclusion: Legitimating Discrimination

While the Indian state sought to portray peaceful protesters as violent threats to law and order, in reality its policing of anti-CAA protesters and responses to challenges to this reveal the ways in which India's judicial machinery has been co-opted to legitimise the discrimination against Muslims embodied by the CAA. That resistance to the CAA by Muslims would not be tolerated by the Indian state, however democratic and peaceful, was apparent even prior to the protests, with the surrounding of the AMU and JMI campuses by the police.

In many ways, as James Baldwin has pointed out in another

context, the police in AMU and JMI were an occupying force, who turned what was once a symbol of participation in a democracy, namely peaceful protest, into means of transforming those who belong to the nation—namely Indian Muslims—into 'insurrectionists', anti-nationals, and outsiders, without equal protection under the law.[67] This process of otherisation has a long history in India, but what makes the actions of the police at AMU and JMI in 2019 and their aftermath so disturbing, against two of the most visible symbols of the contribution of Muslims to the Indian nation-state, is that what was once the domain of vigilantism has been legitimated when performed by agents of the state.

Furthermore, rather than being perpetrated against Muslims who are particularly vulnerable, such as migrant workers, small-scale traders, farmers, and displaced communities and refugees, it was now being perpetrated against the Muslim intelligentsia, or those who were perceived as being merely 'culturally' Muslim.[68] The Indian legal system, moreover, instead of affording protection, redress, and accountability for such crimes, chose instead to support the police in robbing the victims of their human rights.[69]

## Further Thoughts

*Vrinda Grover*

As the Indian Government asserted in Parliament prior to the enactment of three new legal codes to replace colonial-era laws on July 1, 2024—the Bharatiya Nagarik Suraksha (Second) Sanhita (BNSS), the Bharatiya Nyaya (Second) Sanhita, and the Bharatiya Sakshya (Second Bill), which as both the introduction of this book and chapter five reveal, amended and replaced, respectively, the 1973 Code of Criminal Procedure, the 1860 Indian Penal Code, and the 1872 Indian Evidence Act—its aim was to decolonise Indian laws with statutes that would serve the function of 'imbibing the Indian soul'.[1]

The hollowness of this claim is, however, unmasked by the statutory silences that the new criminal codes perpetuate. Documentation in the annual reports of the National Human Rights Commission, the judgements of Constitutional courts, fact-finding reports by human rights organisations, and newspaper reports bear testament to the pervasive and endemic nature of the practice of custodial torture by law enforcement personnel.

However, the offence of torture, recognised as a *jus cogens* norm under international law—namely, a category of peremptory norms of general international law which enjoy universal acceptance, are binding on all states, and cannot be violated—is not reflected in the codification of crimes in India's new criminal laws. Moreover, the colonial continuity of these new laws is exemplified by public servants' inheritance of power, privilege, and legal immunity from criminal prosecution, which was formerly accorded to 'servants of the Crown'. While India signed the UN Convention Against Torture (CAT) in 1997, as noted in the introduction to this book, twenty-seven years later it remains one of only nine nation-states worldwide to have failed to ratify it.[2] The Prevention of Torture Bill, introduced in Parliament in 2010, lapsed, furthermore, in 2014, and the recommendation of the 273rd report of the Law Commission of India to enact a distinct law to prevent torture has elicited no legislative action.[3]

The chapters in this section of *Policing and Violence in India* offer further insights into the diverse and complex reasons for the endemic scourge of custodial violence in India, not least why the police have virtual impunity to enact custodial and other forms of violence.

Jinee Lokaneeta probes the role and responsibility of specific actors in the criminal justice system, particularly medical professionals, key functionaries in the Indian criminal justice system at the time of the arrest and detention of the accused. As Lokaneeta notes, confronted with the intractable and entrenched nature of custodial violence, the Supreme Court in 1997 issued what are commonly referred to as the DK Basu Guidelines on arrest and detention, which were integrated into the Criminal Procedure Code in 2008.[4] This charter of the rights of the accused was codified with the aim of ensuring that the discharge of duties by diverse key functionaries at multiple stages of the arrest and detention of accused persons would provide a bulwark against custodial violence.

Through a close study of the 2020 case of the custodial deaths of the father and son duo Jeyaraj and Bennix in Tamil Nadu, Lokaneeta discloses how the medical professionals tasked with protecting them from custodial violence essentially condoned the use of 'third degree' treatment on them by the police, and deemed the injuries they received through this as not worthy of being recorded or redressed. The undeniable dominance of men in uniform, when paired with societal anxieties about crime, thus ensured that the grievous and fatal injuries inflicted by the police on the two men, arrested allegedly for a Covid curfew violation, found no mention in their medical examination report, either at the time of their arrest or during their admission to prison. Thus, the checks and balances envisaged by the law to protect suspects from custodial violence fell by the wayside as medical professionals, acclimatised to bleeding and injured human bodies being routinely produced by the police, aided and abetted custodial murder while forsaking their professional and ethical duties.

In the face of the failure of legal safeguards to protect suspects from custodial torture, Lokaneeta recommends the adoption of guidelines for medico-legal examination in police custody which would require doctors to fill out a detailed questionnaire on their examination of an accused person.[5] But while this may ensure accurate documentation of injuries sustained in custody I fear it will not, on its own, sufficiently challenge police impunity when it comes to custodial torture.

It is now established legal procedure that in cases of extra-judicial killings, post-mortems must be videoed and a copy of the same handed over to the deceased victim's family. Drawing upon this precedent, and the availability of mobile phones, I propose an additional safeguard, namely that the medical examination of the accused be video recorded (with the prior and informed consent of the accused), deposited with the examining magistrate's court, and also handed over to the accused's family or friends. Moreover, as this has serious implications for privacy, strict rules to protect privacy, as well as to access, control, provide safe custody for, and destroy such recordings will have to be formulated.

Abhinav Sekhri's provocative chapter, on the other hand, suggests that we need to inquire into the role of the Supreme Court to understand the persistence of custodial violence in India. Sekhri astutely argues that sanction for torture is embedded in the criminal investigatory processes ordained by law, which in allowing for investigations to be largely structured around extracting evidence from the accused ensures that custodial interrogation remains at the heart of them. He suggests, furthermore, that against the backdrop of rising crime, graft, corruption, housing scams, low conviction rates, and so on, the Supreme Court is reluctant to grant anticipatory bail, as it believes that without custodial interrogation the police would be handicapped and unable to crack their cases. Interestingly, this heightened anxiety has cumulatively weakened rather than sharpened judicial scrutiny of criminal investigatory processes, as is manifest in India's low criminal conviction rates.[6]

Torture, as a number of the chapters in this book demonstrate, weakens the investigative rigour of the Indian police and encourages them to undertake lazy and misguided investigations. I recall, for example, how the Delhi Police Special Cell, while investigating the 2001 terrorist attack on the Indian Parliament, asked an illiterate Kashmiri fruit vendor to translate a crucial telephone conversation attributed to one of the accused conspirators.[7] In the trial the fruit vendor floundered during cross-examination, as he was unable to explain the English words used in the conversation.

The police have no reason or motivation to sharpen their investigating prowess, especially in regard to serious offences, as the gravity of such crimes, as presented by the police, is sufficient to overwhelm courts. In a case Shalini Gera also refers to in her interview in this book, in 2011 Soni Sori, a prominent Adivasi (indigenous or tribal) leader from Chhattisgarh, was arrested in Delhi on charges of supporting the Maoist Naxalite movement in the state, and transit remand—a form of custody that allows the police to move an accused person from the jurisdiction of one state to another—was sought of her by the Chhattisgarh police.[8]

In seeking transit bail for her I argued before the judicial magistrate hearing the case that bail should be granted because Sori had been attempting to expose police atrocities in Chhattisgarh, and that she was therefore at high risk of being subjected to torture. The magistrate, however, rejected her bail plea and Sori was handed over to the custody of the Chhattisgarh police—during which, as confirmed by a medical examination conducted in a different state, she was subjected to severe sexual torture. However, Sori's writ petition to hold the police accountable and responsible for her sexual torture has never been decided by the Supreme Court.

The Court's zeal to lead a crusade against corruption and tackle the spiralling crime rate has led it, furthermore, to dilute the constitutional protection against self-incrimination for those accused of crimes by Articles 20 and 22 of the Indian Constitution.[9] This has, in turn, exacerbated the longstanding problem of custodial coercion in India. It is particularly alarming to note that in the investigation of grave crimes like rape and murder, the police continue to resort to unreliable, unscientific, and unconstitutional investigative methods such as subjecting accused persons to polygraph tests and narcoanalysis, despite the inadmissibility in court of evidence secured in this manner.[10]

The coming into effect of the BNSS has, furthermore, increased the propensity for custodial violence and coercion, as it allows the police to have an accused in their remand for up to fifteen days within a forty- to sixty-day period following their arrest, depending on the type of offence under investigation. The law thus continues to abed custodial violence. Sekhri's argument that the Supreme Court remains reluctant to acknowledge the coercion and compulsion inherent in police custody compels us to question whether pragmatism rather than constitutionalism governs the Court's denial of personal liberty to accused persons.

Sharib Ali and Ishita Chakrabarty unearth more disconcerting realities about the judicial response to police violence in their chapter, through analysing the egregious police assault on students protesting against the Citizenship Amendment Act, on the 15th of December 2019, at Jamia Millia Islamia and Aligarh Muslim University. Moving beyond the illegality and brutality of the police attack, they argue that abuse, humiliation, cruelty, and excessive use of force marks police action against Indian Muslims when they seek to exercise fundamental freedoms, including the freedom of expression and freedom of assembly and association. They suggest, in addition, that this constitutes a hate crime, although Indian law shies away from framing it as such.

Indian law and jurisprudence have undoubtedly failed to recognise institutional bias in the police force against Muslims despite evidence to the contrary. A 2018 report by the Centre for the Study of Developing Societies and Common Cause, based on a survey of twenty-two states, found that roughly sixty-four per cent of Indian Muslims they interviewed were either 'highly' or 'somewhat' fearful of the police.[11] The main reason for this, the report found, was because of their belief that the Indian police discriminate against them, in particular by falsely implicating Muslims for committing offences.

The study concludes by noting that, in addition to physical brutality by the police, Muslims are subjected to institutional discrimination, which is manifested in a number of different ways and is 'motivated by intolerance towards traditionally marginalised groups, religious communities, caste and class background, and gender'.[12] In the case of communal riots, for example, rather than acting 'as a neutral law enforcement agency', the police instead use unnecessary force against Muslims, in addition to subjecting them to preventive arrests, mistreating them at police stations, and mishandling cases regarding them (including the 'reporting of facts and investigation' as well as their 'detection and prosecution').[13] Inflicting such social marginalisation on Muslims, the report notes, 'is likely to have negative consequences and affect social harmony in Indian society'.[14]

Judicial recognition of targeted violence against Muslims by the police as a hate crime in India is rare. However, two judgements of the Delhi High Court, in which I represented the victims, have made a notable advancement in this regard. In the first of these, in October 2018, Justices Dr S Muralidhar and Vinod Goel convicted a platoon of the Uttar Pradesh Provincial Armed Constabulary (PAC) for the abduction of over forty Muslim men in May 1987 and murder of thirty-eight of them, in what is popularly referred to as the Hashimpura case (which Sanjoy Hazarika also refers to in his interview in this book).

For Justice Muralidhar, a particularly troubling aspect of the case was the targeted killing of Muslim men.[15] The accused,

Justice Muralidhar noted, claimed that the prosecution had not proved a motive for such crimes, since as the 'persons allegedly abducted were total strangers, the accused had no grudge or animosity against them', and that, they argued, 'no sane and prudent person much less than members of the disciplined force like the accused/respondents would commit such [a] gruesome crime'.[16] For Muralidhar, however, what such a claim overlooked was 'that all the victims belonged to a minority community' and that they were killed following a riot in which two PAC rifles were taken by the rioters.[17] Since killing thirty-eight men was a disproportionate response to such an offence, he did not accept that 'the motive for the commission' of such a crime was not proved, and held that it was, instead, 'a case of a targeted killing' that revealed an institutional bias against Muslims by 'the law enforcement agents in this case'.[18]

The second case in which police violence against Muslims has been viewed by the Delhi High Court as a hate crime is the one that Lokaneeta and Heath open with in their introduction to this book, involving the death of a young Muslim man, Faizan, as a result of the treatment to which he was subject by the Delhi police in February 2020. In an August 2024 judgement which transferred the investigation of the case from the Delhi Police to the Central Bureau of Investigation, Justice A Bhambhani held that the case presented allegations of the 'gross violation of human rights', since the actions of the police against Faizan, which were 'driven by religious bigotry', amounted to a 'hate-crime'.[19] Bhambhani based his determination on the Supreme Court's 2018 decision in *Tehseen S Poonawalla* v *Union of India & Ors*, in which the Court elucidated the meaning and 'abhorrent nature of hate-crime…in the context of mob-vigilantism and mob-violence'—

which, as Bhambhani noted, could be perpetrated as much by 'persons in uniform' as ordinary citizens.[20]

The chapters in this section thus persuasively illustrate that any meaningful challenge to impunity for police violence and custodial torture requires the accountability of all key actors in the Indian criminal justice system, which in turn necessitates the reorientation of both Indian law and polity.

PART THREE

# Complicating Understandings of Police Violence

## Chapter 7

# PERCEIVING THREATS AND POLICING CONCERNS

## The Annual Conferences of the Director and Inspector Generals of Police in India

*Pooja Satyogi*

National planning for most of India's post-colonial history has been orchestrated through Five-Year plans which focus on an array of issues, such as agricultural development, rural and urban development, industrial growth, and labour and employment. But such planning in regard to the police has been notably absent, perhaps as a result of their association with executive power and colonial violence.[1] Yet developing a police force that meets the needs of a modern democracy is vital for the wellbeing and prosperity of all Indians.[2] This is not to say that there have been no attempts to plan for, or seek to implement, a modern civil police force in India. But as this chapter will demonstrate, through focusing on the Annual Conferences of the Director Generals of Police (DGsP) and Inspector Generals of Police (IGsP) held regularly in India since early 1947, such planning has, at the national level, taken shape through concerns about perceived threats or insecurities to the state and its citizens—concerns which have, moreover, served to legitimise police violence.

Since the proceedings of such conferences remain classified, this chapter will focus upon what the book *Golden Jubilee: DGsP/IGsP Conference Since 1950,* published in 2015 by the Indian Intelligence Bureau (IB) reveals, through fragments of speeches and addresses by serving prime ministers, home ministers, and directors of the Intelligence Bureau, about the 'national security history' of the Indian state and the role of the Indian police in protecting alleged threats to India's security.[3]

## The 1950s: Early Years of India's Planning

According to the *Golden Jubilee*'s preface, the first 'British India Police Conference' was held at Jubbulpore, Central Provinces, on December 29, 1922, and from 1927 the event, held biennially, was renamed the 'Police Officers' Conference', and post-independence, the 'DGsP/IGsP Conference'.[4] The orientation and priorities of police planning in these conferences in the early post-colonial period can be gauged by the address of Sardar Patel, India's first Deputy Prime Minister, to the conference held in January 1950.

For Patel, the context of policing had changed now that India was an independent democracy comprised of Indian citizens rather than colonial subjects. As a result, a 'psychological' shift, he argued, was needed in the Indian police to enable them to gain the trust of the Indian public, which would not be easy given their role in upholding British colonial rule.[5] While this meant that the police were more likely to be critiqued than any other state institution, they needed to remember, he contended, that 'a democratic government cannot function on the basis of a police state. It can only function on the willing consent and co-operation of the people at large'.[6] The cooperation of the public was necessary, moreover, in everything from the 'prevention and detection of crime' to 'dealing with unruly mobs or recalcitrant assemblies of men'.[7] But once the police gained the trust of the people they would, he was sure, 'retain it'.[8]

But in addition to lauding the Indian police for their service in the partition of India into two separate nation-states in 1947, Patel also warned them not to become complacent in the face of new threats to India's integrity, or what he called 'subversive movements', such as that posed by the Communist Party of India (CPI).[9] What was needed, Patel contended, was a 'complete annihilation' of what he termed such 'subversive forces', for which the police would need to measure up in terms of their 'cleverness, tactical manoeuvrability and secretive methods'.[10] While at the international level it was Mao Tse-tung's establishment of a communist government in China, in 1949, that worried Patel, within India he was concerned about a railway strike, which the CPI launched on 9 May 1949 in the hope of beginning a country-wide working class insurrection.[11]. Lacking support from the railway workers, the strike did not go ahead as planned. However, it, did lead to the arrest of some CPI members.

For Patel, these activities were a sign that the CPI posed a threat to India's security.[12] Such views were emblematic of perceptions in the post-colonial Indian state that leftist politics threatened to undermine the goals of Indian planning, particularly its focus on India's industrial sector.[13] Protecting Indian industries and domestic capital from any kind of leftist politics, from labour unionisation to protests and strikes—and urging the police to see these as subversive—was, then, intimately linked to planning priorities. Policing thus emerged, in the 1950s, as part of the assemblage of legislative and bureaucratic institutions tasked with legitimising Nehruvian industrial policy.[14]

In contrast, the concerns of Prime Minister Jawaharlal Nehru, in his 1954 address to the delegates of the DGsP/IGsP conference, focused not on the security threat posed by political groups in India but on the conduct of the police when faced with a hostile crowd against which they were likely to be outnumbered. The context for such concerns arose from his experience at the historic gurudwara Fatehgarh Sahib (a Sikh temple), in the Patiala District of Punjab, on December 27th, 1953. Following the first elections in independent India, the Indian National Congress had come to power in every government apart from the state then known as Patiala and East Punjab States Union (PEPSU), in which the Akali party formed a government, in 1952, headed by Chief Minister Gian Singh Rarewala.

To secure control of PEPSU, the Congress dismissed the Akali government and imposed a tool inherited from the British, namely Governor's rule, or central control, over it. Nehru went to Fatehgarh Sahib, a place of considerable importance to Sikhs, to give a propitiatory speech to a largely Akali congregation, but despite a large police presence, the crowd turned against him, and he was forced to leave without speaking.[15] The police then attacked the congregation, with the crowd, in turn, attacking the police. The aftermath of this incident, known as the Fatehgarh conspiracy case, resulted in seven people each being sentenced to seven years imprisonment for their role in the events of that day.[16]

Patel's and Nehru's addresses thus reveal the emergence of concerns about both the security of the Indian state, for which policing was responsible, and the security of citizens, which the police could potentially violate. Particularly for Nehru, the management of a *new* Indian crowd, one that was protesting against its own politicians—indeed, its own prime minister—as opposed to a colonial government, would need to be rethought. BN Mullik, the Director of the IB in 1954 and chairman of the DGsP/IGsP conference, held that, rather than 'taking a "firm line"', the police should study such situations and take action that would prevent, rather than exacerbate, the generation of 'bitterness, rancour and violence' among the Indian public.[17]

Not only did the police therefore need to re-think their relationship with the Indian public, but this relationship had to be re-imagined in terms of how the public now related both to its own political leaders and to democracy. For Mullik, the recourse to violence by the police in dealing with the Indian public in incidents such as that at Fatehgarh was, therefore, simply a form of mismanagement that could be overcome with better training and insight, rather than being inherent to the institutional framework and culture of the police.

## The 1960s: The Rising Tide of Communalism

Such understandings of police violence changed little in the following years. The 1960s were a troubled decade for independent India, since it witnessed three prime ministers, two wars (the 1962 Sino-Indian war and the Indo-Pakistan war of 1965), as well as the conservative Swatantra Party's political challenge to the governing Indian National Congress and Congress electoral losses in eastern and western India. It also saw the 'Liberation Struggle', or anti-communist movement in Kerala (1958-59), against EMS Namboodiripad's elected government, the peasant revolts in West Bengal in 1967 (known as the Naxalbari uprising), the widespread participation of students in political movements, a renewed Punjabi Suba movement (namely, the demand for a Punjabi-speaking state), in addition to food shortages and the state nationalisation of banks.[18] Addresses at the DGsP/IGsP conferences during this decade, consequently, gestured towards the difficulties these challenges posed to national integration in India, as well as security and stability, with ethno-religious nationalism, caste, and the protection of minorities as registers through which such concerns were articulated.

The issue of minorities was one that particularly troubled Nehru, who remained India's prime minister until his death in 1964, and who was critical of both exclusivist or separatist nationalism, on the one hand, and the police, on the other, for failing to protect minorities from it. In the 1962 DGsP/IGsP conference, for example, Nehru lamented that what Indians referred to as Indian nationalism was in fact exclusivist ethno-nationalism, namely 'Hindu nationalism… Muslim nationalism or Sikh nationalism'.[19] This, according to him, was 'nationalism…of a particular community'.[20]

The context for this speech was a Hindu-Muslim riot that took place between February 4-9, 1961, in Jabalpur, Madhya Pradesh, in response to which the police committed atrocities against Muslims.[21] In his address, Nehru expressed concern both about the violence perpetrated by the police and that they blamed Muslims for causing the riot. To blame Muslims, for Nehru, was 'arrant nonsense', since just because 'people stand…and shout "*Allah-ho-Akbar*"' this should not automatically be interpreted as a form of aggression; it could also, he claimed, be 'a sign of fear'. For Nehru, therefore, not only was 'the first duty of the police force' to protect India's minorities, but Muslims should not always be assumed to be the guilty party in such conflicts.[22]

Since the 1960s was a decade of considerable communal violence in India, with the police often being held responsible for failing to take appropriate preventive action to put a stop to it, Nehru's critical distance from dominant conceptions of the causes of communal violence and his reminder to the Indian police that it was their duty to protect Muslims is noteworthy.[23] Nehru was, moreover, not alone in expressing such concerns. In the 1970 DGsP/IGsP conference, for example, ML Hooja, the Director of the IB and the chairman of the conference, blamed 'the hardening of the attitude of both Hindu and Muslim communal parties' for heightening 'communal tension in the country', and for fuelling communal riots. This, in turn, had generated a 'lack of confidence in the [Indian] administration' among Muslims and other minority groups, which then encouraged them to 'make their own arrangements to protect themselves'—which further enflamed communal tensions.[24]

That same year, KC Pant, the Home Minister, urged the Indian police 'to keep a strict watch on the activities of communal organisations', act 'promptly, effectively and firmly to put down communal disturbances', and play 'an active role in promoting the cause of secularism'.[25] For Pant, it was thus important to 'fight against communalism' in order to safeguard what he viewed as the 'weaker sections of... society'.[26] Yet Nehru, Hooja, and Pant had little to say about police violence—not least since, when it came to those on the receiving end of it, such as students or peasants, such violence upheld both the state's security interests and its interest in capitalist economic development.[27]

## The 1970s: Executive Authoritarianism, Populist Development, and the Language of Propaganda

The addresses of the DGsP/IGsP conferences of the 1970s must be read considering the growing political resistance, in this decade, to Prime Minister Indira Gandhi from both the far-right and far-left, which culminated in the president of India, Fakhruddin Ali Ahmed, declaring a state of emergency on June 25th, 1975. For the almost two years that the Emergency lasted (until March 21, 1977), India's democratic institutions were suspended and Indira Gandhi governed India by decree. Elections were cancelled, civil liberties suspended, political opponents imprisoned, and the press censored. I will therefore focus, in this decade, on two moments, in the 1975 and 1978 conferences, that demonstrate the ways in which the Indian executive sought to mobilise the police to respond to the particular activities it interpreted as threats to India's security.

The 1975 DGsP/IGsP conference was held on March 21st and 22nd, just three months before the Emergency was declared. In her address to the conference, Indira Gandhi raised concerns about a major railway strike in 1974, the assassination of the Railway Minister, Lalit Narayan Mishra on January 2nd, 1975, and an attempted bomb attack on the Chief Justice of India, AN Ray, on March 20th, 1975—both of whom were her intimate political allies. It was therefore incumbent on the Indian police, for Gandhi, to contain what she saw as the 'the cult of violence' and 'propaganda and intimidation' against the Congress.[28] According to the Prime Minister, it was thus vital that the police be politicised to protect not just the state, but the interests of a particular political party, namely the Indian National Congress.

It was this politicisation of the police, however, that

Indira Gandhi's successor, Morarji Desai, sought to challenge in the 1978 DGsP/IGsP conference.[29] For Desai, who had been a political prisoner during the Emergency and witnessed first-hand the nature of police power in this period, a 'total reorientation of the attitude of the police towards people' was needed.[30] This entailed earning 'the respect of the people not by instilling fear but through being alert and courteous'.[31]

In a much more direct reference to police violence, he also queried 'what right any policeman had to liquidate even dacoits', because governing according to the rule of law was central to the functioning of a democratic society. While he maintained that the police should 'be firm', they should nonetheless 'behave properly' and not obey 'wrong orders even if someone above them were to ask them to do so', since 'authority should never degenerate into authoritarianism'.[32] But as was the case in previous decades, rather than directly critiquing the systemic nature of police violence, Desai reduced such violence to a few bad apples who 'liquidated' dacoits (although he did critique the police for following 'improper orders').[33] He ultimately did little, therefore, to challenge either the politicisation of the Indian police under Indira Gandhi or its institutionalised violence.

## The 1980s: A Growing Crisis of Governance

The end of the 1970s marked the exhaustion of Indian state planning on industrialisation.[34] Moreover, with the collapse of the Janata Government in 1979, a coalition that had been cobbled together in response to the Emergency but struggled to govern in the absence of a clear economic or political ideology, it was clear that no party was yet in a position to seriously challenge the domination of the Indian National

Congress in Indian politics.[35] As a result, the Congress, with Indira Gandhi back at the helm as prime minister, returned to power in 1980—and rather than industrialisation carried out under the aegis of the state, what the Congress now sought was corporate-led industrialisation.[36] In the growing intimacy between the state and private capital that thus emerged, protests against either capital or the state became conceptualised, as the DGsP/IGsP conferences in the 1980s reveal, as 'agitations'.[37]

At the 1980 conference, therefore, for Indira Gandhi, 'agitations'—conceptualised as an attempt to undermine the Indian government's legitimacy through extra-constitutional action—posed critical challenges.[38] The purported agitators were a wide-ranging group, including farmers, left-wing extremists, students and youth groups, gurus and their ashrams (like Ananda Marga, which fostered right wing-extremism), and secessionist and insurgent groups.[39] The rendering of citizens' protests as both undermining the legitimacy of the Indian government and as extra-constitutional cemented ideas that had begun to emerge in the DGsP/IGsP conferences in the 1950s, namely that Indian citizens were the chief threat to the security of the Indian state and that it was the duty of the police to protect the state from such a threat—which, in turn, served to legitimate some forms of police violence.

So, too, did the evolution of new security fears related to regionalism, linguism, and secession, in addition to ongoing anxieties about casteism and communalism in regions such as Assam, West Bengal, Andhra Pradesh, Punjab, Jammu and Kashmir, Manipur, Tripura, and Nagaland.[40] Such concerns led to the evolution of specialised forms of policing, such as new counter-insurgency and anti-terrorist forces, along with exceptional measures such as the denial of bail to those accused of anti-state offences and increases in the period that they could be held in detention.[41]

As the *Golden Jubilee* reveals, however, at times the police themselves pushed back against the proliferation of their growing extraordinary powers. At the 1985 and 1987 DGsP/IGsP conferences, for example, the director generals of police of Bihar, Maharashtra, and Madhya Pradesh critiqued the use of the police to address issues that were a product not of law and order problems but developmental needs, combined with rampant corruption in state bureaucracies.[42] Such critiques were not far removed from academic analyses of Indian political economy during this period, which emphasised that the centralising tendencies of the Indian state were responsible for the growing crisis of governance in the country.[43]

As in previous decades, the DGsP/IGsP conferences in the 1980s, however, reveal little critical reflection on the nature of police violence. Examples of this were evident at the 1980 conference in regard to two separate incidents. In the first incident, which took place at Baghpat, Uttar Pradesh on June 18th, 1980, the police killed three people, gang raped a woman, and paraded her naked.[44] The second was actually a series of incidents in 1979 and 1980 in Bhagalpur, Bihar, in which the police blinded thirty-one under-trial prisoners and convicted criminals by pouring acid into their eyes.[45] The only concern raised about such violence was, however, that it was emblematic of the insufficiency of police training—not, in other words, of wider issues regarding sexual violence and the use of torture by the Indian police.[46] As a result, the suggested solutions to it, such as employing more women in the Indian police to increase the security of women, which was proposed at the 1981 conference, were woefully inadequate. They also served, yet again, to envision police violence as exceptional, namely as a series of isolated incidents, rather than as endemic to India's system of policing.[47]

## The 1990s: Human Rights Violations and Efforts to Protect the State from Criticism

The 1990s is notable for a number of reasons, including the liberalisation of the Indian economy (through a series of policy changes designed to open it up to the world and make it more market-oriented and consumption-driven), the demolition of the historic Babri Masjid mosque in Ayodhya by activists belonging to the right-wing Vishva Hindu Parishad and allied organisations, and the implementation of the findings of the 1979 Mandal Commission, or the Socially and Educationally Backward Classes Commission (which advocated reserving twenty-seven per cent of jobs in the central government and public sector for castes that were deemed to be educationally or socially 'backward').[48]

The effects of these developments are apparent in the DGsP/IGsP conferences in this decade. When it came to the demolition of the Babri Masjid, for example, the main concern for Prime Minister PV Narasimha Rao at the 1993 conference was not the demolition itself, or the riots and other violence that followed it, but the need to rescue the police from the charge of being complicit in such events—or, as he put it, of attempts to malign the Indian police 'by painting them in a communal colour'.[49] The Congress was therefore clearly no longer, as it had under Nehru, seeking police protection for minorities in India.

Rao's desire to protect the Indian state from criticism, rather than deal with pressing communal or security issues, is evident, furthermore, in his discussion of a new concern at DGsP/IGsP conferences, namely human rights.[50] Again, however, his aim was not to protect human rights but to defend the Indian state from critique by international NGOs like Amnesty International and Asia Watch which, he claimed, were 'unleashing' campaigns and 'orchestrating propaganda about human rights violations in India' and thus needed to be properly 'countered'.[51]

Such rhetoric demonstrates a shift in the concerns raised at DGsP/IGsP conferences from internal to external threats, particularly on the purported role of 'outsiders', most notably Pakistanis, in threatening India's security (by sponsoring 'mercenaries' whose aim was to target the 'Hindu community'); militancy itself, furthermore, was being defined as 'religious and fundamentalist-inspired militancy'.[52] Such discourse increased after the Kargil War between India and Pakistan in 1999, which had been triggered by the infiltration of Pakistani troops into the Indian side of the Line of Control separating the two countries.[53] At the 1999 conference, for example, the Director of the IB noted that India had witnessed in Kargil 'an unrivalled form of religious extremism to subserve [the] politico-religious interests of a religion transcending… national ideological interests and geographical boundaries'.[54] In other words, for the IB director, Kargil was a manifestation of a wider global quest among Muslims to advance their religious interests.

Concerns with *hawala*, an informal method of transferring money without any physical money actually changing hands, were also raised in DGsP/IGsP conferences in the 1990s (and beyond), for its role in international crime and terrorist movements.[55] Solutions proposed to deal with these problems, at the 1998 conference, included the issue of photo identity cards and permits in border areas; legislation to check the proliferation of madrassas (Muslim religious schools) and mosques, as well as to curb religious conversion by fraud, inducement or threat; attempts to check illegal migration; the exchange of information on security concerns between various agencies; and the strengthening of the Foreign Contribution Regulation Act to check the use of foreign funds received by NGOs.[56]

Similar views were held, however, by national security systems all over the world in the aftermath of the terrorist attacks carried out by Al-Qaeda (a pan-Islamist militant organisation) against the United States on September 11th, 2001, as was the identification of terrorism with Islam.[57] India's policing and security concerns had become, in other words, global. Yet as the DGsP/IGsP conferences demonstrate, this was simply the culmination of a long history of scepticism about the value of human rights when these were perceived to be opposed to the security—and hence policing—needs of the Indian state.

## The 2000s: Global Terrorism and Civil Society as a Threat to the Nation

By the 2000s, the security concerns of the Indian government, this time under the United Progressive Alliance (UPA), an alliance of the Congress and left-leaning political parties that came to power in 2004, remained focused on combatting global terrorism.[58] But a new anxiety also emerged, which an official at the 2004 DGsP/IGsP conference referred to as the 'increasing mobility of left wing extremism' as a result of the formation of the Communist Part of India (Maoist) on September 21, 2004 (a product of the merger of the Communist Party of India (Marxist-Leninist) People's War with the Maoist Communist Centre of India).[59] In 2005, the Prime Minister, Manmohan Singh, insisted that such Maoists, also known as Naxalites, were the single largest threat to India's security.[60]

It was the UPA government's identification of Naxalism as the biggest threat to India's security that laid the groundwork for the proliferation of the concept of the 'urban Naxal', or urban working-class Maoist, in response to the Communist Part of India (Maoist)'s aim to mobilise the urban working classes—which served, once again, to highlight the supposed danger that *all* of India's citizens, both rural and urban, posed to India's security.[61] Anyone who opposed the Indian state, whether 'religious minorities, Dalits, journalists, or human rights defenders…thus needed to be rigorously policed'.[62] For the Indian state, therefore, what mattered when it came to police violence was not the ways in which the police abused their power—but, instead, the need to ensure that the police were empowered to enact violence to protect the security interests of the state, however these were conceptualised. Such developments reveal that, as Rhys Machold has argued, homeland security, which is 'domestically oriented yet transnational in nature', is in a constant state of fabrication.[63]

## Conclusion

As this chapter has demonstrated, the DGsP/IGsP conferences offer important insights into how not just the police, but the *policed* have been imagined in post-colonial India. But they also reveal the ways in which the police, as well as the Indian government, police themselves. In January 2023, for example, *The Hindu* carried a news report contending that a research paper documenting the Chinese military's incursion into Indian territory, which was authored by a senior police official, had been briefly made publicly available on the 2023 DGsP/IGsP conference website before being withdrawn.[64] *The Indian Express* later reported that papers written by police officials on the rise of right-wing extremism had also been removed from the DGP/IGP conference website.[65] The implication of such acts of silencing, when it comes to police violence, is that the Indian state cannot allow any contradictory or conflicting voices when it comes to conceptualisations of the threats to India's security, and of the right of the police to use whatever methods are necessary to combat them.

Chapter 8

# DISTRUSTED FORCE

## The Police in India's Counterinsurgency in Kashmir

*Ather Zia*

On August 5, 2019, India's governing Hindu right-wing Bharatiya Janata Party (BJP) removed the quasi-autonomy that Indian-occupied Jammu and Kashmir was accorded by section 370 of the Indian Constitution, which it did—in a move of questionable legality—without consulting the Kashmiri legislature (although this has, notably, been suspended since November, 2018).[1] Jammu and Kashmir was also bifurcated into two separate union territories, namely Jammu, and Kashmir and Ladakh. Both are directly administered by the Indian government through two appointed officials, with laws pertaining to domicile, security, and resources in Kashmir enacted through executive orders.[2] While the Indian government has claimed that its aim in taking such actions in regard to the Muslim-majority province was to fully integrate Kashmir into the Indian union, legal experts deemed it an 'unconstitutional deed accomplished by deceitful means'.[3]

In the months that followed, the Indian government laid

siege to Kashmir by deploying thousands of additional troops there, on top of the half million already present, imposing a severe lockdown, including a complete communications blackout, putting Kashmiri politicians (including two former chief ministers of the state, Omar Abdullah and Mehbooba Mufti) and civil society leaders (including human rights activists, lawyers, journalists and others) in preventive custody or under house arrest, detaining thousands of civilians (not least an estimated 13,000 boys), and committing innumerable human rights abuses.[4] For the NGO Genocide Watch, such developments were so concerning that it issued a genocide alert.[5] They were greeted by the Hindu majoritarian voter base of the BJP, however, as well as by much of the Indian media, with euphoria.[6]

In such an operation, the 100,000-strong Jammu and Kashmir Police (JKP) should have played a pivotal role. Instead, they were disarmed and effectively sidelined.[7] Days before the revocation of section 370, which they received no prior warning about, their firearms were taken away and they were transformed, as one JKP officer put it, into 'clerks and helpers…for soldiers'.[8] Sweeping powers for security-related matters in the region were, furthermore, transferred from the JKP to an advisor from New Delhi, while the internal security of Srinagar International Airport was taken from the JKP and handed over to the Central Industrial Security Force—on the purported grounds, in part, of the 'performance deficit' of its top officers.[9] Although the JKP has been increasingly militarised with new technology, weaponry, and gadgets since 2019, it remains subservient to the Indian military apparatus in Kashmir. The Indian government has also taken over the budget of the JKP, which further undermines its authority.[10]

But why was this the case, and what does all this reveal

about the nature of the relationship between the JKP and the Indian state? Since most of the members of the JKP are Kashmiri Muslims, what does it reveal, furthermore, about the relationship between Kashmiris and the Indian state? To begin to answer such questions requires understanding that members of the JKP serve the Indian state as what Gowhar Fazili has termed 'occupied subjects', namely by simultaneously collaborating with and resisting it—a process I will term *strategic complicity*, which is a necessity for many in a region with limited employment prospects.[11] In the context of the siege of Kashmir, however, they had now become, for both Kashmiris and the Indian state, what I will refer to as *distrusted* subjects. This is because, as this chapter will demonstrate, although the coercive nature of the Indian government's longstanding occupation of Kashmir weaponised the JKP against their own community by 'making a Kashmiri fight another Kashmiri', the complicated subjectivity of the JKP means they are unable to gain the trust of either the Indian state or their fellow Kashmiris.[12]

## The Kashmir Question

The origins of the situation in Kashmir can be traced to the partition of India into two separate nation-states, India and Pakistan, in 1947, during which almost 600 semi-autonomous princely states were given the choice of which state to join. As the Hindu head of a state that was sandwiched between both countries and had a population that was largely Muslim, the Maharaja of Kashmir, Hari Singh, wanted his state to remain independent. He was forced, however, to sign an Instrument of Accession to join the Indian union in order to secure military support to fend off an invasion by armed tribesman from the

Northwest Frontier Province of Pakistan, although the United Nations deemed this a temporary measure until a plebiscite was held giving Kashmiris a say in their future.[13]

Following the Indo-Pakistani War of 1947-48 that then ensued, two-thirds of the state, including the valley of Kashmir and the provinces of Jammu and Ladakh, remained under Indian control, with a third under the control of Pakistan. Since the various plebiscite proposals arbitrated by the United Nations failed to win India's approval, Jammu and Kashmir remained a part of India, albeit—thanks to section 370—a semi-autonomous one. As a result, Kashmiris retained territorial sovereignty, a separate constitution, and a separate flag. The Indian government, however, thereafter set about chipping away at such rights through a process of undermining democracy in the province and through what has been termed *occupational constitutionalism*, namely the enactment of legal statues that undermined Kashmir's autonomy and that 'became sedimented through the work of the [Indian law] courts across time'.[14]

Dissatisfaction in Kashmir with such a state of affairs crystallised when a disputed election, in 1987, served as a catalyst for an insurgency against the Indian state, aided by support from Pakistan.[15] In response, in the early 1990s India implemented two emergency counterinsurgency laws: The 1991 Armed Forces (Special Powers) Act 1958 (AFSPA), and the 1992 Jammu and Kashmir Disturbed Areas Act (JKDA), which empower soldiers to arrest, without a warrant, any person who has committed, or is believed to be about to commit, a criminal offence, and to use such force as they deem necessary to effect the arrest, including the power to shoot to kill; they are also accorded legal immunity for any acts committed during the course of their duties.[16]

Such Acts therefore enable human rights violations such as custodial and arbitrary killings, torture, enforced disappearances, rapes, and cruel, inhuman and degrading treatment.[17] In fact, since the implementation of the AFSPA and JKDA, more than 70,000 people have been killed in Kashmir, over eight thousand disappeared, and in excess of sixty thousand subjected to custodial torture.[18] No security force personnel have, however, been tried for such crimes.[19]

Since the Indian army is now free to occupy any land in Kashmir that it designates as 'strategic' (whereas before the revocation of Kashmir's semi-autonomy it had to seek permission to do so from the local administration), what exacerbates such impunity is the sheer number of armed personnel in the region, which equates to roughly one soldier for every eight Kashmiris, giving Kashmir the highest soldier-to-civilian ratio in the world.[20] Kashmir is thus marked by a dense military presence, including checkpoints, barbed wire, bunkers, military convoys, trucks, armoured vehicles, garrisons, and bases. If the area that is militarised in Kashmir was to be aggregated, it would be, at 385.8 square miles, the size of Dallas, Texas.[21]

As a result, it is not only militants who are affected by the Indian government's occupation of Kashmir—civilians, too, live in a state of siege, in which they are at risk of losing their lives, livelihoods, or homes. Take, for example, one of the means through which Indian forces target militants. Instead of apprehending what are generally ill-trained, ill-armed, and often juvenile fighters, Indian forces kill them or burn them in their hideouts, which are often private homes.[22] They bar homeowners, however, from calling fire tenders or putting such fires out themselves. In one district alone, 105 homes were destroyed due to such actions between 2015 and 2018, with forty-eight in Kashmir as a whole in the first half of 2020.[23] As a result, even during the Covid-19 lockdown, many families were left homeless and without shelter.[24]

## The Indian Government's Distrust of the JKP

How, then, does the JKP feature in this difficult history? It has had, to begin with, a complicated relationship with the Indian state. Since members of the JKP have an intimate connection with the population they police, they have served as an important source of counterinsurgency intelligence.[25] They have, nonetheless, always been treated with, at best, condescension by the Indian state, not least by the Indian army, because they are regarded as a second-rate police force that is less competent than Indian forces in maintaining law and order in Kashmir, and at worst with suspicion, because many members of the JKP have, since the beginning of the insurgency in 1989, defected to become militants.[26] This has led to outbreaks of violence by soldiers against JKP members. In 2017, for example, Indian troops assaulted Kashmiri police inside their own police station.[27] The root of the problem, according to a member of the JKP, is that the military 'do not trust us' or 'show any respect' because 'we belong here to Kashmir'.[28]

In 1993 the JKP also mutinied. The origin of the mutiny was the murder of a Kashmiri policeman, who the JKP alleged had been tortured by the Indian army.[29] Kashmiris, in response, protested in large numbers outside the headquarters of the United Nations Military Observer Group in India and Pakistan (UNMOGIP), in the capital city of Kashmir, Srinagar, demanding the right to self-determination.[30] Members of the JKP, brandishing service weapons, also marched to the

UNMOGIP office, and handed over a memorandum seeking global intervention to end what they argued was Indian state terrorism against Kashmiris.[31] Over the following week JKP members staged daily anti-army protests, during which they chanted '*Aadhi roti khayenge, Kashmir ko azad karvayenge*' ('we may starve but we will free Kashmir').[32] The rebels then barricaded themselves in the police control room in Srinagar and took key Indian officials as hostages. After they refused to surrender, a military operation was launched against them, and they were disarmed.

Such incidents threatened to turn the hostility between Indian troops and the JKP into an open and bloody conflict, not least in light of widespread suspicions that the JKP were giving tacit support to Kashmiri militants by helping them in various ways, including by supplying them with arms.[33] While only some members of the JKP, based in Srinagar, mutinied, such an act revealed the extent to which JKP members saw the Kashmir insurgency as legitimate and the Indian army as a brutal occupier.[34] As a result, the Indian government began a crackdown on dissidents in the ranks of the JKP by firing seventy-nine police officers and suspending 110 others who were accused of fomenting the mutiny. The JKP police union, in response, called for a daylong general strike to protest against what it called the 'harassment and victimisation' of law enforcement personnel, although it took no further action.[35]

To ensure the loyalty of the JKP the Indian government also, however, started incentivising its members through awards, gifts, commendations, and out-of-turn promotions. It began, furthermore, to expand the JKP, to which desperate job seekers began flocking.[36] While in 1989 the JKP had roughly 18,000 employees, by the end of the decade it was one of the largest employers in Kashmir, and today, as I have already noted, it has over 100,000 officers.[37] Since the population of Kashmir was approximately six million in the early 1980s and is now approximately 13.6 million, this means that the population of Kashmir has doubled over the last four decades but its police force has increased five-fold.[38] Such expansion has been driven, in part, by the fact that employment in the police generates loyalty to the Indian state, which is why the JKP police advertised for new recruits soon after Kashmir was stripped of its semi-autonomy.[39]

In 1994 the Indian government also began recruiting for a counter-insurgency Special Task Force (STF), later rebranded Special Operations Group (SOG), which worked in tandem with various militia groups, such as the notorious Ikhwan.[40] Culled from former militants, double agents, and thugs who had vendettas or were seeking monetary gain and power, the group was infamous for enacting torture, as well as extra-judicial and custodial killings of both combatants and non-combatants. Although the SOG was disbanded in 2003, it was absorbed into the JKP, which according to critics was to give counterinsurgency operations in Kashmir a more Kashmiri face and to help mitigate the brutality associated with the SOG.[41]

However, it helped to change both the nature and perception of the JKP. So, too, did outfits like Village Defence Committees (VDCs), which like the Ikhwan were founded in the mid-1990s and which consist of both members of the JKP and armed civilians from Kashmir's minority Hindu community, and which are notorious for enacting violence against Kashmiri Muslims.[42] In 2022 the VDCs were re-branded Village Defence Guards and armed with high-tech weapons, which has heightened hostilities in Kashmir between Hindus and Muslims. So have the innumerable discriminatory policies implemented and acts undertaken by the Indian government following the removal of Kashmir's semi-autonomy—which, despite the distrust with which it has been viewed, the JKP has played a key role in implementing.[43]

## Distrust of the JKP Among Kashmiris

It is not only the Indian government, however, which has long distrusted the JKP—so, too, have Kashmiri Muslims, for whom the JKP are *gaddars*, or traitors. Considering their role in counterinsurgency operations in Kashmir, and in implementing divisive and anti-Muslim policies, this should come as little surprise. They have, as a result, been targeted by Kashmiri militants, who have killed approximately 1,700 police personnel since 1989, many while off-duty, including 508 personal security officers (PSOs) deployed in protecting pro-India civil society leaders and politicians.[44]

Yet JKP members are also enmeshed in the Kashmiri resistance movement through their kith and kin. In 2022, for example, a member of the JKP whose son—an engineer turned militant—had previously been killed in counterinsurgency operations was himself murdered by militants.[45] Such complex subjectivities mean that members of the JKP are distrusted by both their own community and the Indian state. In an incident in 2017, for example, JKP officer Ayub Pandith was brutally murdered by a mob after being caught spying during a religious celebration.[46]

As a result of the danger their jobs place them in, JKP members often refrain from divulging what they do for a living to outsiders, and conceal their identities through, for example, changing into their uniforms at their police stations and removing them before they head home (while some JKP personnel in Srinagar stay in a designated and garrisoned locality called Police Colony, since such accommodation is both limited and dependent on hierarchy and rank, most personnel have to live elsewhere).[47] Some also refrain from returning home at predictable times and carry fake identity cards—although in passing as ordinary civilians they run the risk of harassment by Indian soldiers.[48] They are, furthermore, rarely posted to their own neighbourhoods to help keep them from being identified as JKP officers.

Militants are aware, however, that members of the JKP seek to keep a low profile. In 2018, for example, the Hizbul Mujahideen (HM) responded to JKP harassment and arrest of family members by exposing the identities of many of its low-ranking police personnel online, and demanded that such personnel quit their jobs and post videos online of their resignations.[49] About two dozen Special Police Officers (SPOs) did so—although the Indian government tried to prevent such postings going viral and declared that they were propaganda.[50]

## The JKP and Military Humanism

How, then, has the JKP sought to overcome the distrust with which its members are viewed by both the Indian state and Kashmiri population? One key way in which it has tried to juggle doing such a seemingly impossible task is through playing a role in the Indian military's project of military humanism in Kashmir. Though seemingly an oxymoronic term, military humanism, which entails military engagement with civil projects related to healthcare, education, sports, and infrastructure building, has become a key component of global counterinsurgency tactics.[51]

But rather than being altruistic in intent, namely to genuinely improve peoples' wellbeing, such engagement is instead a means of changing perceptions of the state in the eyes of insurgent populations, in particular of the army as munificent as opposed to an occupying force—through, in other words, 'winning hearts and minds'.[52] In the case of Kashmir, the Indian army has, since 1997, undertaken a project of military humanism known as Operation *Sadhbhavana* (Goodwill) in an effort to merge the army with the civil administration.[53]

The Indian army, however, is not alone in such initiatives, since the JKP has, for the past two decades, undertaken a parallel program called the Civic Action Program (CAP). According to the JKP, the CAP is a 'bridge between the Security forces and the local people'.[54] The aim of the program is to win the hearts and minds of Kashmiris, especially Kashmiri youth, to draw them away from anti-India politics and to reframe resistance to the Indian state as deviance and misguidedness. The focus of the programme is what the JKP calls 'deradicalisation', which includes the mentoring and counselling, through sports, educational activities, and entertainment, of those who it designates as misguided youth. Such activities include cricket matches, cycle races, skiing courses, and talent shows, among other events.[55] To change the nature of the relationship between the police and people from antagonism to camaraderie, the JKP also arranges sports matches between civilian teams and the police.[56] However, those who refuse to partake in CAP activities are penalised and harassed by the JKP—which, rather than winning hearts and minds, drives some youth, ironically, into militancy.[57]

## Conclusion

While the JKP have become increasingly oppressive in the course of trying to shed their history of rebelliousness in order to prove their loyalty to the Indian nation-state, they are symbolic of a coercive and oppressive occupation that weaponises Kashmiris against each other.[58] In addition, despite their strategic complicity with the Indian state they remain 'distrusted' subjects. As right-wing commentator Anand Ranganathan recently observed, in regard to the future of Kashmir, were Jammu and Kashmir to be made a state again, with its own government, its police would 'go back to old system' and run with the hare and hunt with the hound—in other words, they would cease to be loyal to the Indian state.[59] As occupied subjects, in other words, for the JKP the quest to gain the trust of either the Indian state or Kashmiris is impossible.

CHAPTER 9

# POLICING AND INTIMACY

## Narratives from Terrorism Trials in Delhi

*Mayur Suresh*

In 2008, when I first began doing ethnographic research of terrorism trials in Delhi's *Tis Hazari* criminal courts, I was confronted with confusing issues involving the police. As someone who comes from a broadly human rights background, I was conditioned to see the police force as an inherently violent institution, and one that oppressed human freedoms. As this book demonstrates, such a belief is not unfounded. In the case of terrorism trials, many people accused of terrorist crimes told me they had been kidnapped by the police and held in illegal custody for days, if not weeks on end. Others informed me that they had been brutally tortured by the police, or subject to various forms of humiliation and psychological torture. I was also aware that, when it comes to terrorism charges, the Indian police target people based on their religious identity or ideological bent, and the overwhelming majority of terrorism trials end in acquittal—either because evidence is weak or has been fabricated.[1] When I first encountered the police in courtrooms, I therefore felt, to put it bluntly, as if they were the enemy, not the terror-accused.

The law and mainstream public opinion, however, as well as some legal scholarship, regards people accused of terrorist crimes as the 'enemies of mankind'.[2] This sentiment exists in Indian courtrooms as well. I was once asked by a court clerk, for example, why I was so interested in terror trials. Something about her tone gave me the sense that she believed that the trials were a waste of time. I said that I was interested in how different people in courtrooms—including herself—experienced and understood these trials, and if there was a difference between how they understood terror trials versus other types of criminal trials. The clerk replied that in her opinion, 'There should be no trial. *Ek ke bad ek, phaansi dena chahiye* [The terrorists should be hung, one after another]'. I was unprepared for the ferocity of this sentiment. When I then asked her if she thought people accused of terrorist crimes ought to be afforded the rights of due process, her response was that 'All of that is fine, but they are only for people who respect our society and country'.[3]

According to such thinking, enmity ought to be the framing motif of the relationship between the police and the public on one side, and the purported terrorists on the other. Yet when I saw terror-accused and police together in courtrooms, it was not a mutual hatred that characterised their relationship. The attitude of such suspects towards police officers was, to begin with, one of trepidation, particularly following their arrest. Terror-accused often told me of how they had faced violence at the hands of certain police officials, such as by being held in illegal detention and beaten, and some even referred to this violence as being serious enough to constitute torture. They also said that they had heard that some police officers were more violent than others or had been advised by other terror-accused of which police officers to avoid, and which ones were *sharif*, or decent and gentle.

But over time, a sort of camaraderie developed between terror-accused and the police. Suspects would sometimes joke with police officials, and suspects' family members would approach such officials as if they were respected guests. While initially their positions as police and suspect framed their relationship hierarchically, with the police dominant and the suspects subordinate, this began to change as their relationship developed.

As anthropologist and policing scholar Beatrice Jauregui (who is also interviewed in this volume) notes, 'one of the insights ethnography of police produces is an understanding that [the] relationships and acts [of the police] may not be reduced to purely instrumental or coercive exchanges, nor to simple patron-client interactions between powerful state representatives and hapless citizens, nor to dominance and violent oppression writ large'.[4] In other words, the relationship between the police and those who come into their orbit, particularly criminal suspects, cannot be understood simply as one of repression.

In my search to find a word or phrase to describe the ambivalent relationship that I witnessed between the police and terror-accused, I settled on the term 'custodial intimacy'.[5] Through this concept, I try to capture the idea that a close relationship grows between the police and terror-accused despite the fact that they are brought together in a milieu in which police violence and stories about police violence are endemic—which would seemingly mitigate against such a relationship developing.

In framing this relationship through the idea of intimacy, I do not mean that it can be framed exclusively through an idea like care. While I did witness how police and terror-accused could express care for one another, in using the idea of intimacy I mean to signal togetherness, since unexpected relationships emerge because police and terror-accused spend so much time together. I am not suggesting, however, that violence is not inherent in such a relationship—but that there is a form of intimacy that is an integral aspect of violence, because being violent to another person involves getting close to them, and knowing their body and what causes them pain.[6]

Through the concept of custodial intimacy, I also want to reveal how relationships between the police and terror-accused are marked by uncertainty. We might assume, for example, that the better we know someone, the better we understand their personality, motivations, and predilections, as well as our place in their life. But when it comes to custodial intimacy, familiarity between the police and terror-accused breeds not clarity but opacity, because in a relationship marked both by acts of care and acts of violence, the more time terror-accused spend with police officers and the friendlier they get with them the more uncertainty they feel about such a bond. They thus experience what anthropologist Michael Taussig calls a space of 'epistemic murk', in which the boundaries between reality and fantasy are blurred.[7]

This chapter will examine these ideas of intimacy through my own relationship with a police official who I will call Bhandari.[8] An officer with the Special Cell, which is the unit of the Delhi Police that investigates terrorist offences, he was the investigating officer in several terrorism cases I was following and a rising star in his unit when I first encountered him during my fieldwork fifteen years ago. In this period, I met with him at least once a week. While I was an observer rather than a terror-accused, I want to examine the relationship I had with Bhandari to give a sense of what the 'custodial intimacy' I am describing might look like.

## Bhandari

Bhandari's role, during my encounters with him, was to serve as the connection between the Special Cell and criminal court—to make sure, in particular, that a prosecutor was briefed about cases against terror suspects. He would often wait outside the court after hearings, where he would join defence lawyers for a cigarette. He was garrulous and loved holding court, during which he would gossip about other lawyers, talk about cases and laugh about what he viewed as the ineptitude of other police agencies. I always felt, however, a bit awkward at these post-hearing conversations as I don't smoke, my spoken Hindi is stilted, and I was uncomfortable with the competitive machismo that often characterised them.

At times, however, I felt that Bhandari took me under his wing. He sometimes made an effort, for example, to explain to me what was going on in court and said that he wanted to tell me what real police work was like so that I could write about it more accurately. He would also often complain to me that the problems with the investigative and judicial processes in India, as he saw them, such as judicial delays and inefficiencies, were 'because this is the system the British left us', and that most of his work involved filling out paperwork. 'This memo, that memo', he would say, 'they make us go crazy with paperwork'. It was such confidences that established the basis of a relationship between us.

One of the first times I met Bhandari was after a hearing against two alleged Maoists. Bhandari oversaw the case, in which the police accused the two defendants of being members of a banned communist organisation and of participating in attacks on Indian paramilitary forces. During the hearings, defence lawyers, and occasionally even the judge, made fun of the prosecutor for the flimsy nature of the evidence of the prosecution's case. After one such hearing, some of the defence lawyers continued to tease Bhandari during their post-hearing smoking session. He became defensive and made allusions to what he saw as the necessity for the police to fabricate evidence. '*Dekho ji* [look sir]', he began, and went on:

> We know the evidence has no strength. But we all know [one of the suspects] is a Maoist. He is a Naxal.[9] You know it, I know it. If someone took my land to build a dam or my fields to dig a mine, *main bhi bandhook uthaoonga* [even I would pick up a gun]. Why not? If I was also dying of hunger like those people, I would also fight. I would also become a Maoist. But how do I bring evidence that he is a Maoist? It's not like they have a central office with records. So, we have to bring whatever we can. This is what we have. What can we do? *Yehi hamara dhanda hai* [This itself is our work]. *Dekho* [see], at the end of it we know what will happen. They will be acquitted. They would have spent seven, eight years in prison but will come out. We wanted them in jail, you wanted them out. *Uske baad, aap bhi khush, hum bhi khush* [after that, we are happy, you are happy].

In making such an argument, Bhandari sought to demonstrate that he could put himself in the place of another person, in this case, someone who becomes a Maoist due to being displaced and hungry. But he was also, simultaneously, asking the defence lawyers to put themselves in his position. Through demonstrating an intimacy and even empathy with the defendant, he was inviting the lawyers to demonstrate the same intimacy and empathy with him.

Other ways in which Bhandari sought to invoke intimacy were, however, more troubling. Two men, who I will call Anwar and Saleem, were accused of being members of a

Kashmiri terrorist organisation. On one of their court dates, while we waited for their case to be called, I was seated at the back of the courtroom behind Anwar, while Saleem was a couple of rows ahead of us. Bhandari came in and asked the constable who was sitting next to Anwar to move aside and sat down next to him. Bhandari and Anwar then engaged in a quiet yet animated conversation for some time before the case was called. While there was some laughter and smiles on both sides, I thought Bhandari was trying to convince Anwar to do something for him. This is because he used a variety of cajoling hand gestures, like putting his hand on Anwar's back and taking Anwar's hand in his own, which Anwar responded to by shaking his head to say 'no' and occasionally letting out a silent, incredulous laugh.

After the hearing was over, I asked Bhandari if he knew Anwar well. Bhandari said that he had known him since he first arrested him. Since I was curious about his conversation with Anwar, I asked him what it was about. Bhandari, with a wink, told me that 'I was telling him that his wife came to me asking for his release. I told him that I told her that if she did some work for me, I would let him off'. Did the wink, I wondered, constitute a threat? Was he intimating to Anwar, for example, that he would help to mitigate the charges against him in exchange for sexual favours from his wife, or that he would rape her? Or was he threatening Anwar—perhaps to uphold false evidence in his case—or trying to scare me, for some reason? Were these potential threats, moreover, serious, or was this his idea of a joke? I had clearly felt friendly enough with Bhandari to ask him about this, but his response made me question whether I had misunderstood the terms of our relationship and left me in doubt about how to characterise it.

Soon after this incident, I googled Bhandari's name. One

website revealed that Bhandari had won a gallantry medal for killing an alleged terrorist in a shoot-out, while a legal database disclosed that he was found to have fabricated evidence in a case and that, in other cases, the courts had held that his version of events was not credible. I also found a High Court case that he had filed against the Delhi government for denying him a promotion. Among his grounds for promotion, he noted his involvement in an 'encounter', or an extra-judicial killing; he said he had 'gunned down a dreaded terrorist' in one case and had 'shot dead a gangster' in another.[10] These discoveries gave me cause for concern. Here was a police officer, who treated me largely with warmth and helped me with my fieldwork, admitting to killing people.

## Intimacy, Menace and Fear

Such discoveries added to my sense of disquiet and uncertainty about Bhandari and my relationship with him, feelings that were exacerbated by another case he was involved in, which I was following. In the late 2000's, several men were arrested for causing explosions in different parts of Delhi. Due to a variety of factors, the police only filed official charges against the defendants roughly two years after they were first arrested.[11] After charges are filed, section 207 of the 1973 Code of Criminal Procedure gives defendants a right to see documents pertaining to their case which will be used as evidence against them during their trial. This is designed to ensure that the defence is familiar with, and is in a position to challenge, the validity of such evidence.

Given the fact that the chargesheet consisted of several volumes of files, each one containing hundreds of pages, the process of making sure the defence lawyers had access to all the evidence in this case took several weeks. During this time, the defence lawyer made a list of documents that were missing from the copy of the chargesheet that he had been given, and asked Bhandari for these.[12] Bhandari and the prosecutor attended the hearings before the trial magistrate during this period. The lawyers for the defence rarely came to these, as they were cursory and nothing much relevant to the case happened in them. On one such occasion, I asked Bhandari, before the case was called, if he thought anything of note would happen that day. 'What will happen? Nothing will happen today', he replied.

After the case was called, however, Bhandari sprang a surprise. He had brought a supplementary chargesheet to file before the magistrate which, the prosecutor for the case informed the magistrate, contained a CD of the 'electronic evidence obtained in this case'. The magistrate was clearly annoyed by this, as she was keen to move the case on, and the supplementary chargesheet would only delay matters further. The prosecutor explained that this was recently discovered evidence, which was why there was a delay in filing it. The magistrate then asked the prosecutor if copies would be given to the defence lawyers, to which the prosecutor replied 'no', on the grounds that if released to the general public it would 'disestablish communal harmony'.

Thinking, perhaps, that I was a defence lawyer, the magistrate then turned to me to ask if I had any objection to not being given a copy of the CD. Since I was caught completely off guard, and stood in stunned silence, the magistrate dictated an order which allowed the prosecution to file the supplementary chargesheet containing the CD and permitted the defence lawyers to only inspect the CD on court premises. In effect, this meant that the defence would have no ability to assess the contents of the CD.

Feeling a rising panic as the hearing concluded, I attempted to interrupt the magistrate to tell her that I was not a lawyer in the case. However, I caught the eye of Bhandari, who signalled for me to keep quiet. As soon as the hearings were over, I rushed to Bhandari to ask him what was in the CD and to look at the documents which were filed along with it, so that I could tell the defence lawyers about their contents. Perhaps sensing my panic, he sought to make light of the situation by replying, 'You know that nothing in law is final. Don't worry, nothing will happen'. Since I persisted, he relented by permitting me to take a quick look at the supplementary chargesheet. My head started reeling as I discovered that the CD contained a number of extremely important and potentially incriminating files, including data ostensibly downloaded from the suspects' mobile phones. Most alarmingly, the CD seemingly also contained CCTV recordings of one of the defendants leaving an area in which an explosion had taken place. This was the evidence, the police would claim, that proved the suspects' guilt.

When I called the defence lawyer—who I will call Azad—and told him what had happened, he told me not to worry. I was, however, wracked by anger and guilt. Why had Bhandari not told me what would happen that day? Why did he not intervene to tell the judge that I was not a defence lawyer? But then why, I wondered, did I expect him to help me at all? And why had I kept silent, instead of preventing what was a clear injustice? Although I used my rudimentary legal skills to help Azad find a way to get a copy of the CD, I was haunted by the fact that my silence had led to this situation, since I imagined that my inability to speak up in the courtroom would result in the defendant being sentenced to death.

That night, I had a nightmare in which I was on the road in

front of Azad's office, where I encountered a smiling Bhandari. He told me, in a sinister way, that he had a special surprise for me and, with his hand on my back, he guided me up the stairs to the office. As I walked up the stairs, however, I noticed that the floor was coated with something sticky and viscous, and when I pushed the door of Azad's office open, I saw one of the defendants lying on a desk with blood pouring out of a slit on his neck, on to the floor and down the staircase. Bhandari was then in front of me, smiling, and inviting me into the office. Bhandari, I realised when I awoke, was no longer merely a casual acquaintance, who I had largely enjoyed interacting with. He was now also a source of menace and fear.

## Conclusion

Several months later, in October (soon after the defence lawyer, Azad, was eventually able to get a copy of the CD), my housemate and I decided to go for a run in Lodhi Gardens, which is a few streets away from the Lodhi Road police station, which also houses the Special Cell. Some terror-accused had told me that they had been beaten at the Lodhi Road police station, although most said that they were generally beaten elsewhere by Special Cell officers before being brought there. During the course of our run, I saw a man whom I recognised, Kirpal Singh, a police officer who I often saw with Bhandari, along with a woman and two children.

When I stopped and said hello, he warmly introduced me to his family and told me that they lived right behind the Lodhi Road police station, in the same compound. I knew that there were official quarters there, but it had not occurred to me that police officers actually lived there with their families. I asked if Bhandari also lived there, and he said that he did, and that his and Bhandari's children went to the same nursery together, and that they were all about to meet in the gardens. 'One minute', he said, 'I'll call him to see where they are'.

As he stepped away to speak with Bhandari, I said to Kirpal's wife that it must be so nice to live near such a lovely garden. She replied that their 'government quarters' were 'not so good', because the only place for the children to play was next to the police station. This made the gardens, therefore, a welcome relief. After Kirpal informed me that Bhandari was in 'an interrogation', and would not be able to come, he signalled to his wife that they had to return home, and they took their leave.

As I jogged away, I wondered what it was like to live so close to a police station. Did Bhandari's and Kirpal's children play close to the interrogation rooms of the station? Could their wives hear what was going on in them? What did such intimacy between violence and domesticity reveal, furthermore, about the daily routines of men like Bhandari and Kirpal? Did they wake up in the morning, buy fresh milk, read their newspaper, go to work, fill out paperwork, illegally detain some men, get a cup of chai, slap the men around, go to court to depose, fill out more paperwork, have an informal chat with the illegally detained men, then go pick up the children from school and buy vegetables on the way home? How, in other words, did they negotiate the boundaries between violence and domesticity? Or was the nature of my encounters with Bhandari, and of the 'custodial intimacy' that he and other police officers fostered, a sign that, instead, these were impossible to maintain?

That would explain the murkiness of my relationship with Bhandari. At times, he felt like a helpful friend, and even seemed to treat me like a younger brother. He took the time to tell me about his work and what he thought about certain cases, to explain things he thought I might not understand, and to give me access to the supplementary chargesheet in the terrorist bombing case, all to help me. This friendliness was intertwined, however, with betrayal, as when he prevented me from speaking up about the CD evidence.

It was also interlaced with menace, as in his account of his conversation with Anwar and the stories terror-accused told about the violence he perpetrated, as well as that reported in court cases and the media—not to mention his legal entanglements, particularly his fabrication of evidence (to which he largely confessed, as I have already noted, in his account about the alleged Maoists). Like the terrorist suspects whose cases I was researching, the fundamental issue I faced, with him, was that I did not know how to approach him, as is evident by the fact that he had a double persona, both friendly and threatening, even in my nightmare. Since he seemed, in short, to be a shapeshifter, my attempt to make sense of my relationship with him felt impossible.

I realised that this, however, was how my main ethnographic interlocutors, the terror-accused, felt about their interactions with Indian police officers. They knew such officers because they had spent so much time with them, first in illegal detention, then in custody, then during the course of trials that generally lasted years. This bred a certain intimacy. But though terrorist suspects might hug the police officials with whom they interacted, and greet them as friends or elders, this relationship of seeming friendship was entwined with stories about and experiences of violence. In their interactions with the police, therefore, the terror-accused had to constantly struggle to make sense of the nature of a relationship in which friendliness and violence were intimately enmeshed.

## Further Thoughts

*V Geetha*

Is there, or can there be, another side to police violence? It is hard to imagine there could be, given the continuing infraction of rights and constitutional obligations by the police across India. As numerous reports put out by civil liberties organisations have noted, policing in India is constitutively brutal, and this is the case even when officers and men are not corrupt or politically compromised. As K Balagopal pointed out nearly four decades ago, the police consider maintaining law and order their chief mandate and when doing so, are not averse 'to teaching the people a lesson', to set them 'right', and so they go about their duties with this end in mind—and if this means beating up people, cordoning off villages, or detaining individuals illegally and torturing them, they do so, with alacrity.[1] This sort of police action might not be within the remit of the criminal law in India, or indeed, in any other country, but the force has vested in itself a spurious moral authority that impels it to punitive action, often of a violent kind.

Given that the police are protected in their illegal acts by their fraternity and the government, policing in India is marked by a remarkable impunity. In this context, it is challenging and intriguing to engage with studies that seek to view policing from unusual perspectives. This section features three such studies, and each comes to its task from a different angle.

Pooja Satyogi draws on an unusual police archive to point to the broad shifts in the Indian state's understanding of policing: speeches made by various prime ministers, home ministers and senior police officers at the annual conferences of inspector generals of police. She examines these from 1947 onwards, starting with Sardar Vallabhbhai Patel's address to independent India's policemen.

From her brief summaries of speeches, it is evident that the police were charged with two contradictory duties: to undertake their tasks in ways that would win them the trust of the Indian citizenry; and at the same time to not demur from identifying and securing troublemakers, of whatever political persuasion, who sought to undermine public peace and the law. Nehru was the most reflective on this subject: while he conceded the right of the so-called troublemakers to their political views, he was anxious that their politics did not polarise the polity and render it riven. His addresses to the police from the 1950s and into the 1960s therefore take note of the difficult conditions under which Indians had to learn to be democratic and exhort them to heed the nation's republican spirit.

However, on the ground, policing did not play out according to the carefully modulated politics he scripted in his police conference speeches. In retrospect, the fine line Nehru sought to draw between managing public restiveness with civility and dealing firmly and fairly with troublemakers appears a notional one. For, in practice, no such distinction was maintained, as was evident in two patently undemocratic acts that were undertaken close on the heels of independence: the banning, in 1948, of the Communist Party of India, and the police action undertaken that same year to secure the integration of the erstwhile Hyderabad state into the Indian Union.

The punishing of militant dissent, however popular, and extra-legal police action, undertaken in the 'national' interest, have since become hallmarks of punitive policing. This has made for a mental habitude that treats political differences, expressed in the form of public protests and agitations, as criminal, with the Indian Penal Code being deployed, as Balagopal noted, to provide statutory reasons for all struggles, whether of a trade union, a political movement, or a civil rights group, to be viewed as illegal. Further, a rhetoric of denunciation emerged, based on beliefs and principles which rendered such struggles as crimes.

Satyogi's article therefore helps us view police violence as being tied to the ambivalences that, historically, have marked the Indian state's understanding and practice of democracy. In this sense, police violence may be viewed as unfolding in a gap that the democratic Indian state has chosen to keep open, between an affective interest in democracy and a punitive intent when it comes to dealing with dissent and political differences.

Mayur Suresh's article, drawn from his research on terror trials as these unfold in the courts, opens up this gap in ways that allow us to take note of all that transpires between the imperative to secure and punish troublemakers, in this case, 'terrorists', and the actual prosecution of their cases, which requires the officers in charge of terrorist investigations to work closely with those accused of such offences. Without taking away from the menace and power that characterise this encounter between the accused and the policeman, Suresh wonders if we might not want to enquire into this phenomenon, which he designates as an instance of 'custodial intimacy'. He is also led to this formulation on account of his own relationship to the policeman he shadows in the course of his field work: he is troubled by the fact that he has to engage with a man whose approach to law and rights disturbs him but who is also 'human' in ways that cannot be overlooked.

Suresh's interrogation of this 'messy' familiarity acquires yet another resonance when he reflects on the possible everyday lives of the police: their 'normal' interactions with spouses and children, and the exceptional violence they exercise when dealing with a prisoner in a lock-up, not far from their residence. How might one understand such behaviour, beyond viewing it as all too human and all too banal?

Reading Suresh's account of the emotional and behavioural ambiguities that structure police-accused relationships, it is impossible not to note the gendered logic that shapes them. For one, the ostensibly well-meaning yet professional policeman's attitude towards the terror accused is airily paternal: he understands the reasons for militancy, he supports development, and he is aware of the emotional toll that the accused experience, and yet he must do his duty, and exercise his authority to secure order and justice. That is, he makes clear that he exercises power not out of malice, but because it is necessary.

This is not unlike how men engage with women over whom they exercise protective control: they are to be disciplined and looked after, for their own good. For women, this has meant that they comply with and are loyal to the demands of family and kin in return for being taken care of. This unequal exchange, secured through affective as well as coercive ties, renders the home space custodial: and makes for a distinctive form of menace and violence that acquires visibility when the custodian turns killer, as happens when the patriarch resorts to 'honour' crimes to redress what he views as the crime of 'inappropriate' conjugality. Like the reluctant policeman, the reluctant father affirms his right to control and violence, even as he plays protector. The point is that intimacy, however it is exercised, is constitutively gendered and in this sense, it problematises the policeman's vocation, by linking it to the life worlds of family and the civil worlds of family and community.

Ather Zia's fine essay on the perils of policing in Kashmir, in turn, examines the relationship between vocation and identity in a context in which a Kashmiri Muslim, even if a policeman, is suspect in the eyes of the custodians of Indian nationhood, be it the army or the paramilitary forces stationed in the Kashmir valley. The Jammu and Kashmir Police force, she notes, has negotiated this situation through what she views as acts of strategic complicity: to survive as a force they have to assent to the overlordship of the armed forces and be part of counter-insurgency operations, yet essay their roles as law enforcers. Zia maps their travails, and the complex political choices they and their families make or fail to make.

This chapter makes us confront a tragic and ironic situation, and the cynical and violent politics that shapes it. Subject to militant control and punishment, on account of their ostensible 'pro-India' positioning, as well as public taunting, and equally to humiliation at the hands of the Indian state, the police in Kashmir cannot claim the authority that is otherwise accorded to their vocation. The Kashmir situation makes it evident that such authority is, literally, a 'gift' of the state, and this is a gift that the state refuses to grant its officers in the region. This has led to the making of a distinctive police lifeworld: uncertain, tentative, and in which the police are bereft of an identity that valorises and affirms their existence. They are also denied that impunity which is the hallmark of their exceptional authority in an everyday sense.

The police in Kashmir thus appear a lost force, and this is also because they are not 'of the people' though their sympathies might lie with the latter. Consigned to a limbo-like existence, which renders their situation unique and deserving of a measure of empathy, their fate opens a window onto that vulnerability that yet attends lives which are granted the right to statutory violence.

# PART FOUR

# Interviews and Reflections on Police Violence and Means of Redress

## Policing and Democracy

### *An Interview with Vikash Narain Rai*

**Interviewer:** What are some of the key challenges in addressing police violence in India today?

**Rai:** The police were the political tool of India's colonial masters. After the colonial masters left India and power was handed over to Indians, a democratic government was formed. If you look at our Constitution, it is very democratic, but a matching administration—including the police—was not provided. But to implement the Constitution requires providing an administration that is responsible to India's citizens. That was not provided, maybe because so many things had to be dealt with after independence. Partition had taken place, which was a tragedy, and India was facing very acute problems like a lack of education, poverty, and unemployment. But dealing with this lack of an accountable administration is a big challenge today, particularly when it comes to the police, because they were moulded to suit colonial interests and the colonial protocols through which they operated persist.

In a colonial mindset there are rulers and ruled. It's an authoritative mindset, which means that violence is built into it. The biggest challenge, then, is to change such protocols into democratic ones—to make the police accountable to the people. So, the crux is that we have to convert our colonial policing protocols into democratic ones. This is difficult because the laws that the colonial masters gave us, which were against the democratic ethos, still exist. In fact, they have been strengthened. Preventive detention. Banning people from assembling. Restricting freedom of expression when it comes to talking about the government or the state. And then there are laws in which bail is denied. All of this is in the name of national security. If there are layers upon layers of authority, then violence is an inevitable part of that.

Police violence is also growing because it is part of political violence, which has increased. This is part of what has happened to democracy, namely growing polarisation between different groups, which can lead to violence. Since the police are part of society, they are part of this process. So, police violence will go away only when political violence goes, I'm sure about it. And for that we need to change the colonial policing protocols into democratic protocols, and that is not being done.

**Interviewer:** What are some examples of police violence as political violence?

**Rai:** The latest is the UP model, the model of bulldozer policing.[1] India's political masters have become very aggressive against minorities and Dalits, and against people who are not in their vote bank. So that has acted as the catalyst for the police to take over and drive that agenda and convert it into a kind of 'encounter' policing, in which the police kill criminal suspects or suspected militants. That is a very naked form of police violence.

**Interviewer:** Can you tell us a bit about your own experience in the police bureaucracy in India, as well as in dealing with the issue of police violence?

**Rai:** I became Director of the Haryana Police Academy in 2005 and I continued in that role until 2010. During the last two years of that period, I was also made the Director General (Law and Order) of Haryana. So, I was simultaneously looking after law and order in the state as well as training the police. That was a golden opportunity for me to combine my two roles and try to work out a democratic protocol for the Haryana police, which I called 'Samvedi Police Sashakt Samaj' (Sensitised Police for an Empowered Society). Sensitised policing involves a rights-based approach towards communities and prioritising police activities in accordance with a community's needs. For instance, at one point in time a lot of the resources of the Madhuban police station in Karnal, Haryana, were focused on quelling the nuisance of drunken, loutish behaviour in public streets at night. This made people feel empowered and generated high public support.

Social empowerment is important because without it the police are not going to gain any respect or cooperation from Indian citizens. I therefore made sensitised policing part of the curriculum at the Haryana Police Academy and then we tried it out at Madhuban police station. We called it 'Samvedi [Sensitive] Police Station'. The police who went to the Academy for training were given the duty to run that police station, which worked very well. It was an experiment, which we carried out for almost two years, but I still feel very proud of it.

We had tremendous cooperation from local people in conducting this experiment. They were so warm and so keen to engage with what we were doing. This is an example of how the police can democratise their protocols. You know, in 1902 the British appointed a commission, known as the Fraser Commission, to recommend ways to reform the Indian police. The report they produced said that the police were inefficient, corrupt, and weren't properly supervised.[2] Jump to the reports produced by the National Police Commission, almost 80 years later (1979-1981), and they say the same things.[3] They talk about the need to change policing structures, the model of supervision, and accountability processes. So, the same problems still exist. But none of these reports talk about democratising policing protocols.

There have, of course, been efforts to reform the Indian police. Take, for example, the reforms recommended by the Supreme Court in its judgement on the Prakash Singh case in 2006.[4] Those reforms are about who should supervise the police and who they should be accountable to. The problem is, there are so many complaints committees. If I want to complain about the police, I can go to a supervisory police officer. I can go to the courts. I can go to the Human Rights Commission. There are so many avenues through which to make complaints. But how does this help? It doesn't, because there is still no real accountability. The reforms recommended by the Supreme Court have been introduced in at least ten states, but their policing hasn't changed. Maybe there has been some marginal difference, but this is because of larger cultural shifts, not because of these reforms.

**Interviewer:** What was the outcome of the Haryana experiment?

**Rai:** I think it died a natural death. After I left it was continued for some time, but failed because it did not suit the political establishment. And so, the moment I was not in charge, it was nobody's baby and it withered away. I wish that somebody would chronicle their experiences of it—I don't have the energy or resources to do it. The people who benefited from it, though, they're still there.

**Interviewer:** What are some of the broader proposals that you think might bring about the kind of democratisation that you are talking about?

**Rai:** What needs to be done, to really democratise the police, requires a massive effort at the governmental level. But the Indian government is not interested in this, and nor are any political parties. There's a big gap, as I have said, between the constitutional mandate and the administrative machinery which is there to carry out that mandate. Now we have to bridge that gap. My son is a doctor in the USA—every two or three years he's required to sit an exam to show that he's still in touch with the latest protocols in his profession. Lawyers have to do this, and chartered accountants have to do it in some countries. But in our country, once a police officer passes their exam and puts on a uniform, that's it. They don't have to be tested again. If they are not seen to be behaving adversely, they are considered to be doing a fine job.

**Interviewer:** What about police training?

**Rai:** There are some promotion and training courses, but they actually cement the values which police officers already have—they don't change anything or create anything new. So, that gap has to be filled. The gap between our democratic Constitution and our authoritative police can, however, be bridged through training, testing, and through surveys and other things. There could be periodical commissions to find out whether that gap is being filled or not. What I am saying is, a police officer should be more than someone who is wearing a police uniform, has cleared a certain examination, or is good at controlling mobs. They should be something more, namely constitutionally conditioned. The values of our Constitution, in other words, should be the values of our police. We will also have to change our laws. All those authoritarian laws must go—lock, stock, and barrel they must go. But we are actually going in the reverse direction. Governments are becoming armed with more and more authority and are exercising that through the police. They are transferring their authority to police officers. That is why the police look so brazen, so violent, so aloof from democratic protocols.

**Interviewer:** So, you are saying the police need to be made more constitutionally aware?

**Rai:** I am saying that only when police protocols change will police attitudes change. And you cannot change these attitudes without making it mandatory that the police demonstrate that they are following Constitutional protocols. If they're not displaying those features, then they should not be in the police force.

**Interviewer:** So, once the police put on a uniform then there are certain kinds of protocols and values or Constitutional features that they have to embody regardless of what they think about them?

**Rai:** Exactly. What I am saying is this can be ingrained through training, periodical testing, and periodically appointing commissions to find out how much has been accomplished and how much remains to be accomplished—in addition to changing our laws, our protocols, and our training methods.

**Interviewer:** Globally, I am sure you are aware, the Black Lives Matter movement, and in India the Dalit Lives, Adivasi Lives, and Muslim Lives Matter movements have demonstrated that discrimination is felt much more specifically by certain communities over others. This has led to calls to defund or abolish the police. How would you respond to these in the Indian context?

**Rai:** Well, this idea of defunding or abolishing the police may not be relevant in our context because in India, most of the population wants the government to come to their aid because they don't have any resources. People don't have private lawyers or attorneys to approach authorities or the courts, or other mechanisms of redress for their problems. So, they want the government to help them. They therefore welcome the police in their hour of need. But the relationship between the police and society is not one between government and citizens, as I have mentioned, but between authorities and subjects. Defunding or abolishing the police is not the solution to this.

Actually, the police need more funds in order to modernise, not less. But what has happened is that over the years, while funds have been released by the Government of India to modernise the police—because the states were not spending enough on this—instead of being modernised, they have instead undergone a massive militarisation. The Indian police were modelled, by the British, on military lines as a second line of defence, after the 1857 Revolt, as they were not sure they could rely on the Indian army to maintain their control over India.[5] But that colonial model of policing is no longer required. What we're spending in the name of modernisation is mostly on hardware—on arms and ammunition, vehicles, and so on—not on things like democratic sensitisation and community-orientated software, which needs to be modernised, and there needs to be training on how to use such software to help the Indian police to tackle twenty-first-century challenges. Defunding is therefore not a solution to the problem of police violence: putting funding to use in the right direction is the solution.

## Better Training, Representation, and Capacity Building as Keys to Addressing Police Violence in India

*An interview with Sanjoy Hazarika*

**Interviewer:** Based on your wide-ranging experience as a human rights activist (notably, from 2016-2022, as the International Director of the Commonwealth Human Rights Initiative), as well as an academic, journalist, author, filmmaker, and policy analyst, what do you think are some of the key challenges in addressing police violence in India today?

**Hazarika:** The first and most fundamental issue is the need for political reforms, because without these it is not possible to reform the Indian police. The police cannot be held accountable for the very simple reason that politicians don't think it's important enough for them to be, or rather, they want the police to be accountable to them. This is the root of the problem, because there are a lot of good policemen who do their work well, and competently, and with dedication, and at times to the point of exhaustion. I know some of them. But the police force in India was designed as a colonial institution, so its primary function has been to protect the political and economic system, to protect the Raj—and the Raj, now, is whoever is in power. So, it's a major problem when there are people at all levels, whether constables or director generals, looking over their shoulders constantly, wondering how the political dispensation would want them to react in response to a calamity, crisis, emergency, or just a normal law and order situation—and needing to get political approval in order to act.

There are, of course, many other issues that need to be addressed to deal with extra-legal violence by the Indian police. Take education, class, and corruption. Traditionally, the people who get selected for the national police service, at a senior level, often come from privileged families, and have had a reasonable education. Many of the others, namely constables, and even up to the level of superintendents of police, are often from a different income group, and may be less well-educated. Their recruitment path is also different, since it tends to be shaped by influence, including corruption—which, in turn, shapes how they will police. The effects of these issues play out in a variety of ways, particularly when it comes to the understanding of the subordinate police, or their lack of understanding, of peoples' constitutional rights, and the importance of accepting and upholding them. There are also few competent, rigorous training programmes that will actually enable the subordinate police to understand what they're supposed to be doing, and how to uphold such rights.

The police also have a very thankless task. Most of them work very long hours and their living conditions are poor. These have improved in the past decade or so, but they are still poor, especially for those who have quarters at the *thana* (police station).[1] The police also feel that people don't understand them. Take the traffic police, who don't have anything to do with things like custodial violence. They have to stand for eight to ten hours a day in burning heat and heavy rain without appropriate clothing. In cities like Delhi, where the pollution conditions are toxic, and they don't wear proper masks, such a job is enough to adversely impact their health. So, we have to also empathise with the fact that they are doing a tough job in impossibly difficult conditions. Their stress levels, as in all branches of the Indian police, are therefore very high.

They are also on the frontline during emergencies. Think about the Covid pandemic, in which there was a high death toll among the Indian police.[2] This is because they were completely unprepared, and untrained, for an emergency of that sort. In the initial days, they were operating with very little experience, very little knowledge, and little understanding of what they were getting into. The Indian police are trained to meet a law-and-order problem, like rioting or mob violence. But suddenly people were dying in large numbers and needed to be rescued and taken to hospital. That was a major challenge, then, for the police to deal with.

We have to remember that the police are also rooted in the society that they're dealing with, and so hold all of its prejudices, likes and dislikes. This includes issues to do with caste, religion, and ethnicity. Even though there are now people of different castes, religions, and ethnicities in the senior ranks of the Indian police, these all still shape how the police operate. So, a chap at the bottom of the police hierarchy might, as a result of these things, not think very highly of his boss. The boss, of course, thinks very poorly of his subordinates. All of this affects, in turn, how the police interact with the public.

**Interviewer:** So, are you saying that the structural issues in the Indian police haven't essentially changed from the colonial period?

**Hazarika:** No, they have not really changed. If anything, they have become harder to handle because the rigidities in relation to religion and caste have become sharper since the destruction of the Babri Masjid mosque in Ayodhya the early 1990s by right-wing Hindu groups.[3]

Such political issues have played out in ways ranging from a lack of will for police reform to how the police respond to crises. Custodial deaths are declining, but the ones that take place are pretty horrific, like those of Bennix and his father in Tamil Nadu during the height of the pandemic, which Jinee Lokaneeta discusses in this book. They were beaten virtually to death because they did not respond well to an order to close their shop.[4] Henri Tiphagne, executive director of the human rights organisation People's Watch, has spoken a lot about the severity of custodial violence in Tamil Nadu.[5]

There are two National Police Academies, one in Hyderabad, and The North Eastern Police Academy, at Umiam, near Shillong. Once when I was taking a class for new entrants to the North Eastern academy, I asked the trainees whether custodial violence, particularly the use of 'third degree methods' (mental or physical torture), was justifiable under any circumstances. Only four people out of over 200 said it wasn't. I told them that by using third degree methods they were committing a crime. But most of them didn't even think this was a crime. They were not even aware that when a person is in custody he or she is under the protection of the police.

**Interviewer:** What was their rationale for using 'third degree' methods?

**Hazarika:** One chap said, 'how are we supposed to get a confession out of them [suspects] if we don't'? This showed their lack of training, and the lack of capacity building in the Indian police. They need to build skills. There are enough senior, skilled police officers who could teach non-violent interrogation methods—not the sort depicted in Bollywood or Hollywood films.

**Interviewer:** What is your experience in regard to police violence from your work with the Commonwealth Human Rights Initiative (CHRI)?

**Hazarika:** I learnt a lot from my colleagues at CHRI about police violence. But many of them feel that we won't be able to reform the police until we get political reform. I agree, as I've said, that we need political reform in order to reform the police. But there are other social issues that need addressing as well, relating to the ways in which the police treat Dalits and Muslims, especially in places like Rajasthan, Madhya Pradesh, and UP (Uttar Pradesh), and women as well.

I was greatly concerned about these issues before I joined CHRI. In 2000, I founded the Centre for North East Studies and Policy Research at Jamia Millia Islamia, in New Delhi, and beginning in 2012 we carried out a study on the perceptions and experiences of women who had migrated from northeast India to four Indian metros (Delhi, Mumbai, Kolkata, and Bangalore) in relation to sexual harassment and racial abuse. It was commissioned by the National Commission for Women.[6] Among the questions that we asked the women we surveyed was, 'if you came across a problem of prejudice or abuse would you go to the police for help'? The overwhelming response was 'no', because the police would blame the women for whatever problem they were facing, they wouldn't know how to handle it, and the women wouldn't feel safe. So, they sought help from peers and support groups and dealt with whatever the situation was as best as they could. In other words, they did not trust the police.

This has also been borne out by a report we published at

CHRI towards the end of my term as its director, in 2020—in collaboration with the Association for Advocacy and Legal Initiatives, a women-run human rights organisation that works to tackle gender violence in UP—on the experiences of fourteen rape survivors from the state.[7] Their complete distrust of the police was evident in everything they told us. They said that the police didn't take them seriously, and thought they were lying—they used the Hindi word, *phasaao*, which means 'to trap', to say that they were just trying to frame a man for something. Or they would say things like, 'Oh, you're like that only', meaning that if a woman had had sex with a man who wasn't her husband she was immoral. This lack of trust is apparent in the relationship between society and the police, however, across India, and the police are very aware of this.

There are, of course, very good reasons for such distrust. I'm sure you've heard of what's been called the Hashimpura massacre, in 1987, in which nineteen middle- and upper-caste members of an armed police unit in UP, the Provincial Armed Constabulary, rounded up forty-two Muslims from Hashimpura, in Meerut, took them to the outskirts of the city, shot them, and dumped their bodies in an irrigation canal.[8] But what we found at CHRI, in cases like this, was that the perpetrators of such terrible violence did not see themselves as doing something particularly bad—and hence they were convinced that they wouldn't be punished for it. There were cases that we came across from Maharashtra, Gujarat, Rajasthan, UP, the South and also eastern states of policemen who were completely confident that, whatever awful things they did, they wouldn't be hauled up for them.

**Interviewer:** The police obviously feel invincible because they face virtually no accountability. But there's a flip side to public attitudes towards the police in India, because despite the distrust and, we could add, fear that they generate, particularly for marginalised groups, they're also seen as people who get things done. So, if you're having trouble with a difficult neighbour, you might use the police as a resource, by asking them to intimidate the neighbour or do some mediation.

**Hazarika:** Yes, the police do get used. A high court judge in Patna recently rebuked the police and local officials for destroying somebody's home with a bulldozer, saying that they had violated the law. But what was most notable was that he said they'd done it on behalf of some political party or a politician.[9] For a judge to actually speak his mind so clearly and fearlessly is rare. But the Hindu right is so supportive of everything the police do, and vice versa, that this further emboldens the police. Take the example of the *gau rakshaks*, or cow vigilantes, who try to stop cows being stolen or slaughtered in places like Rajasthan, Haryana, UP, and Madhya Pradesh—the police are hand in glove with them.[10]

But let me also share with you something from my experience at CHRI, which shows that the police realise that there are other ways of negotiating difficulties than using violence, or involving the law, by looking at how local social dynamics work and working with them—which they frequently do. There was a young woman from the United States who had come to work with CHRI, who was being harassed by the landlord's son in the place she was staying in as a paying guest. I wanted to get the police to take legal action against the young man, so I consulted a friend of mine, who was a very senior officer in the police. He was about to retire but I had known him all my life and I trusted his judgement. He said, 'No, don't do that. Let me talk to the local SHO [Station

House Officer, or head of a police station] because he may know the family'. So, the SHO talked to the young man's father, the landlord, who put a stop to his son's behaviour. This underlines the informal networks that exist between the police and public. Since the police are inundated with investigating cases, they would naturally prefer using their influence to mediate resolutions to some of these rather than pursuing long, tedious legal resolutions to them. But people need access to networks to connect to those in influence or power for this process to work.

**Interviewer:** Do you have any reflections on the role of the Indian legal system in making the police feel invincible?

**Hazarika:** The law has certainly enabled the police to become more powerful, especially a law like UAPA (the 1967 Unlawful Activities (Prevention) Act), which gives them absolute impunity to commit extra-legal violence. A political leader, minister, or chief minister just has to say that certain people are working against the state, they're terrorists, and that's sufficient to use UAPA against them. So, the law enables anyone to be put away who is regarded as being inconvenient, like students at JNU (Jawaharlal Nehru University), who have been charged under UAPA for protesting. One of them, Umar Khalid, who was arrested in 2020 for leading peaceful protests against the CAA (Citizenship Amendment Act), is still in prison.[11]

But while the police are armed with tremendous powers, under a law like the UAPA, they also lack powers in other areas, such as in relation to cybercrime. The police are completely unable to deal with this. I've been trying to deal with a case, for example, in which I was attacked online. But it's been six years since it happened and the police still haven't been able to deal with it. My bank account was also hacked, and I lost some money. When I went to the police, a senior officer responsible for handling such crimes in Delhi said to me, 'Sir, nobody in the police understands this type of crime'.

A few years ago, the then Home Minister, Rajnath Singh, unveiled a 25,000-crore project for strengthening police infrastructure, for things like body armour, and better cars, Wi-Fi, and digital surveillance technology.[12] But what about training the police, improving their capacity, their knowledge of the law, etc.? How many times do the police go through refresher courses? How many times are they supposed to? I wonder who is paying attention to such basic things. The same is true regarding training the police about gender equality and gender sensitivity. Training on this is better in places like Delhi, Mumbai, Chennai, and even Hyderabad, I would say, than in other parts of India.

The police also need better gender representation, in terms of more female officers. Women make up less than twelve per cent of the Indian police.[13] This is a particularly serious problem in places like Kashmir and the Northeast, where the Armed Forces Special Powers Act is in operation, because female police officers are supposed to go with the armed forces when they arrest a female insurgent and often, they're not there.[14] So, they make such arrests without them.

Tackling this means changing mindsets, because what woman would want to apply for a job in the Indian police? CHRI did a study on the challenges female police officers in India face, and part of the problem was that women are unwilling to put in the long hours that the police in India must work, and for a measly salary and working conditions in which they face harassment. They also have to deal with difficult conditions at home, including unsupportive husbands. That's a quadruple whammy for female officers. So, better representation for under-represented groups—which includes a range of minorities as well as women—along with better training (so that the police understand that they can't break the law if they want to uphold it) and very rigorous capacity building are the simple but fundamental things that need to be done to help address police violence in India.

# The Impunity of Police Encounters in Uttar Pradesh

*An interview with Mangla Verma and Vipul Kumar*

**Interviewer:** In your work as human rights advocates, how did you come to publish a report, in 2021, with Citizens Against Hate and People Watch, on the extra-judicial executions of suspects, or what are commonly referred to as 'encounters', in Uttar Pradesh (UP) under the BJP government of Hindu monk Yogi Adityanath—of which 10,900 took place between March 2017 and April 2023, resulting in 5,046 injuries and 183 deaths?[1]

**Verma:** To understand this escalation of police encounters in UP requires, firstly, going back to the BJP's campaign for the 2017 UP state elections. To help mobilise Hindu support, the party released lists of Hindu families it claimed had fled from the town of Kairana, in which half the inhabitants are Muslim, due to threats from Muslim criminal gangs—particularly that headed by one Mukim Kala. The party vowed to take a tough stand against such crime. While these claims were later debunked, it was after the BJP came to power in the state that this spree of encounter killings began.[2] These included the brother of Mukim Kala, Wasim, who was only seventeen, a juvenile, when he was killed. In 2021 Mukim was also killed while in custody in Saharanpur District Jail.[3]

We did not initially set out to investigate encounters in UP. We came to focus on them, however, when we came across many cases of extra-judicial killings in Haryana while we were documenting the lynching of Muslims by Hindu mobs there in 2017-2018.[4] These were, according to family members, police encounters, but the police denied this—they blamed such deaths on things like gang warfare. We started reading of similar things happening in UP, although in contrast to Haryana the UP police were admitting to undertaking such encounter killings. So that shifted our attention to UP.

**Kumar:** Prior to this, I was mainly working on custodial torture cases for those accused of terrorism-related offences. But I saw a very clear linkage between police impunity in regard to custodial death cases and in those involving extra-judicial killings. Yet while there is discussion in India on the ethics of judicial murder—namely state executions of those convicted of criminal offences—there is little in regard to extra-judicial murder, which we felt was a big problem. We are also big fans of the prominent lawyers, human rights activists, and authors K Balagopal and KG Kannabiran, and their tradition of human rights documentation, which motivated us to investigate extra-judicial killings.[5]

While Mangla approached these from a legal angle and I approached them from a human rights perspective, we both agreed that evidence gathering and documentation were crucial. It was such concerns that led us to form Youth for Human Rights Documentation (YHRD) in 2020, which is designed as a platform for young people to undertake fact-finding and evidence building on human rights and social justice issues. In regard to extra-judicial killings, we started with fact-finding, first through contacting activists in UP who had been collecting news clippings on such killings, and then speaking to the families concerned. They told us that the police went to their homes, picked up a male family member, and then they heard news about their deaths in an 'encounter'. So, the families also wanted justice.

In 2014 the Supreme Court issued sixteen guidelines to make the police accountable for encounter killings, in the *People's Union for Civil Liberties* v. *State of Maharashtra*.[6] These are a good set of guidelines but there are problems with them, not least that they do not stipulate that an external investigatory body should investigate such killings—instead, the police are expected to do this. So, although we decided that we needed to rigorously document fifteen to twenty cases against the police and then pursue these, we knew that little would realistically come of them.

But once we started doing this, the families of encounter victims began to be harassed by the police, including by bringing false charges against them, which drew our attention to how weak witness protection laws are in India. We realised, then, that while we were unlikely to succeed in bringing cases against the police, recording them would, at least, be a good addition to the field of human rights documentation in India. We also realised that we needed to scrutinise the role of all institutions in regard to such killings, from the magistracy to the National Human Rights Commission (NHRC), since they all, in various ways, facilitated them.

**Interviewer:** What, then, were the key findings of the report?

**Verma:** With the help of Supreme Court lawyer and legal activist Prashant Bhushan, among others, we brought two complaints to the NHRC—one from nine families of encounter victims and the other from a group of civil society organisations. These related to violations of the 2014 guidelines in regard to encounter killings. Within days the NRHC ordered a detailed investigation into the seventeen cases that we brought to them. It was also very cooperative with us in regard to the first few cases. It informed us, for example, when it was meeting with victims' families, so that we could be present when their testimonies were recorded.

But then such cooperation stopped. While we were initially told that the NHRC investigation would take four weeks, it took three to four years for our cases to be addressed—and at the end of this process the NHRC determined that there had been no foul play in any of them, except for one, in which it recommended only that the family receive compensation for the wrongful death of one of its members. This family and the others, however, were also persecuted by the police throughout this process—usually before NHRC meetings with them. We documented all of this in around a dozen letters to the NHRC but received no response.

But once the NHRC closed the cases we had brought, we started submitting a series of RTIs (right to information requests) asking for details of the NHRC's investigation of them. We took that RTI process right up to the CIC (Chief Information Commissioner) in Delhi, who granted us permission to inspect the NHRC files in nine cases—which includes the police records on these cases. Our report is an analysis of these documents, along with information on our engagement with the NHRC.

At the same time that we were undertaking this process, the PUCL (People's Union for Civil Liberties) filed a public interest litigation in the Supreme Court in regard to police encounters in UP. We put all of the evidence we had gathered before the Court to help support this. While dozens more people were killed in police encounters during the course of the case, the Supreme Court did not, notably, pass an interim order to stop them.

**Interviewer:** Was there a pattern in the nature of the encounters?

**Verma:** The sequence of events in all of the encounters that we investigated was virtually identical. The FIRs (first information reports), or chargesheets, all appeared to conform to the same template, with just the names of the encounter victims changed. There were always two suspects involved, one of whom died and the other of whom escaped, and the police were never able to identify the person who escaped. There was also always a motorbike involved, and a chase, and in most cases the bike skidded, after which the alleged criminals started to shoot at the police and the police fired back in self-defence.

**Kumar:** There is one sentence that is used in every FIR. It's a Hindi proverb, *so hum ko yaad ho gaya* (I have now memorised it): '*Adamya sahas aur shoorveerta ka pradarshan karte hue, kanoon ka dhyan rakhte hue, training mein di gayi saari baton ka dhyan rakhte hue, hum ne apne bachaav mein, self-defence ke naam pe hum ne firing kiya* [With great courage, keeping the law and our training in mind, we protected ourselves, in the name of self-defence]'. So that's essentially the rationale given for encounter deaths in the FIRs we've seen.

**Verma:** In all of the cases the police also made maps of the scene of the encounter, as is required by law. These also looked identical. There is a *chauraaha* (crossroad), and just after the *chauraaha* there is a slip road down which the suspects flee, and that's where the encounter takes place. So, these scenes looked fabricated and the sequence of how encounters happened very similar.

**Kumar:** The encounters also always happened at night, so there was never a public witness to them, and while the police were always injured, they were never seriously injured.

**Verma:** Another trend we found in the documents is that while the police initially claimed they were not able to identify the other accused involved in an encounter, since he fled the scene, a few days later there would be another encounter and the police would say that the person killed was the missing absconder.

In addition, in each of these encounter cases the police would file three FIRs. Generally, in criminal law, there is one FIR number for every incident. But in encounter cases there are three, numbered sequentially (in other words, 82, 83, 84, etc.), although their contents are very similar. They relate, however, to different charges. One would be charged under section 307 of the IPC (Indian Penal Code) for attempted murder, because the encounter victim was supposedly trying to kill the police. Another would be for an offence under the 1959 Arms Act, such as carrying illegal arms. A third would be for a charge against the suspect who the police claimed had absconded—and when the police close each case, the FIR relating to the missing person is kept open. They can then insert anyone's name into it, at a later date, to frame them for an offence. Further, all the FIRs that we looked at were registered against the deceased person, meaning that the person who died in the encounter was made an accused in all these FIRs. This never happened, however, to the police officers involved in the shooting.

It is therefore the police narrative of events that is recorded in these FIRs. Ideally, in law, there should be an investigation into whether the police can claim self-defence in a case. But police claims of self-defence are just accepted by superior officers and the judiciary. There is another gap in the 2014 Supreme Court guidelines on encounters, which is that they do not clearly spell out who an FIR should be filed against in such cases. It should also be understood that the criminal offence in these cases is that a person has been killed. Therefore, the police officers who do the killing should be listed as the accused and the people who they kill should be understood as victims. Instead, the opposite happens, which helps the police to cover up their crimes.

**Kumar:** Another major gap in Supreme Court guidelines is that it is not clear whether a judicial magistrate or an executive magistrate should investigate extra-judicial killings. It is required, in Indian criminal law, that an inquiry be carried out by a judicial magistrate (a district court judge) for every case of death, disappearance, or rape inside a jail or while an individual is in police custody. In other cases of unnatural death, an inquiry by an executive magistrate (district or sub-divisional magistrates), which is set up by state governments and is administrative in nature, may be conducted to determine the cause of death—although this is limited in scope.

But executive magistrates are the administrative heads of their districts and are appointed by state governments. For this reason, the Supreme Court, while discussing instances of police encounter killings in Manipur, remarked that inquiries by executive magistrates in such cases could not be given much credence, as they were conducted at the behest of the state government and were purely administrative inquiries.[7] It's not possible for such an inquiry to be independent when state politicians, state police and the state chief minister publicly support encounter killings. Despite this, the practice in UP is for executive magistrates to conduct inquiries into police extra-judicial killings, which shore up the police version of events.

This system of inquiries, as it operates in regard to encounter killings, therefore serves only to protect the police.

**Interviewer:** Just to clarify, when there are deaths in custody, either police or jail custody, the inquiry into these is done by judicial magistrates?

**Verma:** Yes—that's what the law specifies. However, when it comes to police encounters, there seems to be a bizarre understanding among police officers that such deaths do not qualify as custodial, since they haven't happened within the confines of a jail or a police lockup. This is also fuelled by gaps in the guidelines laid down by the Supreme Court regarding encounter killings.

The Supreme Court guidelines on encounters also state that when an encounter has happened, a senior officer should immediately put together a new team of officers from a different police station to investigate it. But what instead tends to happen is that police officers from the same police station involved in an encounter initiate the investigation into it, so they secure the scene of the crime and collect evidence—which means, of course, they can manipulate the evidence.

A few days or weeks later the local superintendent of police then orders the investigation to be transferred to another police station. Since it has already received the evidence in such cases there is, again, no chance of a fair investigation being carried out in regard to them. While there is therefore compliance with the Supreme Court guidelines on paper, this is a direct violation of their spirit. What then happens is that after two or three months the police file a very short, three-line closure report before a judicial magistrate, which states the encounter was a case of self-defence.

Ideally the judicial magistrate, at this stage, should look

through all the evidence collected and seek further investigation or documentation as necessary (such as CDRs, or Call Detail Records, along with forensic and ballistic reports) in order to determine whether the use of force by the police was justified and proportionate. But this is generally not what happens.

What happens, instead, is that the judicial magistrate issues a notice to the complainant of the case—which as we've described, in the case of encounters, is a police officer from the team that carried out the encounter—asking whether the officer has any objections to the case being closed. This is required according to the Supreme Court guidelines once a closure report is filed. The police, of course, reply, 'No, we have no objections, please close the case'. The judicial magistrate then orders that the case be closed. This was the process followed in all of the seventeen cases we have examined. When we first approached the NHRC—in other words, before we saw their files on the case—we had already documented these issues in our complaints. The NHRC, however, never responded to them.

**Kumar:** In the report, we call such practices 'permissive lawlessness'. What's so distressing is that the practice of encounter killings and their subsequent cover-up have become increasingly normalised in India. So, when four men accused of gang raping and murdering a young woman were killed in a police encounter in Hyderabad in 2019, this was widely celebrated not just in Hyderabad but across India, as you observe in the introduction to this book. People set off firecrackers, distributed sweets, and sent hundreds of thousands of supportive tweets.[8]

When in UP former Chief Minister Mayawati tweeted that the UP police should 'take inspiration' from their Hyderabadi counterparts in dealing with criminals, the police responded by saying they had nothing to learn from Hyderabad, and supplied data on the number of purported criminals killed or injured in encounters in the state.[9] UP is, in fact, being held up as a model for other states to follow even by courts. The Punjab and Haryana High Court, for example, advised the police in Punjab and Haryana to learn from the UP police on how to deal with gangsters.[10]

But those being killed are mostly from disadvantaged communities, whether economically or socially. In western UP, for instance, most victims are from minority communities, while in eastern UP caste and political dynamics shape the profiles of victims. So extra-judicial killing is a way of stigmatising and criminalising certain kinds of people. There is also a strong communal nature to it.

Yet it has a wide public mandate, which is a product, in part, of our cinema, since there have been so many films, in India, which romanticise and celebrate trigger-happy cops. Killing by the police is therefore accepted. Socially and culturally, we are also a very Brahminical country, so many of our religious festivals celebrate the killing of 'enemies'. When it comes to encounter killings, we are still living in a demonical age in which people from certain communities can be racialised, criminalised, and demonised—and killing demons is not, according to popular sentiment, wrong.

# The War Against Adivasis in Chhattisgarh

## *An Interview with Shalini Gera*

**Interviewer:** What do you regard as some of the key challenges in addressing police violence in India today?

**Gera:** One of the main challenges is the politicisation of the police. They are no longer there to just maintain what we understand by law and order. Rather, their purpose has become to enforce a particular kind of order that those in power desire, by which I mean that the political establishment has come to dominate the police administration. So, people who do not toe a particular political line then end up being the enemies of the police. Police violence is therefore no longer being directed at people who are challenging law and order but those who are challenging a certain political narrative.

But I want to concentrate, in answering this question, mostly on police violence in Bastar, Chhattisgarh, with which, as a human rights lawyer, I am very familiar. Such violence is mainly directed against three targets. The first is Naxalites, which the Indian state is at war against.[1] I'm talking of a war against a certain kind of political order. The enemy, in this war, is not just those people who are in the Naxalite *dalams* (squads), but anyone who is directly or indirectly, willingly or unwillingly, supporting the Naxals. So, the relatives of supposed Naxalites get picked up by the police—brothers, sisters, husbands, wives—as a way to put pressure on Naxals.

Shopkeepers have even been picked up and charged with terrorism for having supplied the cloth from which Naxal uniforms have been made. In the case of the 2017 Burkapal Naxal ambush, in Dantewada, for example, in which twenty-three members of the Central Reserve Police Force died, every male in the area who was between fifteen to thirty-five years of age—all Adivasis (indigenous or tribal peoples)—was picked up by the police, and 121 people were eventually charged under the draconian Unlawful Activities (Prevention) Act (UAPA).[2]

The second type of police violence that we see in Bastar is against those movements or people who are challenging the forced acquisition of their land or resources by the state, particularly for iron ore mining—fifty-one mining leases have been given just since 2022.[3] The leaders of movements against such mining, which threatens the lands and livelihoods of Adivasi communities, have been targeted and many of them have been either 'encountered'—namely extra-judiciously killed—or picked up by the police. But the people continue to protest.

Many *aandolans,* or peaceful public protests, for example, have taken place in recent years against the opening of new police camps, some 250 of which have been set up in what the Indian Government refers to as 'Left Wing Extremism' (LWE)-affected states.[4] In Bastar there is a camp every two to five kilometres, making it one of the most militarised regions in India.[5] While the government claims that these camps are necessary to control the spread of the Naxalite movement, local communities believe that they are to ensure the safety of mining companies, and fear they will restrict their freedom of movement and lead to harassment, murders and rapes. But since this sort of protest is always treated as anti-state and anti-establishment they are subject to police violence. On the 17th of May 2021, for example, the police fired on protestors at the Silger camp and four people were killed.[6]

The third type of police violence that we see in Bastar is against Christian communities—part of the saffronisation of the police and administration, or their increasing adherence to right-wing Hindu ideology, that is happening all over the country. In 2021 the SP (Superintendent) of Sukma, for example, sent out a circular asking all police *thanas* (stations) in Bastar to put Christian missionaries and converts under surveillance because they caused unrest.[7] In Kanker there was also a campaign by the RSS (Rashtriya Swayamsevak Sangh) to oppose the burial of Christian bodies in the village.[8] So the villagers said they wouldn't allow this.

But the police are actually enabling this kind of violence. Recently, for example, a Christian convert died and the body was buried on the family's private land in their village. When the villagers protested that it had to be exhumed and thrown out of the village the police facilitated the exhumation. Christian tribals are often targeted for eating beef and charged with trafficking cattle, so there was clearly a communal colour to such events.

**Interviewer:** Can you talk a little bit about your own experience with police violence?

**Gera:** I was a part of the Jagdalpur legal aid group, started by myself and two other female lawyers to provide legal aid to people in south Bastar (namely Dantewada, Sukma and Bijapur), that operated in Jagdalpur from 2013 to 2016. Bastar has a largely poor population that has long been caught in the middle of the conflict between the Indian government and the

Naxals. So, most of my encounters with police violence have been in this context.

When we started the Jagdalpur group, we were all novice lawyers, who didn't have much lawyering experience. But we were supported by the local district magistrate, who wrote us a letter of appreciation and sent some legal aid matters for us to deal with. Yet most of the cases we dealt with revealed, at best, how callous the local administration and police were to Adivasis and at worst how such officials used torture and violence against them. We rapidly, therefore, came to be viewed as enemies of the state, and there was a campaign to get rid of us. We also, like those we were trying to help, became subject to police harassment, intimidation, and threats, which forced us to leave Bastar in 2016.[9]

When I say 'police' I am referring to a number of different entities. These include the state and the district police, the DRG (District Reserve Guard), the CRPF (Central Reserve Police Force), which is referred to as a paramilitary force but is actually a police reserve force, the BSF (Border Security Force), the ITBP (Indo-Tibetan Border Police Force), and the SSB (Sashastra Seema Bal). These all either directly enact violence or facilitate it. The worst form of direct violence we encountered was cases in which the security forces were basically raiding villages, in exercises they call 'Area Domination Exercises'—the very term itself is revealing.

These were very brutalising affairs. Battle forces of two or three hundred armed personnel would comb through designated areas and brutalise people. The men would see the police coming and they would scatter and run because if they didn't and were caught, they would be taken to the local *thana*. There were villages where almost every house had a family member who was or had been locked up in the *thana*.

Women and older people would also, sometimes, run, but there were some cases in which if a village was completely empty the police would just break into homes, set them on fire, and destroy everything.

There were also cases of sexual violence by the police against women who remained in their villages, and encounters in which people were killed—many of whom were not armed and posed no danger to the police. These were often people who, according to police informers, had been Naxals in the past but had given up their Naxalism and were living peacefully in their villages. In 2017 alone, there were 197 such killings, with a similarly high number of 166 in 2018.[10]

Of those arrested in such raids, most end up being acquitted, but the long years of incarceration they often experience is also a form of violence—not least since they are commonly subjected to torture, particularly young men. This isn't really to extract information but to teach them a lesson for, as the police see it, supporting Naxals. In other words, it's just brutal, sadistic, punitive violence.

There were also, of course, cases of sexual violence in police lockups. Soni Sori, for example, as Vrinda Grover also notes in this volume, was arrested in 2011 for supporting the Naxals, tortured, and subjected to sexual violence during her detention in police custody.[11] She ended up spending two years in jail (though she was acquitted in all eight cases filed against her). This horrific experience transformed her into an activist who fights on behalf of other women who have experienced such ordeals, including fifteen-year-old Kawasi Hidme, who was detained for eight years in 2008 on false charges for playing a role in the Dantewada police ambush and relentlessly beaten and raped following her arrest.[12] Although these cases are well-documented, nothing has happened to the police who perpetrated such violence.

Another kind of police violence we have seen in Bastar is the endless harassment of Adivasis by the police. This ranges from things like pressuring them to become police informers to turning themselves in to the police. An example of the latter was the '*Lone Varatu*' (return home) campaign, launched in Dantewada in 2020, in which the police plastered images in public places of the faces of people they claimed were Naxalites, or their supporters, along with their names, and invited them to surrender at the local *thana*.[13] Yet most of them, from what we could find, were not involved in any way with the Naxal movement. They were just villagers. But this campaign generated a lot of fear in those identified, which led at least one person, a young woman, to commit suicide.[14]

I've already mentioned some ways in which the police have facilitated violence against the people of Bastar. Other ways have included sponsoring groups committing what appear to be non-state acts of violence, which the police would stand by silently and watch instead of putting a stop to them. Salwa Judum (Peace March), for example, which was a state-sponsored militia formed in 2005 and disbanded after the Supreme Court directed the Chhattisgarh government, in 2008, to stop supporting it, carried out arson, looting, and killings.[15]

But it reappeared in other forms. In 2015, a group of civil society lawyers, journalists and tradesmen formed the *Samajik Ekta Manch* (unity society) vigilante group, which *India Today* revealed in 2016 was working in close association with the local police.[16] It did things like organise rallies, burn the effigies of people it accused of being Naxalites, or supporters of them, along with harassing and intimidating them. Journalists like Malini Subramaniam, academics including Nandini Sundar and Bela Bhatia, activists such as Soni Sori and Himanshu

Kumar, political leaders like Manish Kunjam, and lawyers, including my colleague Isha Khandelwal and myself, were all subjected to such treatment—and all under police protection.[17] The Manch yelled threatening things outside our houses, threw stones into our houses, and damaged our cars, in addition to harassing lawyers who were involved in cases with us. The local bar association, it's worth noting, also passed a resolution prohibiting us from appearing in court.[18]

When we complained, no real action was taken, and in one instance, when we tried to lodge a complaint at the *thana*, the police came and picked up our landlord and pretty much forced him to evict us from our house. The police also picked up the young maidservant of a local journalist on the pretext that they were investigating a complaint of violence regarding her, tortured everybody associated with us, and essentially forced us to leave Bastar.[19]

After they were exposed, the group then dissolved, but the same people formed another vigilante group, called the Action Group for National Integration (AGNI). In January 2017, thirty men from the group barged into the house of the scholar and activist Bela Bhatia in Parpa village, threatened to burn it, and told her to leave the state within twenty-four hours or face the consequences.[20] The police, again, facilitated such harassment by failing to take any action to protect Bhatia.

So, there is virtual impunity for such violence. There is no inquiry into such actions, or even so much as a blemish on the records of the police who are guilty of committing extra-legal violence. Even worse, the police are lauded for such violence—indeed, they have even been given awards and medals for it. In 2012, for example, an 'encounter' happened in Sarkeguda in which the police gunned down seventeen tribals, including six children, and claimed that they were all Maoists. Sixteen were killed on the spot and one was hunted down and killed the next morning. So that was clearly a case of cold-blooded murder. The judicial inquiry set up in the aftermath of this case, before which we represented the families of the deceased villagers (with the help of advocate Yug Mohit Chaudhry, from Mumbai), found that that there was no evidence that those killed were Naxals or that they posed any threat to the police.[21] But S Elango, the DIG (Deputy Inspector-General) of the CRPF in command of the police who carried out these crimes, was given a medal by the Home Minister. Perhaps even more incredibly, the CPRF publishes comic books on its supposed heroes, and it published one in 2016 entitled *Jaanbaaz Elango* (Brave Elango), which lauds Elango as a hero for such acts.[22]

In a similar vein, Ankit Garg (now an Inspector General of Police), who Soni Sori has held responsible for ordering the torture and sexual violence to which she was subject when in custody, has been awarded the Police Medal for Gallantry, while the Inspector General of Police in Bastur, SRP Kalluri, who has many, many human rights complaints against him, has been given the Police Medal for Meritorious Service.[23] At least Ankit Garg's gallantry award wasn't given because of what he did to Soni Sori.

But there are cases in which police officers have been promoted because they were part of a 'successful' encounter. A few DRG officers have told us openly that the more Naxals you kill the better off you will be in terms of promotions. So, such things incentivise the police. There are, however, other incentives for them to commit extra-legal violence, at least in LWE-affected states, because they get a lot of slush funds for this, such as for developing intelligence sources, for which there is hardly any record keeping.

But there are other reasons the police in Bastar commit

such violence, to do with their general poverty and terrible working conditions. Most CRPF officers are from poor families and are alien to Bastar. They come from Bihar and UP (Uttar Pradesh). Their situation is really, really bad. They're on the front lines all the time, in hostile areas, where they don't know the local population. They are hated and viewed as an occupying force. They also lack sufficient protection, since not all of them are issued bulletproof vests or helmets. The authorities also tend to treat them as expendable manpower and have little sympathy for the conditions under which they live. When security camps were first built in Bastar, they did not have toilets. It was only after Naxals started attacking camp residents when they went for their morning ablutions that toilets were constructed.[24]

The security forces are, in addition, essentially caged behind barbed wire in such camps, and can't step out without protection, since hundreds of them have been killed by Naxals. So, they're very scared. They think that everybody is out to kill them. This is what leads to Sarkeguda-like encounters, which was really a result of the police firing in panic—they were walking in the dark, thinking they were sitting ducks for Naxalites, came across a group of people and thought 'that's it, they're going to kill us', and opened fire.

**Interviewer:** What do you think can be done to combat such violence?

**Gera:** First, when an area is heavily militarised, police violence is inevitable. There's no way to have large numbers of men armed to the teeth, in the conditions I've described, and expect that there will be no violence. So, we need to ask whether demilitarisation is possible. But in the case of Naxal violence, this cannot be dealt with entirely as a law-and-order situation which can be solved by sending in troops of armed men. Naxal violence is a form of political violence, and the solution to it must also, therefore, be a political one. What we sorely need is a coordinated effort to establish political dialogue between the government, the Maoists, and representatives of the Bastar branch of the *Sarva Adivasi Samaaj* (all-Adivasi society), which represents tribals. This must be done unconditionally, with a ceasefire being one of the first things negotiated.

Second, we also really need a law that holds commanding officers responsible for the violence enacted by their forces. There is a concept enshrined in international law known as *command responsibility*, according to which a commanding officer is liable for the crimes committed by their subordinates.[25] Such a concept, however, is missing in Indian criminal law.

Third, we need to ensure that there is accountability for police violence. In 2009, a full bench of the Andhra Pradesh High Court, while hearing a petition by the AP Civil Liberties Committee on extra-judicial killings, ruled that in every case in which a person was killed in a police action, an FIR (first information report), or chargesheet had to be registered, and an independent investigation conducted, in addition to an inquest by an executive magistrate.[26] It also ruled that an investigating officer is not competent to close an investigation into an extra-judicial killing by recording a plea of self-defence. While this was a landmark judgement that was welcomed by human rights groups, the Andhra Pradesh Police Officers' Association challenged it before the Supreme Court, which put a stay on it on the grounds that the registration of an FIR could cause problems to an honest police officer carrying out his duties against hardened criminals.[27]

In a 2014 judgement on another case, however, the court reiterated that an FIR should be lodged for every extra-judicial killing—but it did not spell out against whom such an FIR should be lodged.[28] So, the police get away with lodging an FIR against the person they've killed, rather than against themselves, on the grounds that the deceased attempted to murder them. Although a magisterial inquiry is sometimes held if there is enough public outrage against a killing, this is done by an executive magistrate, who is not an independent authority and hence largely rubberstamps the investigating officer's report.[29]

**Interviewer:** Lastly, how would you respond to recent demands for police reforms by the Black Lives Matter, Dalit Lives Matter, Adivasi Lives Matter, and Muslim Lives Matter movements to defund or abolish the police?

**Gera:** It's clear that existing means to address police violence aren't working. In 2006, for example, the Supreme Court, in what's referred to as the Prakash Singh case, directed all states and union territories to undertake a series of police reforms.[30] This included setting up Police Complaints Authorities to inquire into public complaints against police officers. At Jagdalpur we tried to find the relevant authority in Chhattisgarh, which goes under the name of the Chhattisgarh State Police Accountability Authority, and although Raipur contains a building with an appropriate sign on it, we were never able to figure out whether it was functional. We never saw it open or functioning like an office, with a staff. But if it does actually exist, I don't know if it would be of any use, since it is only supposed to investigate heinous crimes committed by police officers within the previous six months. So, police reforms haven't gone very far in Chhattisgarh.

# A Reflection on Living with Violence in India's Northeast

*Santana Khanikar*

About two decades ago, when I was in the last years of high school in a small town in Assam, I had a friend who was originally a year senior to me, but later joined my class. One day when we were chatting, he mentioned that he had lost a school year because his books were burnt by the army just a couple of weeks before his class ten board exams, along with half of his thatched mud house. Apparently, one of his distant relatives was 'underground' with the secessionist United Liberation Front of Assam (ULFA), formed in 1979 and disbanded in 2023, which aimed to make Assam a sovereign state for indigenous Assamese people through armed struggle. The incident before his exam was connected to a search operation by Indian security forces for ULFA members, as Assam and neighbouring states were designated Disturbed Areas under section 3 of the 1958 Armed Forces Special Powers Act (AFSPA).

Since guns embellished the rural and urban landscapes where I grew up, violence was always close. As a result, I do not remember being shocked by my friend's experience. It was one of many similar stories that children in Assam in the last two decades of the twentieth century grew up with—simply part of 'normal' life. Such 'normality' reveals a lot about the role of violence in constructing North-east India, as well as about how people have responded to it, since places are not stagnant or homogenous entities; they transform over time, and in different ways across connected locations.

Conflict, violence and the mechanisms and practices around it, in other words, are shaped by and continuously reshape the place itself, since places are socially constructed by the people who live in them, namely by their experiences as individuals, groups and communities, which are connected through specific relations of power. How a place is located within such relations of power and how individuals are located within these therefore shape how a place comes to be understood or constructed.

But the places that we inhabit in India have also been constructed through relations of domination forged by colonialism, particularly practices of mapping, which made it possible to visualise places in new ways in order to exert power over them. The anti-colonial movement, in turn, re-imagined India as national space, and with it transformed power dynamics in particular places. But place is neither coterminous with territory nor experienced homogeneously. In post-colonial India this can be seen not just in the diversity of languages and cultures that exist side by side but also in perceptions and policies, including in relation to who is inside or is perceived to belong to a given place and who is regarded as being an outsider to it.

Northeast India, or the Northeast as it is commonly known, is one such place. Let's begin with this term, since it is of very recent coinage. In contrast, for example, to Norway, the name of which means *north way*, or the Magreb, which means *west*, the term *Northeast* was coined by the post-colonial Indian state in the 1970s to designate a place in need of particular kinds of intervention.[1] This was a product, in many ways, of the role of the colonial imaginary in rendering swathes of the north-east of India as an inhospitable frontier inhabited by 'natives' or 'savages' who were in need of civilising. A place like Manipur, therefore, which had been an ancient kingdom with a distinct history, became conceptualised by the post-colonial state as simply a strange, backward and remote part of the union of India.

Such othering and exoticisation, however, applied to most of the Northeast, which became envisioned, on the one hand, as a place full of barbaric practices, and on the other, as a haven of exotic food and dance. Such perceptions remain prevalent in Indian society at large, as revealed by the 2019 film *Axone*, directed by Nicholas Kharkongor, which focuses on the challenges a group of friends from the Northeast face when trying to make Axone, a regional dish, for a wedding.

These constructions of a place called *Northeast* were accompanied not only by policies that aimed to 'develop' the region, but also to discipline and control it. This brings me back to AFSPA, which Bhavani Raman, Ather Zia, and Sanjoy Hazarika talk about elsewhere in this book. I want to focus, however, on *why* what were essentially colonial anti-insurgency powers were applied to pacify parts of what was purportedly decolonised national space. The AFSPA, as Zia and Raman detail, is unique in the way it enables the operation of emergency powers and military rule without defining this as such under the emergency provisions delineated by the Indian Constitution in articles 352, 356 and 360. As a result, it is not subject to legislative scrutiny.

Once AFSPA is promulgated, moreover, an area can be called a *disturbed area* under the 1976 Disturbed Areas (Special

Courts) Act and a state of permanent emergency can thereafter operate indefinitely, as has been the case, for decades, for much of the Northeast. As Member of Parliament Nuashir Bharucha queried, in a spirited speech prior to the passage of AFSPA, what type of policy was 'shoot to kill' to 'win the hearts of the people whom you are trying to incorporate and integrate as part of India'?[2]

Such concerns were clearly not shared by the Indian government, which went on to launch the career of the AFSPA by imposing it on Naga areas of Manipur, before extending it to other parts of the Northeast. States such as Nagaland, Manipur, Arunachal Pradesh, and Assam have come under its remit for almost three decades now, which was the case for Tripura until 2015 and Meghalaya until 2018. The Act continues to be in operation in the Northeast, furthermore, despite a decline in separatist politics over the past decade—although as I will discuss, the Act has spurred an increase in ethnic violence.

Human rights organisations, local, national, and international, including the UN High Commissioner for Human Rights, have protested against the widespread human rights violations committed by Indian security forces under the AFSPA, from shootings and killings to torture and rape—to little effect. Since, furthermore, the sanction of the central government is required to initiate prosecutions for such crimes, and it rarely accords this, they can be carried out with impunity. According to the People's Union for Democratic Rights, between 1991 and 2015, of thirty-eight requests the Indian government received to sanction prosecution for crimes committed under the Act, thirty were denied and eight were still pending in 2015.[3] Similarly, the Jammu and Kashmir government was not given sanction from the Indian government to prosecute a single AFSPA-related case from 1990 to 2011.[4]

In my book *State, Violence and Legitimacy*, I examine two forms of state violence in India.[5] One of these is generally deemed 'ordinary', since it is enacted by the police under civilian control, and the other 'extraordinary', since it is enacted by security forces under laws like the AFSPA. But the distinction between what is routine and what is extraordinary, I argue, is blurred, since what might theoretically seem exceptional can become part of the everyday. In such 'zones of abandonment' the state abandons its duty to protect its citizens—via processes ranging from othering (through, for example, the inflammatory and derogatory accusations by the Chief Minister of Assam, Himanta Biswa Sarma, that Muslims are illegal immigrants and criminals) to direct violence (such as custodial killings of Assamese Muslim men), all of which are legitimated by the Indian political establishment and met with either mass support or indifference by much of the public.[6] Many places in India qualify as such zones of abandonment.

But what happens in these zones in the long run? How do people respond to and cope with incessant, everyday violence? In *How to Tell the Story of an Insurgency*, Aruni Kashyap observes that when people in violence-ridden areas write about their lives, they talk about facets of their lives that have nothing to do with violence; those facets, however, are still shaped by violence. As the story I began with shows, life neither stops in zones of abandonment, and nor is it completely annihilated. Rather, behaviours, practices, routines, and habits are shaped, in myriad ways, not only by direct experiences of violence, but an awareness of its omnipresence—which in turn remakes the places that people inhabit.

In *State, Violence and Legitimacy,* for example, I talk

about the inhabitants of two villages in Assam, Laupoti and Kenduguri, which were located at the forefront of the Indian government's anti-insurgency war against ULFA. How they chose to live, pursue their livelihoods and forge friendships were dictated by the constant threat of death, which led affective bonds and affinities to crumble in what had been close-knit communities. So, a neighbour's house being surrounded by Indian security forces during a search operation could fuel suspicion and gossip throughout the neighbourhood, which could then erupt into violence. The politics of othering that is at the heart of nation-building processes thus found a place in the nooks and crannies of the Northeast in multiple competing nation-making discourses.

Such challenges were compounded by the emergence, in 1992, of Surrendered ULFA, or SULFA, which consisted of ULFA members who had surrendered to authorities, or in some cases of civilians who had been pressured to inflate SULFA numbers. Between 1998 and 2001 the security forces used some of the SULFA cadres to kidnap and murder not just ULFA members but even their entire families. The newspapers in this tense, terrifying period in Assam were therefore rife with violent, gory stories about masked gunmen, who they dubbed 'secret killers'.

Youth growing up in places like Lakhipathar, which was at the centre of such violence, therefore wanted, not surprisingly, to move to places outside of it, where they could lead depoliticised, peaceful and secure lives. Such a desire for mobility was not limited just to Lakhipathar, or for this specific period, or to young people. In the 1990s and 2000s, large numbers of people fled from the violence-ridden Northeast to other parts of India—although a considerable number of these were young.

This did not, however, stop the proliferation of processes of othering and fear—of hill versus valley, indigenous versus non-indigenous, and linguistic and religious majorities versus minorities—and with it, a burgeoning of inter-ethnic violence. The violence that was embedded in AFSPA, which Dolly Kikon has argued should be viewed as a security framework instead of just a legal act, became inscribed, therefore, over the body politic of the Northeast as a whole, forming what she calls an 'AFSPA culture'.[7]

In such a culture, everyday citizenship practices, socio-political vocabularies, livelihood goals and interpersonal relations became shaped by an atmosphere of violence and terror. This is not to say that inter-ethnic violence was absent from the Northeast before the implementation of the AFSPA, thanks to problematic colonial and post-colonial efforts to govern the region. But the kind of violence that accompanies such ethnic politics has come to mirror the brutal forms of violence enacted by the police and paramilitary forces under AFSPA, in both its forms and targets.

This includes sexual violence against women which, as human rights organisations have documented well, has long been a feature of AFSPA-related violence. The stripping, molestation and beating of an Adivasi (indigenous or tribal) girl in Guwahati in 2007, for example, as she was participating in a rally to demand Scheduled Tribe (indigenous people officially regarded as socially disadvantaged) status for her community, was carried out by members of a competing group seeking the same status.[8] Such violence has since become more normalised, as revealed in the conflict between the Kuki and Meitei that broke out in May 2023 in Manipur. While provoked by the latter being awarded Scheduled Tribe status and entitled to the same benefits as Kukis—which provoked fears among the minority Kukis about the loss of their livelihoods and security—Meitei men have responded by perpetrating widespread and brutal sexual violence against Kuki women. Although a video of two Kuki women being paraded naked by a mob on 4 May 2023 in Manipur, one of whom was later gang raped by a group of Meitei men, drew widespread attention to such horrors, innumerable other incidents, such as two women being raped and tortured to death that same day by a braying Meitei mob armed with knives and sticks, have provoked less interest.

So, too, has the fact that the men who committed such acts have, at times, been goaded on by Meitei women. What makes such behaviour particularly shocking is that Meitei women have historically engaged in brave protests against AFSPA-related sexual violence by Indian security forces. In July 2004, for example, in response to the abduction, torture, rape and murder of thirty-year-old Thangjam Manorama, falsely accused by the Indian army of being a militant, twelve middle-aged and elderly Meitei women stripped naked in front of Kangla Fort, where the 17th Assam Rifles were stationed, and held signs across their bodies with exhortations such as 'Indian Army Rape Us'. What the role of Meitei women in the brutalisation of Kuki women therefore reveals is the ways in which the decades of sexual violence perpetrated with impunity by the Indian security forces in Manipur have normalised such brutality, and rendered its perpetration speakable, imaginable, and ultimately acceptable.

Levels of militarised violence within the Northeast have, however, on the whole declined in recent years. Of the dozens of armed groups formerly in operation, only seven are currently still active.[9] That AFSPA continues to operate in various parts of the Northeast is a sign that for the Indian government, its inhabitants are still viewed as outsiders, and not as part of the nation-state. An Indian army commander who I interviewed, for example, from a camp in the Tinsukia district in Assam, justified the presence of the army there on the grounds that anyone who opposes the state is automatically an 'outsider', and not a rightful citizen. This may explain why in recent years there have been dozens of police 'encounters', or executions of purported criminal suspects—although in reality such encounters involve the murder of members of minority communities while they allegedly attempt to flee arrest—and why the Chief Minister of Assam, in a 2021 seminar on 'Redefining Police Standards in Assam', advocated that the police shoot suspects in the leg if they attempted to flee.

While such incidents raise serious questions about civil and human rights, justice, about assumptions of innocence before being proven guilty, and about the distinction between the judiciary and executive, the fact that a democratically elected politician could propose committing violence against citizens in the course of arresting them, without any repercussions, reveals the extent to which violence against the inhabitants of the Northeast has become normalised—as well as the ways in which such normalisation perpetuates the othering of entire groups of citizens in the Indian imaginary.

## What Makes Police Violence Possible in India

*An interview with Abdul Wahid Shaikh*

**Interviewer:** Since you were incarcerated for nine years and tortured by the police, for a crime you didn't commit and were acquitted for—namely the 2006 Mumbai train blasts, which led to the deaths of 189 people—what is your understanding of the nature of police violence in India?

**Shaikh:** Brutal police violence is now common, such as killing people through extra-judicial 'encounters' or torturing them at police stations—as well as outside them. In Gujarat in 2022, for example, police beat up a group of Muslim men in broad daylight, while members of the public shouted '*Jai Shri Ram*' (hail Lord Ram), a Hindu chant that has been used to intimidate Muslims.[1]

And they do all of this with impunity. During my time in custody, I overheard police officers saying that nothing could prevent them from abusing their power, by torturing or even killing an accused.[2] Cases like the encounter killings of Ishrat Jahan, a nineteen-year-old woman, and three men in Gujarat, in 2004, have emboldened them, because although seven police officers were charged with these deaths, the case was discharged without trial.[3] They cite such incidents to claim, with confidence, that nothing will happen to them if they abuse their power.

There are other issues that foster police violence in India, especially against particular groups of people. One is the caste system. Because Brahmins dominate the higher ranks of the police, they shield the upper castes from justice at the expense of the lower castes. In 2022, for example, the Supreme Court acquitted a Dalit man, Ramanand, after he had been sentenced to death and spent twelve years in jail for five murders he didn't commit—he had been framed by the Uttar Pradesh police for killing his wife and four daughters but they had actually been killed by Brahmins, who had been protected from prosecution by the police.[4]

The caste system helps to explain the attitude of the police towards groups like Muslims in India. According to a 2019 study, almost fifty per cent of Indian police officers feel that Muslims are likely to commit criminal offences, including terrorism.[5] I talk about this study on my YouTube channel, 'Acquit Undertrial'.[6] The police therefore have an anti-Muslim mentality, which predisposes them against Muslims.

What exacerbates these problems is the flaws in the Indian judicial system. There is a tendency in members of the Indian judiciary not to use their own judgement in regard to cases, or to do anything that challenges the police, out of concern that this will lower police morale—even when the police are clearly in the wrong. So, the judiciary largely upholds the police version of events in criminal cases. In Ramanand's case, for example, the Supreme Court clearly stated that a group of Brahmins had framed him for the murder of his family that they committed.

The judges should, therefore, have ordered a special investigation team (appointed for cases in which the police investigation has not been carried out appropriately) to reopen the case, investigate who killed Ramanand's wife and children, and prosecute those responsible. Instead, the Court noted that Ramanand had been in jail for many years and sentenced to death due to his poverty and lack of a good lawyer, so it ordered all legal aid committees in India to appoint experienced, competent lawyers to provide legal aid to accused people who were poor. The core issue, of convicting those who murdered Ramanand's family, was not addressed.

But judges often have no choice but to accept the police version of events, particularly in regard to terrorism-related offences. Since the passage of amendments to the Unlawful Activities (Prevention) Act in 2019, for example, particularly section 43(D), getting bail has become almost impossible for those charged with such offences, since judges no longer have the power to grant it in terrorist cases unless the prosecution agrees to this—and the prosecution never agrees.[7] The section also overturns the assumption that an accused person is innocent until they are proven guilty, since the accused essentially has to prove they did not commit the crime they have been charged with, which is very difficult to do, since the police often file false chargesheets and affidavits (written statements from individuals which they swear are true). As a result, people can end up being in jail indefinitely—which is a form of violence, aside from the fact that they may be subjected to torture.

Police violence is also enabled, however, by things like new technologies, often from elsewhere. The Indian police, or the Indian Intelligence Bureau, through their close connections with Israel, have adopted technologies to police minorities from it—such as what we could call 'bulldozer genocide'.[8] So when our police see how Israel is treating Palestinians or the USA has treated the inmates of Guantanamo Bay or Abu Ghraib—including things like isolating and torturing them—

they adopt such techniques. They think that if Israelis, for example, can get away with bulldozing people's houses, so can we. So, the similarities in the methods of policing minorities in Israel, the US, and India are not a coincidence.

**Interviewer:** Can you speak a bit more about your personal experiences in regard to the police?

**Shaikh:** My experience with the Indian police has not been good. I used to think that the police were servants who maintained peace and law and order—that they did good work. But they lack accountability, so when they do bad things, there is no stopping them. If they wrongly arrest someone and nothing happens to them, tomorrow they will go and do that to ten more people. If they kill one person in an encounter and there are no repercussions, tomorrow they will kill ten more people in encounters. Because they lack accountability, the tyranny of the police, in other words, keeps increasing.

They lack accountability for a number of reasons. One is the nexus that exists between doctors and the police. This was highlighted in 1996, in the DK Basu case.[9] In its judgement on this case the Supreme Court laid out guidelines that must be followed in regard to arrest or detention in order to prevent custodial violence, including on the medical examination of the bodies of those accused of crimes. These guidelines are beautifully articulated. As Jinee Lokaneeta discusses in this book, doctors do not, however, generally follow them. They largely, instead, provide false medical reports on the condition of those held in custody, either by giving incorrect information or by suppressing and withholding evidence, which protects the police by hiding custodial violence.[10] They often, for example, write 'NAD', which means 'no abnormality detected', on their reports in such cases, even though there may be many signs of torture on the bodies they have examined. Being a doctor is supposed to be a noble profession. Doctors should feel compassion upon seeing someone in distress and should work to alleviate their suffering, but that is not what happens in regard to custodial violence.

The police also lack accountability because of the nexus between the police and judiciary. Now there is a saffron, or right-wing Hindu, government at the helm in India, it is normal to see judges who pass orders or enact judgements that suit the present regime. However, even back in 2006, when I was arrested, there were some judges who were saffron-minded, and hence biased against Muslims. Since I am a Muslim, as were my co-accused, such judges never listened to us, never believed our statements that we were being tortured or threatened with being killed in an encounter, or that the police were threatening to rape our family members or bring false charges against them.[11] They said that we were lying, as a result of which we were forced to suffer imprisonment and torture.

**Interviewer:** Can you suggest any legal reforms to redress such issues?

**Shaikh:** According to Indian law, the police must file a chargesheet within a stipulated time, and if they fail to do so, the accused automatically gets bail. I believe we need a similar law that mandates bail for those accused in all cases, including murder, rape, and minor offenses, if a trial isn't undertaken within a set timeframe. It's crucial to implement a law, therefore, that ensures that criminal trials conclude within a reasonable period of time, with bail granted to the accused if this period is exceeded by even a day. This would reduce the huge backlog of legal cases in India and provide relief to many long-term detainees.[12] While there may be concerns that those on bail would abscond, these are unfounded, since bail conditions are quite strict, including the need for surety. I discuss these issues in my book, *Innocent Prisoners.*

Other judicial changes are needed to address the problems I've identified. The law needs to be amended, for example, to ensure judges do not accept information provided in the chargesheets police file as being *prima facie* true without a proper investigation of these. This would undermine the information provided by the police in criminal cases being deemed sacrosanct.

But other changes need to be made beyond the law. The working conditions of the police, for example, are very poor. Their shifts are twelve hours long, and the police-to-population ratio is poor. Police departments are also very hierarchical, so lower-ranking officers must bow to their superiors. The police are therefore constantly stressed, which is evident in their high suicide rates.[13] I believe this situation can be improved by implementing eight-hour shifts and recruiting more officers. Reducing their workloads will, in turn, lead to less pressure on the police to prove themselves by enacting violence to secure suspects. This could make the Indian police, in other words, more respectful towards their fellow human beings. To ensure this, however, the institutionalisation of the caste system within the police must end, which can be facilitated by members of the lower castes, Dalits, and Muslims being appointed and promoted to higher police positions.

I have already mentioned, furthermore, that there needs to be more institutional accountability for police violence. One reason for this lack of accountability that I haven't yet mentioned is that, in each state, the police report directly to the state's Home Ministry. The problem with this is that the ministries go out of their way to protect the police because police violence reflects poorly on them. So, responsibility for the police should be transferred to the judiciary, or else the police should be reorganised as an independent body with clearly defined accountability—since there will be accountability issues no matter which ministry they are transferred to.

This is evident in the ways in which agencies like the Central Bureau of Investigation (India's domestic crime investigating agency), the National Investigation Agency (its central counter-terrorism law enforcement agency), and the Directorate of Enforcement (tasked with investigating money laundering and violations of foreign exchange laws) are utilised to harass and intimidate political opponents, who are then subjected to false charges by the police. Shiv Sena MP Sanjay Raut, who a Mumbai court declared in 2022 had been illegally arrested for money laundering, is an example of this problem.[14]

**Interviewer:** Recent movements like Black Lives Matter, Dalit Lives Matter, Adivasi Lives Matter, and Muslim Lives Matter have demanded that the police be reformed or defunded. What is your opinion on this?

**Shaikh:** A lot of money is being spent in India to strengthen the police. The Home Ministry is spending a lot of money to build large police stations—inside which torture cells are constructed—along with sophisticated cars and weapons, and other kinds of equipment. Gyms are also being built inside police stations so that the police stay fit. It is true that the police are, mostly, very unfit, and overweight. They can't chase criminals like that. When it comes to male police officers, they are also being made fit so that a common person is awed by their tall, strong, and macho looks.

But I think that money should be spent, instead, on

reforming the police, in particular on changing their mindsets. They should be taught how to treat Indian citizens, and how to communicate with them. Today, no one wants to go to the police because they know that if they do, they will be abused, beaten, and humiliated, and not listened to. Think about how the police treated people in the protests over the passage of the Citizenship Amendment Act and the National Register of Citizens in 2019.[15] In some places they used batons, or water cannons. In others, they used rubber bullets. And they misbehaved with women, particularly at JNU (Jawaharlal Nehru University) and Jamia Millia Islamia.

When I was in jail, when the police were treating us very badly, I wrote a letter asking them not to consider people who are in jail as animals, and to learn how to talk to and treat us. The jail administration often asserts that its objective is to reform prisoners. But since the way the police treat prisoners is not meant to improve their behaviour but to dehumanise them, their behaviour, when they leave jail, is worse than when they went in. A change in attitudes would therefore be a big step towards addressing these issues.

There have, of course, been many reports and recommendations for police reform, including by High Court and Supreme Court judges. There has, however, been no real follow-up to these. So, while the need for police reform is urgent, who will address it? I don't think it will come unless civil society takes up the cause and engages in discussions with the government or the Home Ministry. Activists could, for example, engage with politicians like Sanjay Raut, Nawab Malik, and Jitendra Awhad, who have all been recently jailed and whose experience of the realities of jail life might motivate them to advocate for reform.[16] Meetings should also be arranged with chief ministers, and with influential individuals who can sway the authorities. While civil society organises public protests on issues to do with police violence and the criminal justice system, and holds meetings, it often fails to engage with individuals who have connections to the authorities who hold power. What we need is the political will to achieve this.

## How the Dehumanisation of the Police and Dehumanisation they Enact Work in Tandem

*An interview with Beatrice Jauregui*

**Interviewer:** The Indian police are forced to work in very complex situations, with a great many pressures and expectations on them—to which they, however, can, and do, respond with extra-legal violence. Considering your expertise as an anthropologist who works, among other subjects, on the Indian police, what do you think are the challenges to addressing this?

**Jauregui:** Police violence in India takes so many forms. There's everyday violence, such as beating somebody on the streets, or slapping them, but also more systemic, or structural forms of violence, such as who gets helped because they happen to be connected and have influence, and who doesn't. But members of the public do the same thing to the police, if they have a personal connection they can use—for example, a family member or a caste affiliate who can use their influence to put pressure on particular officers. The police often, however, feel obligated to serve people who they feel need their help, whatever their status might be. This can even include egregious forms of violence like (extrajudicial) 'encounter' killings, when villagers say to them, 'we're being harassed and the courts don't work and, we need immediate justice'. People do call upon the police to enact this type of violence. I call these social pressures a form of 'social demand'.

What's interesting here, is what the police view as 'real' police work, and what isn't—and for many of them enacting such summary justice is the sort of work they are meant to do. The flip side of this is that there's work they're supposed to do but that they don't see as part of their job, especially when it comes to things like gender violence or intimate partner violence. Regarding such forms of violence, the police I have talked to will say things like, 'Oh, that's a private family matter and that's not what we do'.

In the last decade or so there has been a lot more attention given to gender-based violence in India and how the police respond to it, particularly since the brutal gang rape and murder of a twenty-two-year-old woman in Delhi in 2012, now known as the Nirbhaya case and, more recently, the 2020 gang rape and murder of a nineteen-year-old Dalit woman in Hathras district, in Uttar Pradesh (UP), by four upper-caste men—and the acquittal of three of them.[1] So institutional reforms have been introduced at police stations, including in places like UP, where I have carried out much of my research on Indian policing.[2] These include police stations staffed by female police officers.

These reforms seem to have had some beneficial effects. In conversations that I have had with young women, they say things like, 'I am glad something is being done; I feel like I can call a line if somebody is harassing me'. They know that maybe the police will do something about it, maybe not, but they're relieved by the fact that some attention is being given to gender-based violence.[3] Yet on the day-to-day level, not much has changed. The UP government recently announced that seventy-nine new police *chowkis*, or outposts, run by female officers would be set up in rural areas, but it's not clear how much of this has or will be done.[4] Women who approach regular police stations in regard to gender-based issues are told things like 'you have to go over to the *mahila* [women's] police station' to lodge a complaint about them. So, issues relating specifically to women tend to be siphoned off to stations staffed by female officers, which makes officers at other stations think they don't have to deal with them. This ghettoisation of how gender-based violence is dealt with is not unique to India. Brazil, for example, tried to institutionalise a systemic response to gender-based violence, but it was largely ghettoised.[5]

**Interviewer:** You're talking, then, about potential ways to tackle what in your research you call the routinisation of police violence—whether that be through violence the police directly commit or, as is often the case with gender-based violence, facilitate—namely, targeting a particular issue which involves various agencies and is made a focus of reform?

**Jauregui:** Yes. It also involves a division of labour, and coordination between the state police and other agencies. But such an approach can also be problematic if the solution to a particular problem, such as gender-based violence, is seen as something that only certain police officers have to deal with, because then it's not integrated into the whole policing system. So, while, for example, gender-sensitisation training has been introduced in UP and other states, as well as human rights training, the cops, after doing it, generally go back to their *thanas* (stations) and everything they've learned seems abstract and philosophical, and not applicable to real life—so they don't apply it. The social pressures that the police face remain very strong, and these work against such reformist efforts.

**Interviewer:** In your work you talk about police death rates and the horrific working conditions the police are subject to, including various kinds of violence. Since the dehumanisation of the police and the dehumanisation they enact clearly work in tandem, do you see any possibility of addressing these issues?

**Jauregui:** This is a really tricky question to answer in light of social movements, in recent years, to defund and abolish the police—such as Black Lives Matter, globally, and in India movements like Muslims Lives Matter or Dalit Lives Matter. The issue of police violence—and, indeed, of policing in general—has therefore become very polarised.[6] These days people seem to be pigeonholed as either 'anti-police' or 'pro-police'. If you are not arguing that the entire system of policing as it operates should be completely transformed or abolished, then you can be seen as pro-status quo.

It's a real conundrum because at least some of the rank-and-file police I have come to know in UP are genuinely trying to find ways to change how they work, as well as to improve police working conditions—not least since their working conditions affect how they police. The police I've met feel so beaten down, though, and so incapable of affecting change, particularly for their own well-being—not least because there are laws preventing or banning unionisation of police in most Indian states. I am not, of course, suggesting that police unions are the answer to the issues we're talking about because police associations and unions can become really problematic, obstructionist interest groups when it comes to police reform.[7]

But there needs to be a lot more attention given to the kinds of structural violence that the Indian police suffer, since it's a cause of the routinised violence that they deploy against members of the public.[8] It dehumanises them. They also feel demonised—that, as they see it, 'everyone loves to hate us'—which heightens their disregard for the wellbeing of the people they're supposed to serve. Yet there's so little awareness about the wellbeing of the Indian police, or about their lack of wellbeing.[9] The Indian government, for example, doesn't track suicide rates among the police. This therefore needs to be integrated into public debates around what needs to be done in terms of police reform. I am not saying that police lives are more valuable than other people's lives, but that their lives are routinely devalued and dismissed. That's not only bad for the police; it also inhibits imaginative and progressive ways of addressing police violence.

In early 2020, for example, during the Covid pandemic, some exceptionally outspoken constables were saying on social media that 'the government is not taking care of us', and that on top of their poor living and working conditions they lacked decent personal protective equipment, were expected to harass people who evaded the lockdown curfew and were 'out here completely exposed'. But nothing was done to help or support them, which is why so many police feel beaten down.

**Interviewer:** Are there statistics for the numbers of Indian police who died during the pandemic?

**Jauregui:** The Indian Police Foundation did keep some statistics, although I am not sure how accurate these were.[10] I was working with a research assistant and we struggled to find definitive numbers, but there was some data that showed that the police were hyper-exposed to Covid early in the pandemic—so it's highly probable that it wasn't just healthcare workers who were getting sick and dying at higher rates than the general Indian population, but the police as well.

**Interviewer:** It's not possible for the police to strike in many Indian states, but are there any movements from within the Indian police to challenge the sorts of things we're talking about?

**Jauregui:** Yes, there are. I got interested in the issue of police attempts to organise in India because of an insurgency by members of the police paramilitary reserve, the Provincial Armed Constabulary, over grievances in relation to pay, working conditions and the right to organise a trade union in UP in 1973.[11] It was very violent—the police took over armouries, and dozens of people died.

The situation now is that a few states like Kerala have police unions that are very well entrenched. They are almost like a shadow police, since every single station has a union representative in it. Most other states, however, have ratified the 1966 the Police-Forces (Restriction of Rights) Act, which prohibits the police from associating or affiliating with any organisation that could be considered political, like a trade union. But there are associations that have been working underground, or informally. They usually just say that their association is a 'welfare' organisation, or an NGO (non-governmental organisation) so they can register it with the Registrar of Societies under what's known as the 1860 Societies Registration Act.[12] Even that can be difficult if the association has the word 'police' in its name, since the state registration office will say, 'no, this is a union, you're not allowed to do that'. But the police find workarounds to these challenges.

Several years ago, when I was in UP, I came across at least five groups that were vying to represent the rank-and-file police. They tended to be headed by men who are either (high) 'general caste' or Yadavs, one of the dominant OBC (Other Backward Caste) castes in UP.[13] Some of these groups have tried to take a more anti-corruption and pro-worker approach, like the Uttar Pradesh Police Association (formerly UP Police Welfare Association), led by Subodh Yadav, and aim to fight alleged corruption driven by senior officers and to undertake collective bargaining for things like salary increases.[14]

Brijendra Singh Yadav—after initially attempting to form another union first called the *Kalyan Sangathan* (Welfare Organisation) Uttar Pradesh, then the *Rajya Kalyan* (State Welfare) Trust/*Arajpaatrit* (Non-gazetted) Police Welfare Association—eventually went ahead and formed his own political party, the *Rakshak Jan Morcha Party* (guardian of the people), because the legal ban on police unions made operating even as a 'welfare association' too difficult.[15] Other police organisers have claimed they are attempting to form alliances with workers in other sectors, like public school teachers and farmers. But the place of police unions and associations in the broader labour movement globally, including in India, remains troubled, because many workers in other sectors do not want to associate with police unions.[16]

It remains to be seen, however, whether such efforts can accomplish anything. There have, of course, been a lot of commissions in the last fifty years that have made innumerable recommendations for reforming the Indian police.[17] But nothing much ever comes of them and their perspectives also tend to be very elitist, since their remit, and reports, are framed by top-level bureaucrats in the IPS (Indian Police Service) and IAS (Indian Administrative Service). They give no voice to, nor convey any sense of the issues that concern, the vast majority of the police rank and file.

**Interviewer:** You're saying that the police are not humanised in discussions about reform—that they're just seen as an inchoate mass?

**Jauregui:** Absolutely. I have had a senior police officer say to me, 'We [senior officers] need to make the decisions, and we know what's good for our [rank-and-file] men'. That's why efforts at police reform, such as the guidelines the Supreme Court issued to state governments in 2006 in what's commonly known as the Prakash Singh case, focus on issues mostly of concern to people in the top ranks of the police.[18] There is not only a belief, as another senior member of the Indian police said to me, that such changes will 'trickle down' to the lower ranks, but there's also, it seems, little desire to bring the police rank and file to the table and ask them what they feel is needed in terms of institutional changes.

Such views reveal another structural problem that relates more broadly to questions of police violence, namely that there is class warfare within the Indian police. For the subordinate ranks, senior officers are just petty tyrants who boss them around and force them to do their bidding. I'm not saying this is the actual case. But in many parts of UP, you will still see constables living in tents outside the house of a senior officer who they're basically acting as domestic servants for. Such a scenario reveals a lot about the structural violence of class, inequality, and caste too, depending on the context, within the police in India.

**Interviewer:** One of the interesting things you've shown in your research, however, is that despite the dehumanisation that those on the lowest rungs of the police hierarchy are subject to, they can show surprising compassion to the people they police. You've given examples, for instance, in which it's possible for the police to extort, say, fifty rupees from someone, but they instead choose to be altruistic and help them. There are spaces, then, that seem to open up sometimes in which the human prevails over institutional or social dynamics.

Do you have any thoughts on what makes those spaces possible?

**Jauregui:** Definitely. I've seen many instances in which the police will express real sympathy with people that they encounter through their work—they are not always just out there doing *laathi* charges.[19] So they do things like mediate disputes, comfort people—say when their house is robbed, or a child dies. At times this is due to caste affinity. Cops will think, 'Oh, this is a person from my community, and I know how oppressed I have felt'—so they want to help the person. Beyond that, the police see people struggling in all sorts of ways, which may resonate with them. They may, for example, see that someone is being abused in a household, which can remind them of abuse they may have suffered in theirs—so they try to put a stop to it.

There are all kinds of ways in which these spaces can open up. What needs to be done is to find ways to encourage that or make it a central part of conversations regarding police reform—and for this, again, it's vital to talk to the rank and file themselves. There's a lot of 'us versus them' sensibility when it comes to police reforms, with civilians thinking that they should be the ones to decide what needs to be done, because of a belief that the police will only act in their own self-interest. But if the police are not included in discussions about what needs to be changed or transformed then there's no real democratic sensibility in the whole process.

But how do we even talk realistically about something like police reform, be it in relation to systemic violence or whatever the case may be, in the current political context? The possibility seems ever more remote, because existing governance institutions and laws are being weaponised to target critics of the Hindu right—not just people from minority communities, but people who are speaking out against the ideology of the Hindu right and its impact on governance institutions. It's therefore getting harder and harder to speak openly about anything that's perceived to undermine the political establishment in India at the moment—which is how police reform is unfortunately perceived. So, something needs to change, on the political front, before we can talk meaningfully about change when it comes to the police in India.

# Contributors

**Sharib A Ali** is a doctoral student at the Institute of Social Anthropology, University of Bern. He is associated with several human rights initiatives in India and abroad, and works on issues in relation to justice, peace, and restitution.

**Ishita Chakrabarty** is an international legal researcher and holds an MA in International Law from the Graduate Institute of International and Development Studies, Geneva (IHEID). She is currently working on issues related to development finance and accountability.

**Veena Das** is Research Professor of Anthropology at Johns Hopkins University. Her most recent book is *Slum Acts* (Polity Press, 2022). She is a Fellow of the American Academy of Arts and Sciences and a Corresponding Fellow of the British Academy.

**V Geetha** is a feminist historian and publisher from Chennai, Tamil Nadu, who writes in English and Tamil on caste, labour, gender, education, and civil rights.

**Shalini Gera** is an advocate who practices in the Chhattisgarh High Court as part of the Janhit Legal Resource Centre, a voluntary group of lawyers providing legal aid to groups and movements on issues relating to social justice and societal change. She co-founded and worked in the Jagdalpur Legal Aid Group from 2013 to 2020, which provided legal assistance to the indigenous community in conflict-torn regions in Bastar.

**Vrinda Grover** is a lawyer, researcher, and human rights and women's rights activist. As a lawyer, she has appeared in prominent human rights cases and represented women and child survivors of domestic and sexual violence; victims and survivors of communal massacre, extrajudicial killings and custodial torture; sexual minorities; trade unions; and political activists.

**Sanjoy Hazarika** is an author, columnist, and research and policy analyst specialising in the Northeast of India and its neighbourhood. He is the founder and Managing Trustee of the Centre for North East Studies and Policy Research, Jamia Millia Islamia, and former international director of the Commonwealth Human Rights Initiative.

**Deana Heath** is Professor of Indian and Colonial History at the University of Liverpool. She has written widely on issues relating to policing and violence in colonial India, particularly on torture and sexual violence. Her latest book, *Colonial Terror: Torture and State Violence in Colonial India*, was published by Oxford University Press in 2021.

**Beatrice Jauregui** is an Associate Professor in Anthropology and Criminology at the University of Toronto who specialises in policing in India. She is the author of, among many other works, *Provisional Authority: Police, Order and Security in India*, published by the University of Chicago Press in 2016.

**Santana Khanikar** is an Assistant Professor in Political Geography at Jawaharlal Nehru University, New Delhi. Her areas of interest include policing and violence, spatial politics, and gender studies. She is the author of *State, Violence and Legitimacy in India*, published by Oxford University Press in 2018.

**Radha Kumar** is Associate Professor of History at Syracuse University, New York and is the author of *Police Matters: The Everyday State and Caste Politics in South India, 1900-1975*, published in 2021 by Cornell University Press.

**Vipul Kumar** is a researcher specialising in criminology and justice. He has widely documented the criminalisation of disadvantaged and minority groups and has co-founded Youth for Human Rights Documentation (YHRD), a network dedicated to documenting human rights violations and advocating for state accountability.

**Jinee Lokaneeta** is Professor in Political Science and International Relations at Drew University, New Jersey. She is the author of *The Truth Machines: Policing, Violence, and Scientific Interrogations in India*, published in 2020 by the University of Michigan Press and Orient Blackswan, and *Transnational Torture: Law, Violence, and State Power in the United States and India*, published by New York University Press in 2011 and Orient Blackswan in 2012.

**Abhinav Sekhri** is a graduate of the National Law School of India University, Bangalore (LLB) and Harvard Law School (LLM), and is a practising advocate in New Delhi focusing on issues to do with criminal law and procedure. He has written for various law reviews, newspapers, magazines, and also runs *Proof of Guilt*, a blog on Indian criminal law, procedure, and evidence.

**Vikash Narain Rai** is former Director General of Police (Law and Order), Haryana. He also headed the training academies of Haryana Police and Border Security Force and served as Director of the National Police Academy, Hyderabad.

**Bhavani Raman** is an Associate Professor of History at the University of Toronto. She is the author of *Document Raj: Writing and Scribes in Early Colonial South India*, published by the University of Chicago Press in 2012 and Permanent Black in 2015, and is currently working on a book on early colonial security laws in South Asia.

**Pooja Satyogi** teaches at the School of Legal and Socio-Political Studies, Dr B R Ambedkar University. Her research focuses on the interconnections between the pedagogy of police training, the bureaucratic nature of policing, and technologised policing. She is currently working on a book entitled *Intimate Public Spaces: Policing 'Domestic Cruelty' in Women's Cells, Delhi*.

**Abdul Wahid Sheikh** was falsely charged for playing a role in the 2006 Mumbai train blasts and incarcerated and tortured for nine years, along with other innocent Muslims. He is a lawyer and the author of *Begunah Qaidi* (Innocent Prisoners, 2017), runs a YouTube channel, Begunah Qaidi, which advocates for those who are falsely accused of crimes in India, and is currently pursuing a PhD.

**Mayur Suresh** is a Reader at the School of Oriental and African Studies, University of London. He is the author of *Terror Trials: Life and Law in Delhi's Courts*, published in 2023 by Fordham University Press and OrientBlackswan in 2023, and was awarded a Leverhulme Research Leadership Award in 2022.

**Mangla Verma** is a practicing human rights lawyer and researcher, working on issues to do with identity-based violence and state violence perpetuated against disadvantaged communities. She has co-founded Youth for Human Rights Documentation (YHRD), a network dedicated to documenting human rights violations and advocating for state accountability.

**Ather Zia** is an Associate Professor of Anthropology and Gender Studies at the University of Northern Colorado and is the author of *Resisting Disappearances: Military Occupation and Women's Activism in Kashmir*, published by the University of Washington Press in 2019. She is also a political anthropologist, poet, short fiction writer, and columnist, co-editor of the journal *Cultural Anthropology*, and the founder-editor of Kashmir Lit.

# Notes

## Introduction: Policing and Violence in India

1 For an overview of the Act, as well as the protests against it and the response of the police to these, particularly in Delhi, see Sharib Ali and Ishita Chakrabarty, 'Hate Crimes as the New "Legitimate": Anti-CAA protests and Policing in Aligarh Muslim University and Jamia Millia Islamia, 2019', Chapter 6 in this volume. See also Lindsay Maizland, 'India's Muslims: An Increasingly Marginalized Population', *Council on Foreign Relations*, 18 March 2024, available at https://www.cfr.org/backgrounder/india-muslims-marginalized-population-bjp-modi (last accessed 18 August 2024). The Delhi High Court passed this judgement in a writ petition, or request, filed by Kismatun, Faizan's mother (represented by advocates Vrinda Grover and Soutik Banerjee), that the Court transfer the investigation into Faizan's death to an independent agency in view of the partisan and biased actions of the Delhi Police.

2 'Delhi Riots: HC Orders CBI Probe into Death of Muslim Man Beaten, Forced to Sing National Anthem', *The Wire,* 23 July 2024, available at https://thewire.in/law/delhi-riots-hc-orders-cbi-probe-into-death-of-muslim-man-beaten-forced-to-sing-national-anthem. See also Jinee Lokaneeta, 'Faizan's Custodial Death Is the Collective Failure of Our Society and the Judiciary', 8 August 2024, available at https://thewire.in/society/faizans-custodial-death-is-the-collective-failure-of-our-society-and-the-judiciary (both last accessed 16 August 2024).

3 'Delhi Riots: HC Orders CBI Probe into Death of Muslim Man

Beaten, Forced to Sing National Anthem'; and Nupur Thapliyal, 'Faizan's Death A "Hate Crime", Delhi Police's Probe Has Been Sketchy: High Court In National Anthem Case', *Lawlive.in,* 23 July 2024, available at https://www.livelaw.in/high-court/delhi-high-court/faizans-death-a-hate-crime-delhi-polices-probe-has-been-sketchy-high-court-in-national-anthem-case-264262. On the value of CCTVs in police stations see Sneha Bharti, 'The Role of CCTV Surveillance in Mitigating Custodial Violence in India', *The Amikus Qriae,* n.d., available at https://theamikusqriae.com/the-role-of-cctv-surveillance-in-mitigating-custodial-violence-in-india/ (both last accessed 18 August 2024).

4 For more on the deaths of Jeyaraj and Bennix see Jinee Lokaneeta, 'Justice in Custody: Doctors as Semi-State Actors', Chapter 4 in this volume.

5 See Aditi Phadnis, 'Story in numbers: 5 people die in judicial custody every day, shows data', *Business Standard,* 11 September 2022, available at https://www.business-standard.com/article/current-affairs/story-in-numbers-5-people-die-in-judicial-custody-every-day-shows-data-122091100677_1.html; and 'Nearly 5 deaths daily in judicial custody in the last three years: MHA', *The Times of India,* 30 July 2021, available at https://timesofindia.indiatimes.com/india/nearly-5-deaths-daily-in-judicial-custody-in-the-last-three-years-mha/articleshow/84902683.cms (both last accessed 16 August 2024).

6 While the contributions to this book are informed by theoretical understandings of policing, not least of Michel Foucault's conception of policing as a form of discipline enacted by a variety of institutions (both state and non-state, such as the family), in addition to social norms, they focus largely on the police as a state institution. See, for example, *Discipline and Punish: The Birth of the Prison* (Alan Sheridan, tr., New York: Vintage Books, 1979); and *Security, Territory, Population: Lectures at the Collège de France 1977-78*, ed. M Snellart (Graham Burchell tr, New York: Palgrave Macmillan, 2007).

7 See Deana Heath, *Colonial Terror: Torture and State Violence in Colonial India* (Oxford: Oxford University Press, 2021).

8 'Briefing on The Armed Forces (Special Powers) Act', Amnesty International, 8 March 2004, available at https://www.amnesty.org/en/documents/asa20/025/2005/en/; and '"Misused, abused": India's harsh terror law under rare scrutiny', *Al Jazeera,* 16 August 2021, available at https://www.aljazeera.com/news/2021/8/16/india-uapa-terror-law-scrutiny (both last accessed 18 August 2024). The militarisation of policing is, however, a wider global phenomenon, in many cases as a result of colonial roots. See, for example, Anil Kalhan et al., 'Colonial Continuities: Human Rights, Terrorism, and Security Laws in India', *Columbia Journal of Asian Law,* 20, 1 (2006): 93–234.

9 Boniface Gaigulung Kamei, 'Nagaland Civilian Killings: AFSPA Is An Archaic Law That Has No Place In Modern India', *Adivasi Lives Matter,* 16 December 2021, available at https://www.adivasilivesmatter.com/post/nagaland-civilian-killings-afspa-is-an-archaic-law-that-has-no-space-in-modern-india. The UAPA has also been increasingly used, in addition, against human rights lawyers, activists, journalists, academics, and students 'as a tool of psychological warfare'. See Alpa Shah, *The Incarcerations: BK-16 and the Search for Democracy in India* (London: HarperCollins, 2024); Suchitra Vijayan and Francesca Recchia, *How Long Can the Lion Be Caged? Voices of Indian Political Prisoners* (London: Pluto Press, 2023); Sreejayaa Rajguru, 'The Strangling Grip of UAPA: Silencing Arundhati Roy and the Voices of Dissent', *The Wire,* 17 June 2024, available at https://thewire.in/law/the-strangling-grip-of-uapa-silencing-arundhati-roy-and-the-voices-of-dissent/?mid_related_new; and 'Seven Kashmiri students charged under UAPA for raising pro-Pak. slogans during World Cup final', *The Hindu,* 27 November 2023, available at https://www.thehindu.com/news/national/seven-kashmiri-students-charged-under-uapa-for-raising-pro-pak-slogans-during-world-cup-final/article67580372.ece. On undertrial prisoners, who constitute an astonishing seventy-five per cent of detainees in India, see Shreehari Paliath, 'Despite campaign, India saw number of prisoners increase in 2022', *Scroll.in,* 15 December 2023, available at https://scroll.in/article/1060246/

despite-campaign-india-saw-number-of-prisoners-increase-in-2022 (all last accessed 18 August 2024).

10 Saqib Wani, 'The Armed Forces Special Powers Act (AFSPA): Legal impunity to kill', *The Public Sphere: Journal of Public Policy,* 10, 1 (2022):187, available at https://psj.lse.ac.uk/articles/120 (last accessed 18 August 2024); and Dolly Kikon, 'The Predicament of Justice: Fifty Years of Armed Forces Special Powers Act in India', *Contemporary South Asia,* 17, 3 (2009): 271-282. See also chapter 10 in this volume.

11 Andrew Metheven, 'Militarism and the police: How our streets became battlefields', The Transnational Institute, 16 May 2021, available at https://www.tni.org/en/article/militarism-and-the-police (last accessed 18 August 2024).

12 Andrew Metheven, 'Militarism and the police'. See also Swati Parashar, 'Discursive (in)securities and postcolonial anxiety: Enabling excessive militarism in India', *Security & Dialogue*, 49, 1-2 (2018): 123 –135.

13 'What is the Rule of Law', United Nations, available at https://www.un.org/ruleoflaw/what-is-the-rule-of-law/ (last accessed 18 August 2024).

14 Upendra Baxi, 'The Rule of Law in India', *Sur: International Journal on Human Rights*, 6 (2007): 7-26 (last accessed 23 August 2024).

15 Baxi, 'The Rule of Law in India'. On how the rule of law and the constitutional protections have been eroded in India since the coming to power of the BJP in 2010, see Tarunabh Khaitan, 'Killing a Constitution with a Thousand Cuts: Executive Aggrandizement and Party-state Fusion in India', *Law and Ethics of Human Rights,* 14, 1 (2020): 49-95.

16 See Eklavya Vasudev and Thomas Blom Hansen, 'Citizens and the State: Policing, Impunity, and the Rule of Law in India', The Hindu Centre for Politics and Public Policy, *Policy Watch,* no. 18, 1 March 2024, available at https://www.thehinducentre.com/incoming/citizens-and-the-state-policing-impunity-and-the-rule-of-law-in-india/article67887312.ece (last accessed 18 December 2024); and Pratiksha Baxi, *Public Secrets of Law: Rape Trials in India* (New Delhi: Oxford University Press, 2007).

17 See Abhinav Sekhri, 'Confessions, Police Officers and Section 25 of the Indian Evidence Act, 1872', *NUJS Law Review,* 7, 1 (2014), available at chrome-extension://efaidnbmnnnibpcajpcglclefindmkaj/https://docs.manupatra.in/newsline/articles/Upload/E53B970C-C35A-4FB4-B3E3-F17CB9A8BB1B.pdf; and Neetika Vishwanath, 'Criminal Justice and the Death Penalty in India: An Opinion Study with 60 Former Supreme Court Judges', Oxford Human Rights Hub, 14 February, 2018, available at https://ohrh.law.ox.ac.uk/criminal-justice-and-the-death-penalty-in-india-an-opinion-study-with-60-former-supreme-court-judges/ (both last accessed 18 August 2024).

18 Nazifa Alizada et al., 'Autocratization Turns Viral: Democracy Report 2021', University of Gothenburg: V-Dem Institute, 2021, available at chrome-extension://efaidnbmnnnibpcajpcglclefindmkaj/https://www.v-dem.net/documents/12/dr_2021.pdf. See also 'Chasing accountability: The case of custodial deaths in India', *The Polis Project,* 21 July 2023, available at https://www.thepolisproject.com/research/chasing-accountability-the-case-of-custodial-deaths-in-india/. India is not alone in such a democratic decline, since according to the V-Dem report, as of 2020 sixty-eight per cent of the world's population was living under autocracies. The 2023 World Press Freedom Index report, however, ranks India as one of the lowest in the word—161 out of 180 countries—for press freedom, a situation the report deems 'very serious'. See '2023 World Press Freedom Index—journalism threatened by fake content industry', Reporters Without Borders, available at https://rsf.org/en/2023-world-press-freedom-index-journalism-threatened-fake-content-industry (all last accessed 28 August 2024).

19 *Report of the Indian Police Commission, 1902-03* (Simla: Printed at the Government Central Printing Office, 1903), p. 115.

20 See *Broken System: Dysfunction, Abuse, and Impunity in the Indian Police* (New York, NY: Human Rights Watch, 2009), available at https://www.hrw.org/report/2009/08/04/broken-system/dysfunction-abuse-and-impunity-indian-police; and Rituparna Bhattacharyya, 'Living with Armed Forces Special Powers Act

(AFSPA) as everyday life', *GeoJournal*, 83,1 (2018): 31-48. In 2024 India ranked fourth in the top 10 list of countries with the highest number of police killings in the world. See 'Police Killings by Country 2024', World Population Review, https://worldpopulationreview.com/country-rankings/police-killings-by-country (all last accessed 18 August 2024).

21 See Beatrice Jauregui, 'Police work and the politics of expendability in India', *Security Dialogue* (2024), https://doi.org/10.1177/09670106241230431; and Shemin Joy, '35,398 police personnel killed on duty since independence; 264 in past one year', *The Deccan Herald*, 21 October 2020, available at https://www.deccanherald.com/india/35398-police-personnel-killed-on-duty-since-independence-264-in-past-one-year-905158.html (both last accessed 18 August 2024).

22 According to the 2022 Global Peace Index report, India ranks in the top thirty least peaceful countries. See 'Global Peace Index 2022', Institute for Economics and Peace, available at chrome-extension://efaidnbmnnnibpcajpcglclefindmkaj/https://www.economicsandpeace.org/wp-content/uploads/2022/06/GPI-2022-web.pdf (last accessed 18 December 2024).

23 Sidharth Bhatia, 'Why Indians Don't Come Out on the Streets Against Regular Police Brutality', *The Wire*, 1 June 2020, available at https://thewire.in/rights/george-floyd-protests-india-police-brutality (last accessed 26 August 2024). See also Hannah Ellis-Petersen, '"We are not safe": India's Muslims tell of wave of police brutality', *The Guardian*, 3 January 2020, available at https://www.theguardian.com/world/2020/jan/03/we-are-not-safe-indias-muslims-tell-of-wave-of-police-brutality; Jayshree Bajoria, 'India's Police Found Complicit in Anti-Muslim Mob Violence', *Human Rights Watch*, 17 July 2020, available at https://www.hrw.org/news/2020/07/17/indias-police-found-complicit-anti-muslim-mob-violence; Anand Dutta, 'Custodial deaths, claims of torture—how Adivasis suffer "police repression" in Jharkhand', *The Print*, 27 March 2022, available at https://theprint.in/india/custodial-deaths-claims-of-torture-how-adivasis-suffer-police-repression-in-jharkhand/888743/; and Gagan

Preet Singh, 'Caste and Policing', *Society & Space*, 22 April 2024, available at https://www.societyandspace.org/articles/caste-and-policing (all last accessed 18 August 2024).

24 Jeffrey Gettleman and Sameer Yasir, 'Hundreds of Police Killings in India, but No Mass Protests', *The New York Times*, 20 August 2020, available at https://www.nytimes.com/2020/08/20/world/asia/india-police-brutality.html?auth=login-google1tap&login=google1tap&login=smartlock&auth=login-smartlock (last accessed 18 August 2024).

25 Bhatia, 'Why Indians Don't Come Out on the Streets Against Regular Police Brutality'.

26 Jeffrey Gettleman, 'In India Tech City Shocked by Gang Rape, Vigilante Justice Gets Praise', *The New York Times*, 21 December 2019, available at https://www.nytimes.com/2019/12/21/world/asia/india-rape-hyderabad.html (last accessed 18 August 2024).

27 PTI, 'What Assam CM said on shooting at criminals trying to fle' *Deccan Herald*, 6 July 2021, available at https://www.deccanherald.com/india/what-assam-cm-said-on-shooting-at-criminals-trying-to-flee-1005404.html (last accessed 18 August 2024).

28 '"Thok Denge": We will knock down criminals in UP, says UP CM Yogi Adityanath in Aap Ki Adalat', *IndiaTV*, 3 June 2017, available at https://www.indiatvnews.com/politics/national-thok-denge-we-will-knock-down-criminals-in-up-says-up-cm-yogi-adityanath-in-aap-ki-adalat-384587 (last accessed 18 December 2024).

29 Protesting against the state in India can be met with considerable reprisals. See, for example, 'India: Deadly Force Used Against Protesters: Police Target Anti-Citizenship Law Demonstrators', *Human Rights Watch*, 23 December 2019, available at https://www.hrw.org/news/2019/12/23/india-deadly-force-used-against-protesters; and Abrary Fayaz and Mehran Firdous, 'India's massive farmer protests spark police brutality claims', *Nikkei Asia*, 24 February 2024, available at https://asia.nikkei.com/Politics/India-s-massive-farmer-protests-spark-police-brutality-claims (both last accessed 18 August 2024). See also Gettleman and Yasir, 'Hundreds of Police Killings in India, but No Mass Protests'.

30 'Custodial Torture Continues Unabated in India Amidst Culture of Impunity: Report', *The Wire*, 8 July 2020, available at https://thewire.in/rights/custodial-torture-continues-unabated-in-india-amidst-culture-of-impunity-report (last accessed 18 August 2024).

31 See G Haragopal and K Balagopal, 'Civil Liberties Movement and the State in India', in Manoranjan Mohanty, Partha Nath Mukherji, and Olle Tornquist (eds), *People's Rights: Social Movement and the State in the Third World* (New Delhi: Sage Publications, 1998), pp. 353-372; Ajay Gudavarthy, 'Human Rights Movement(s) in India: State, Civil Society and Beyond', in Ujjwal Singh (ed.), *Human Rights and Peace: Ideas, Laws, Institutions and Movement* (New Delhi: Sage, 2009), pp. 252-275; and Usha Ramanathan, 'Human Rights in India: A Mapping', 7 June 2001, available at https://www.ielrc.org/content/w0103.pdf (last accessed August 24, 2024).

32 See, for example, *NTR's One Year: A Report on the Democratic Rights in Andhra Pradesh* (Delhi: Andhra Pradesh Civil Liberties Committee and People's Union for Democratic Rights, 1984), available at chrome-extension://efaidnbmnnnibpcajpcglclefindmkaj/http://www.unipune.ac.in/snc/cssh/humanrights/02%20STATE%20AND%20ARMY%20-%20POLICE%20REPRESSION/A-%20Andhra%20pradesh/8.pdf (last accessed 18 December 2024).

33 The APDP website is available at https://apdpkashmir.com/ (last accessed 18 December 2024).

34 The APDR website is available at https://apdrwb.in/apdr/about (last accessed 18 December 2024).

35 The CPDR website is available at https://www.cpdrindiahumanrights.com/ (last accessed 18 December 2024).

36 See https://nagaaffairs.org/contributor/naga-peoples-movement-for-human-rights/ (last accessed 18 December 2024).

37 The PUCL website is available at https://pucl.org/ (last accessed 18 December 2024).

38 The PUDR website is available at https://www.pudr.org/ (last accessed 18 December 2024).

39 See, for example, Amnesty International, *India: Torture, Rape & Deaths in Custody* (New York: Amnesty International,

1992), available at https://www.amnesty.org/en/documents/asa20/006/1992/en/#:~:text=This%20report%20describes%20in%20detail,been%20beaten%20or%20otherwise%20tortured; '"We Have No Orders to Save You": State Participation and Complicity in Communal Violence in Gujarat', Human Rights Watch, 2002, available at https://www.hrw.org/report/2002/04/30/we-have-no-orders-save-you/state-participation-and-complicity-communal-violence; and '"Bound by Brotherhood": India's Failure to End Killings in Police Custody', Human Rights Watch, 19 December 2016, available at https://www.hrw.org/report/2016/12/19/bound-brotherhood/indias-failure-end-killings-police-custody (all last accessed 28 August 2024)

40 'India: Laws Misused to Crack Down on Peaceful Dissent: Raids on Activists, Blocking of Online Criticism', *Human Rights Watch*, 8 February 2024, available at https://www.hrw.org/news/2024/02/08/india-laws-misused-crack-down-peaceful-dissent#:~:text=(New%20York)%20%E2%80%93%20India's%20Bharatiya,Human%20Rights%20Watch%20said%20today (last accessed 15 December 2024).

41 See 'Amnesty International India halts its work on upholding human rights in India due to reprisal from Government of India', Press Release, 29 September 2020, available at https://www.amnesty.org/en/latest/press-release/2020/09/amnesty-international-india-halts-its-work-on-upholding-human-rights-in-india-due-to-reprisal-from-government-of-india/ (last accessed 15 December 2024).

42 See the NHRC website at https://nhrc.nic.in/about-us/about-the-Organisation#:~:text=The%20National%20Human%20Rights%20Commission,(Amendment)%20Act%2C%202006 (last accessed 18 December 2024).

43 See '"Bound by Brotherhood": India's Failure to End Killings in Police Custody'; Baljeet Kaur, 'India's Silent Acceptance of Torture Has Made It a "Public Secret"', *Economic and Political Weekly*, 53, 36 (8 September 2018), available at https://www.epw.in/engage/article/indias-silent-acceptance-torture-has; 'India needs a standalone law on custodial torture', *The New Indian Express*,

3 June 2023, available at https://www.newindianexpress.com/states/tamil-nadu/2023/Jun/03/india-needs-a-standalone-law-on-custodial-torture-2581467.html; and Vasudev and Hansen, 'Citizens and the State' (all last accessed 18 August 2024).

44 See Ankita Pandey, 'Left turn to legalism: Fact-finding inquiries as political critique in 1970s India', *Third World Quarterly*, 42, 3 (2021): 525-542. The civil liberties and democratic rights movements have, however, been critiqued for their disconnect from the women's and anti-caste movements in India. See Uma Chakravarti, 'Archiving Disquiet: Feminist Praxis and the Nation-State', in Singh (ed.), *Human Rights and Peace*, pp. 49–73; and Kancha Illaiah, 'Caste or Class or Caste-Class: A Study in Dalitbahujan Consciousness and Struggles in Andhra Pradesh in 1980s', in Manoranjan Mohanty (ed.), *Class, Caste, Gender* (New Delhi: Sage, 2004), pp. 227-255.

45 See Ankita Pandey, 'Left turn to legalism: fact-finding inquiries as political critique in 1970s India', *Third World Quarterly*, 42, 3 (2021): 525-542. The civil liberties and democratic rights movements have, however, been critiqued for their disconnect from the women's and anti-caste movements in India. See Uma Chakravarti 'Archiving Disquiet: Feminist Praxis and the Nation-State', in Singh (ed.), *Human Rights and Peace*, pp. 49–73; and Kancha Illaiah, 'Caste or Class or Caste-Class: A Study in Dalitbahujan Consciousness and Struggles in Andhra Pradesh in 1980s', in Manoranjan Mohanty (ed.), *Class, Caste, Gender* (New Delhi: Sage, 2004), pp. 227-255.

46 Amrit Dhillon, 'India's police stations are human rights threat, says chief justice', *The Guardian*, 10 August 2021, available at https://www.theguardian.com/world/2021/aug/10/india-police-stations-human-rights-threat-chief-justice (last accessed 18 August 2024).

47 See Sarasvati NT, '7,500 CCTVs in Police Stations Across Haryana to Check Police Abuse, Steps to Implement Apex Court Order: Report', *Medianama*, 17 January 2024, available at https://www.medianama.com/2024/01/223-7500-cctvs-police-stations-haryana-police-abuse/#:~:text=Supreme%20Court's%20directions%20regarding%20CCTVs,recording%20both%20video%20and%20audio; and Swasti Chaturvedi, 'Installation Of CCTVs In Police

Stations: SC Grants 3 Months' Time To Centre, States & UTs To Comply With Its Directions', *Verdictum*, 26 April 2023, available at https://www.verdictum.in/court-updates/supreme-court/cctv-in-police-stations-sc-grants-three-months-time-to-centre-states-ut-1473620?infinitescroll=1. In January, 2024, the Punjab and Haryana High Court followed suit by ordering the Punjab Director General of police to submit a report detailing the functioning of CCTV cameras in police stations throughout the state. See 'HC seeks report on functioning of CCTVs at police stations from DGP', *The Hindustan Times*, 23 January 2024, available at https://www.hindustantimes.com/cities/chandigarh-news/hc-seeks-report-on-functioning-of-cctvs-at-police-stations-from-dgp-101705951281979.html (all last accessed 18 August 2024).

48 Sudarshan Varadhan, '"India's George Floyds": Father-son death in police custody sparks outrage', *Reuters*, 27 June 2020, available at https://www.reuters.com/article/world/india-s-george-floyds-father-son-death-in-police-custody-sparks-outrage-idUSKBN23Y0FA/ (last accessed 28 August 2024).

49 On the Dalit, Adivasi, and Muslim Lives Matter movements see Dalit Lives Matter at https://dalitlivesmatter.org/; Adivasi Lives Matter at https://www.adivasilivesmatter.com/; India Civil Watch, 'This Has Happened Before', *Antipode Online*, 30 October 2020, available at https://antipodeonline.org/2020/10/30/dalit-lives-matter/; ANI, 'Students, activists protest against Rajasthan hacking in Delhi', *Business Standard*, 10 December 2017, available at https://www.business-standard.com/article/news-ani/students-activists-protest-against-rajasthan-hacking-in-delhi-117121000029_1.html; and Sumedha Pal, 'Tripura Violence: UAPA Charges Levied Against Lawyers From Fact-Finding Team', *The Wire*, 4 November 2021, available at https://thewire.in/communalism/tripura-violence-uapa-charges-levied-against-lawyers-from-fact-finding-team (all last accessed 18 August 2024).

50 See Arun Ferreira, *Colours of the Cage: A Prison Memoir* (Delhi: Aleph Book Company, 2014); Mohammad Aamir Khan and Nandita Haksar, *Framed as a Terrorist: My 14-year Struggle to*

*Prove my Innocence* (New Delhi: Speaking Tiger Publishing, 2016); Essar Batul et al, *Do You Remember Kunan Pushpora* (New Delhi: Zubaan, 2016); Abdul Wahid Shaikh, *Begunah Qaidi* (Delhi: Pharos Media, 2017); Sunetra Choudhury, *Behind Bars: Prison Tales of India's Most Famous* (New Delhi: Roli Books, 2017). See also a rare police testimonial on police violence, Anand Teltumbde, 'Cruel, Colonial and "High on Theatrics": Why India's Police Are The Way They Are', *The Wire,* 20 July 2024, available at https://thewire.in/books/india-police-quagmire-book-sunil-ramanand (last accessed 28 August 2024).

51 This includes issues relating to arrests, remanding suspects to police or judicial custody, indefinite detention, bail, legal representation, evidence, and the condition of lockups and prisons.

52 See, for example, Alpa Shah, *The Incarcerations: BK-16 and the Search for Democracy in India* (London: HarperCollins, 2024); and Ajaz Ashraf, *Bhima Koregaon: Challenging Caste* (Self-published, 2024).

53 'Police brutality as heroism: 8 Tamil films we didn't question', *The News Minute,* 27 June 2020, https://www.thenewsminute.com/tamil-nadu/police-brutality-heroism-8-tamil-films-we-didnt-question-127458; Omkar Khandekar, 'Rethinking the angry young cop in Indian cinema', *Mint Lounge,* 13 July 2020, available at https://lifestyle.livemint.com/how-to-lounge/movies-tv/rethinking-the-angry-young-cop-in-indian-cinema-111634476144273.html; and 'Supercops in cinema: Breaking the law in real life?', *Citizens for Justice and Peace,* 7 December 2022, available at https://cjp.org.in/supercops-in-cinema-breaking-the-law-in-real-life/ (all last accessed 18 August 2024).

54 See Sowmya Rajendran, 'In wake of Ambasamudram case, tracing Tamil cinema's portrayals of police brutality', *The News Minute,* 7 April 2023, available at https://www.thenewsminute.com/tamil-nadu/wake-ambasamudram-case-tracing-tamil-cinema-s-portrayals-police-brutality-175613; Stephen McCarty, 'Indian crime drama Paatal Lok dives into police brutality and offers a considered comment on world's largest democracy', *South China Morning Post,*

7 June 2020, available at https://www.scmp.com/magazines/post-magazine/arts-music/article/3087647/indian-crime-drama-paatal-lok-dives-police; and Rahul Desai, 'Kohra series review: The most captivating series of 2023 so far', *Film Companion,* 15 July 2023 (all last accessed 18 August 2024).

55 Anurag Tiwary, 'The unlawfulness of police brutality in India', *The Leaflet,* 26 October 2021, available at https://theleaflet.in/the-unlawfulness-of-police-brutality-in-india/ (last accessed 18 August 2024).

56 Bharti Jain, 'MHA to Lok Sabha: 2152 cases of deaths in judicial custody, 155 in police custody', *The Times of India,* 22 March 2022, available at https://timesofindia.indiatimes.com/india/mha-to-lok-sabha-2152-cases-of-deaths-in-judicial-custody-155-in-police-custody/articleshow/90380779.cms (last accessed 18 August 2024).

57 See 'What the surge in criticism of the three new criminal laws is all about', *The Leaflet,* 30 June 2024, available at https://theleaflet.in/what-the-surge-in-criticism-of-the-three-new-criminal-laws-is-all-about/; and Project 39A's extensive analysis of the new acts at https://p39ablog.com/category/analysis-of-bills/ (both last accessed 18 August 2024).

58 Rebecca Root, 'Criminal law: New legislation leaves Indian lawyers confused and ruing missed opportunities', International Bar Association, 5 August 2024, available at https://www.ibanet.org/criminal%20law-new-legislation-leaves-iIndian-lawyers-confused-and-ruing-missed-opportunities (last accessed 18 August 2024).

59 Semi-state actors are closely connected to a state but are not part of it.

60 See Maja Daruwala, 'A specific anti-torture law needs to be detailed, comprehensive and conform to international standards', *The Indian Express*, 27 September 27 2019, available at https://indianexpress.com/article/opinion/columns/exorcising-third-degree-torutre-police-force-amit-shah-6032055/ (last accessed 10 September 2024).

61 See Nikita Sonavane, 'Everyday policing is casteist', *Times of India* blog, 22 July 2023, available at https://timesofindia.indiatimes.com/blogs/developing-contemporary-india/everyday-policing-is-

casteist/. See also Nikita Sonavane, Mrinalini R, Aditya Rawat, Ramani Mohanakrishnan, and Vikas Yadav, 'Building Blocks of a Digital Caste Panopticon: Everyday Brahminical Policing in India', *Logic(s)*, 20 (13 December 2023), available at https://logicmag.io/policy/building-blocks-of-a-digital-caste-panopticon-everyday-brahminical-policing/ (both last accessed on September 10, 2024).

62 See '"Bound by Brotherhood': India's Failure to End Killings in Police Custody'; and '"We are humans in uniforms": Delhi police stage protest after assault by lawyers', *The Indian Express*, 6 November 2019, available at https://indianexpress.com/photos/india-news/tis-hazari-clash-delhi-police-protest-against-lawyers-6104180/ (last accessed 18 August 2024).

63 See, for example, David Arnold, *Police Power and Colonial Rule: Madras 1859-1947* (Oxford University Press, 1986); Essar Batool Ifrah Butt, Samreena Mushtaq, Munaza Rashid, and Natasha Rather, *Do You Remember Kunan Poshpura? The Story of a Mass Rape* (New Delhi: Zubaan Books, 2016); Pratiksha Baxi, *Public Secrets of Law: Rape Trials in India* (New Delhi: Oxford University Press, 2014); Upendra Baxi, *The Crisis of the Indian Legal System* (New Delhi: Vikas Publishing House Pvt Ltd, 1982); Saroj Kumar Bhowmik, *Rural Police, Local Justice in Bengal (1772-1870)* (Calcutta: Nalanda Publications, 1991); Anuj Bhuwania, '"Very Wicked Children": "Indian torture" and the Madras Torture Commission Report of 1855', *Sur: Journal on Human Rights*, 10 (2009): 6-27; David A Campion, 'Authority, Accountability and Representation: the United Provinces police and the dilemmas of the colonial policeman in British India, 1902-39', *Historical Research* 76, 192 (2003): 217-237; Uma Chakravarti (ed.), *Fault Lines of History: The India Papers II* (New Delhi: Zubaan Books, 2016), Rajnarayan Chandarvarkar, *Imperial Power and Popular Politics: Class, Resistance and the State in India, c. 1850-1950* (Cambridge University Press, 1998); Basudev Chatterji, 'The Darogah and the Countryside: The Imposition of Police Control in Bengal and its Impact (1793-1837)', *The Indian Economic and Social History Review* 18, 1 (1981): 19-42; KS Dhillon, *Defenders of the Establishment: Ruler-Supportive Police Forces of*

*South Asia* (Shimla: Indian Institute of Advanced Study, 1998); Nandini Gooptu, *The Politics of the Urban Poor in Early Twentieth-Century India* (Cambridge: Cambridge University Press, 2001); Prashant Kidambi, '"The ultimate masters of the city": Police, public order and the poor in colonial Bombay, c. 1893-1914', *Crime, Histoire & Sociétés /Crime, History & Societies*, Vol. 8, no, 1 (2004): 27-47; Dolly Kikon and Duncan McDui-Ra, *Ceasefire City: Militarism, Capitalism, and Urbanism in Dimapur* (New York: Oxford University Press, 2021); TK Vinod Kumar and Arvind Verma, 'Hegemony, Discipline and Control in the Administration of Police in Colonial India', *Asian Criminology* 4 (2009): 61-78; Anupuma Rao, 'Problems of Violence, States of Terror: Torture in Colonial India', in Steven Pierce and Anupama Rao (eds.), *Discipline and the Other Body: Correction, Corporeality, Colonialism* (Duke University Press, 2006), pp. 151-185; Douglas Peers, 'Torture, the Police, and the Colonial State in the Madras Presidency, 1816-55', *Criminal Justice History: An International Annual*, 12 (1991): 29-56; Anastasia Piliavsky, 'The Moghia Menace, or the Watch Over Watchmen In British India', *Modern Asian Studies* 47, 3 (2013): 751-779; Arnaud Sauli, 'Circulation and Authority: Police, Public Space and Territorial Control in Punjab, 1861-1920', in Claude Markovits, Jacques Pouchepadass and Sanjay Subrahmanyam (eds), *Society and Circulation: Mobile People and Itinerant Cultures in South Asia, 1750-1950* (New Delhi: Permanent Black, 2003), pp. 215-274; Navsharan Singh and Patrick Hoenig (eds), *Landscapes of Fear: Understanding Impunity in India* (New Delhi: Zubaan Books, 2014); Arvind Verma, 'Consolidation of the Raj: Notes from a Police Station in British India, 1865-1928', *Criminal Justice History* 17 (2002): 109-32; and Rachel Wahl, *Just Violence: Torture and Human Rights in the Eyes of the Police* (Stanford: Stanford University Press, 2017).

64 See Sharib Ali, 'Politics of Terror: The Mecca Masjid Blast Case', *Economic and Political Weekly*, 48, 34 (24 August 2013): 36-46; Veena Das, *Life and Words: Violence and the Descent into the Ordinary* (Berkeley: University of California Press, 2006); V Geetha,

'On Impunity', *Economic and Political Weekly,* 48, 2 (January 12, 2013): 15-17; V Geetha, *Undoing Impunity: Speech After Sexual Violence* (New Delhi: Zubaan Books, 2016); Vrinda Grover and Saumya Uma, *Kandhamal: Introspection of Initiative for Justice 2007-2015* (Media House, 2015); Sanjoy Hazarika, *Strangers of the Mist: Tales of War And Peace from India's Northeast* (New Delhi: Penguin, 1995); Sanjoy Hazarika, *Writing On The Wall: Reflections on the North-east* (New Delhi: Penguin, 2008); Deana Heath, 'Torture, the State and Sexual Violence Against Men in Colonial India', *Radical History Review*, 126 (2016): 122-133; Deana Heath, *Colonial Terror*; Deana Heath, 'Some "nameless, dreadful wrong": Reading the Silencing of Police Rape in the Indian Colonial Archive', in *Intersectional Encounters in the Nineteenth-Century Archive,* ed. Rachel Bryant Davies and Erin Johnson-Williams (London: Bloomsbury, 2022); Beatrice Jauregui, 'Law and Order: Police Encounter Killings and Routinized Political Violence', in I Clark-Decès (ed.), *A Companion to the Anthropology of India* (Oxford: Wiley-Blackwell, 2010), 371-388; Beatrice Jauregui, 'Beatings, Beacons and Big Men: Police Disempowerment and Delegitimation in India', *Law & Social Inquiry* 38/3 (2013): 643-669; Beatrice Jauregui, 'Just War: The Metaphysics of Police Vigilantism in India', *Conflict and Society* 1/1 (2015), 41-59; Beatrice Jauregui, *Provisional Authority: Police, Order, and Security in India* (New Delhi: Permanent Black, 2016); Santana Khanikar, *State Violence and Legitimacy in India* (New Delhi: Oxford University Press, 2018); Radha Kumar, *Police Matters: The Everyday State and Caste Politics in India, 1900-1975* (Cornell: Cornell University Press, 2021); Jinee Lokaneeta, *Transnational Torture: Law, Violence, and State Power in the United States and India* (New York: New York University Press, 2011); Jinee Lokaneeta, *The Truth Machines: Policing, Violence and Scientific Interrogations in India* (Ann Arbor: University of Michigan Press, 2020); Bhavani Raman, 'Law in Times of Counter-insurgency', in Aparna Balachandran, Rashmi Pant and Bhavani Raman (eds), *Iterations of Law: Legal Histories from India* (New Delhi: Oxford University Press, 2018), pp. 120-146; Pooja

Satyogi, 'Law, police and "domestic cruelty": Assembling written complaints from oral narratives', *Contributions to Indian Sociology*, 53, 1 (2019): 46–71; Abhinav Sekhri, 'From "Bully Boys" to "Willing Servants": Police, the Third Degree, and Indian Courts: 1861-1961', SSRN, 5 May 2018, available at https://papers.ssrn.com/sol3/papers.cfm?abstract_id=3174042 (last accessed 18 December 2024); Abdul Wahid Shaikh, *Innocent Prisoners: Begunah Qaidi* (New Delhi: Pharos Media, 2021 [2018]); Mayur Suresh, *Terror Trials: Life and Law in Delhi's Courts* (New York: Fordham University Press, 2023); and Ather Zia, *Resisting Disappearance: Military Occupation and Women's Activism in Kashmir* (Seattle: University of Washington Press, 2019).

65 Rachel Kushner, 'Is Prison Necessary? Ruth Wilson Gilmore Might Change Your Mind', *The New York Times Magazine*, 17 April 2019, available at https://www.nytimes.com/2019/04/17/magazine/prison-abolition-ruth-wilsongilmore.html#:~:text=%E2%80%9CI%20think%20the%20fact%20that,and%20in%20grass%2Droot%20circles. (last accessed 18 August 2024).

66 While established in 1993 to protect human rights in India, at the time of writing this book the National Human Rights Commission's accreditation status by the Global Alliance of National Human Rights Institutions, a UN-linked body, has been deferred for a second time based on its lack of independence, pluralism, diversity, and accountability—not least for overlooking human rights violations by the state, including the police, by police officers, and for failing to engage effectively with human rights defenders in India (who are widely viewed, by the Indian government, as 'anti-nationals'). See Aakar Patel, 'After NHRC Loses Its UN Links, India Might Lose Vote at Human Rights Body', *The Wire*, 21 May, 2024, available at https://thewire.in/rights/after-nhrc-loses-its-un-links-india-might-lose-vote-at-human-rights-body (last accessed 18 August 2024).

67 See also Josy Joseph, *How to Subvert a Democracy: Inside India's Deep State* (London: Hurst, 2022).

68 See also, however, the interview with Shalini Gera and reflection by Santana Khanikar, in section four of this volume.

69 See United Nations Sustainable Development Goal 16 at https://www.un.org/sustainabledevelopment/peace-justice/ (last accessed 28 August 2024).

## PART I: FROM THE COLONIAL TO THE POST-COLONIAL

### Chapter 1. The Colonial Origins of Police Violence in India

1 Note: This chapter is derived from my book *Colonial Terror: Torture and State Violence in India* (Oxford University Press, 2021), which offers a theoretical analysis of the nature of police violence in colonial India and draws upon a wide range of archival material from colonial and pre-colonial India. It thus addresses a number of the suggestions made by Veena Das in her 'further thoughts' on this section of *Policing and Violence in India* that I do not have the space—or, since this book is intended for a general readership—opportunity to develop here.

2 IOR/F/4/1930/82995, British Library (BL).

3 Jason Burke, 'Delhi gang-rape accused were tortured by police, lawyer claims', *The Guardian,* 10 January, 2013. Available at https://www.theguardian.com/world/2013/jan/10/delhi-gang-rape-accused-claim-torture (last accessed 28 August 2024).

4 National Campaign Against Torture, *India: Annual Report on Torture, 2019*26 June 2020, available at http://www.uncat.org/wp-content/uploads/2020/06/INDIATORTURE2019.pdf (last accessed 28 August 2024).

5 The marginalisation of Chinoo and Govindoo, however, is complex, since Chinoo belonged to a sub-group of an artisanal caste, the *Kammālan,* that claimed Brahman status, while Govindoo was a Reddy, which while part of the ruling castes of southern India had a complex and contested place in the caste system, since during the colonial era the British classified them—as well, notably, as the Vellala group of castes—as *Sat*-shudras, or high-caste Shudras. They were both, however, poor, and their out-of-wedlock, inter-caste cohabitation undoubtedly increased their marginality.

6 Human Rights Watch, 'Broken System: Dysfunction, Abuse and Impunity in the Indian Police', 2009, available at https://www.

hrw.org/report/2009/08/04/broken-system/dysfunction-abuse-and-impunity-indian-police (last accessed 28 August 2024).

7 National Campaign Against Torture, *India: Annual Report on Torture, 2019.*

8 KS Subramanian, 'The Sordid Story of Colonial Policing in Independent India', *The Wire,* 20 November 2017, available at https://thewire.in/government/sordid-story-colonial-policing-independent-india (last accessed 28 August 2024).

9 'Eight years and numerous decisions taken by the Modi Govt to erase India's colonial past', *The Organiser,* 8 September 2022, available at https://organiser.org/2022/09/08/93437/bharat/eight-years-and-numerous-decisions-taken-by-the-modi-govt-to-erase-indias-colonial-past/ (last accessed 28 August 2024).

10 *Status of Policing in India Report 2019* (New Delhi: Common Cause and CSDS, 2019), available at https://www.commoncause.in/uploadimage/page/Status_of_Policing_in_India_Report_2019_by_Common_Cause_and_CSDS.pdf (last accessed 28 August 2024).

11 Praveen Swami, 'UP Police's brutality shows Indian law enforcement remains true to its colonial heritage', *The Print,* 15 June, 2022, available at https://theprint.in/opinion/security-code/up-polices-brutality-shows-indian-law-enforcement-remains-true-to-its-colonial-heritage/996914/ (last accessed 28 August 2024).

12 Martha K Huggins, Mika Haritos-Fatouros, and Philip G Zimbardo, *Violence Workers: Police Torturers and Murderers Reconstruct Brazilian Atrocities* (Berkeley: University of California Press 2002).

13 *Report of the Indian Police Commission, 1902-03* (Simla: Printed at the Government Central Printing Office 1903), p. 115.

14 Frantz Fanon, *Concerning Violence,* tr. Constance Farrington (London: Penguin [1963] 2008), p. 8.

15 Mike Davis, *Late Victorian Holocausts: El Nino Famines and the Making of the Third World* (London and New York: Verso, 2001), p. 302.

16 Talal Asad, 'On Torture, or Cruel, Inhuman and Degrading Treatment', in Arthur Kleinman, Veena Das, and Margaret Lock (eds), *Social Suffering* (University of California Press, 1997), p. 293.

17 Achille Mbembe, 'Necropolitics', *Public Culture,* 15, 1 (2003): 23.

18 *The Calcutta Review*, no. 157, 1884, 23-33; and *Report of the Proceedings of the Fourth Session of Indian National Congress, 1888* (Vintage Books, 1993), p. 52.

19 The Cornwallis code was a body of legislation that governed the administration of the police, judiciary, and civil administration in Company-administered India.

20 IOR/P/311/47, 13945, BL. The first legislation penalising police torture were Regulations XI of 1816 and XX of 1817.

21 Ranjan Chakrabarti, *Terror, Crime and Punishment: Order and Disorder in Early Colonial Bengal 1800-1860* (Kolkata: Reader's Service, 2009), pp. 95, 77.

22 Robert Carstairs, *The Little World of an Indian District Officer* (London: Macmillan and Co., 1912), p. 30.

23 *First Report of the Police Commission* (Calcutta: Government of India, 1860), p. 9.

24 TK Vinod Kumar and Arvind Verma, 'Hegemony, Discipline and Control in the Administration of Police in Colonial India', *Asian Criminology,* 4 (2009): 67.

25 KS Dhillon, *Defenders of the Establishment: Ruler-Supportive Police Forces of South Asia* (Shimla: Indian Institute of Advanced Study, 1998) 18.

26 'The Character of the Police', *The Modern Review* 5, 2 (Calcutta, February, 1909): 183.

27 John Bruce Norton, *The Administration of Justice in Southern India* (Madras: Athenaeum Press, 1853), pp. 111, 113.

28 Ibid, p. 8.

29 'The Madras Constabulary', *The Calcutta Review,* LXX (December 1860): 357. They were also, at various times in different provinces, required—along with the police—to act as revenue collectors.

30 Douglas Peers, 'Torture, the Police, and the Colonial State in the Madras Presidency, 1816-55', *Criminal Justice History: An International Annual,* 12 (1991): 47-48.

31 Act VIII of 1869.

32 '*Reports of Cases Determined in the Court of Nizamat Adawlut at*

*Calcutta for* 1855. Calcutta, Thacker, Spink and Co.', *The Calcutta Review*, LVI (June 1857): 479.

33 Act I of 1872.

34 Act V of 1898.

35 Regulation of XI 1816; Act I of 1872; and IOR/L/PJ/6/1368, File 1823, BL.

36 Norman Chevers, *A Manual of Medical Jurisprudence for Bengal and the North-Western Provinces* (Calcutta: Bengal Military Orphan Press, 1856), p. 26.

37 Major HWV Cox, *Medico-Legal Court Companion: A Complete Vade Mecum for Magistrates, Police Officers, Students and Members of the Legal and Medical Profession*, 2nd ed. (Calcutta: RL De, 1928), p. vii.

38 Home, Police, B, December, 51-53. 1909, National Archives of India (NAI).

39 *Report of the Committee Appointed by Government to Consider Certain Questions Connected with the Police Administration of the Punjab, Lahore, November 1899 to February 1900* (Lahore: Punjab Government Press, 1900), p. 113.

40 *History of the Police Training College, (Northern Zone), Phillaur*, n.a., n.d., 1, IOR Mss. Eur. F.161/184, BL.

41 Arvind Verma, 'Consolidation of the Raj: Notes from a Police Station in British India, 1865-1928', *Criminal Justice History*, 17 (2002): 114.

42 Cited in Appendix, in Norton, *The Administration of Justice in Southern India*, p. 8.

43 Anastasia Piliavsky, 'The Moghia Menace, or the Watch Over Watchmen in British India', *Modern Asian Studies*, 47, 3 (2013): 754.

44 *Report of the Indian Police Commission, 1902-03*, p. 87.

45 Such legislation included, for example, the 1899 Official Secrets Act, the 1901 Frontier Crimes Regulation, the 1901 Frontier Murderous Outrages Regulation, and the 1901 Frontier Law and Justice Regulation.

46 Frederic Mackarness, *The Methods of the Indian Police in the 20th Century* (London: National Press Agency, 1910), p. 15.

47 JC Madan, *Indian Police: Its Development up to 1905 an Historical Analysis* (New Delhi: Uppal Publishing House, 1980), p. 180.

48 *Report of the Committee Appointed by Government under Resolution (Police Dept). No. 373/VIII-186A-2, dated 6th June 1890 to Enquire into Certain Questions connected with the Police Administration of the North-Western Provinces and Oudh* (Allahabad: North-Western Provinces and Oudh Government Press, 1891), pp. 60, 99.

49 Ranajit Guha, *Elementary Aspects of Peasant Insurgency in Colonial India* (New Delhi: Oxford University Press, 1983), p. 18.

50 Huggins, Haritos-Fatouros, and Zimbardo, *Violence Workers*, p. 257.

51 Home, Police, A, January, 27-29, 1869, NAI.

52 David Canter, 'The Violated Body', in Sean T Sweeney and Ian Hodder (eds), *The Body* (Cambridge: Cambridge University Press, 2002), p. 59.

53 Sarah Solangon and Preeti Patel, 'Sexual Violence Against Men in Countries Affected by Armed Conflict', *Conflict, Security & Development*, 12, 4 (2012): 428.

54 IOR/F/4/1930/82995, BL.

55 Jinee Lokaneeta, *Transnational Torture: Law, Violence, and State Power in the United States and India* (New York and London: New York University Press, 2011), p. 191.

56 'The Madras Constabulary': 351.

57 *Abhydaya* (Allahabad), 11 Oct 1907, cited in David Campion, 'Watchmen of the Raj: The United Provinces Police, 1870-1931 and the Dilemmas of Colonial Policing in British India' (PhD Diss., University of Virginia, 2002), p. 140.

58 Chevers, *A Manual of Medical Jurisprudence*, p. 46.

59 IOR/L/PJ/6/1237, File no. 1499, 461, BL.

**Chapter 2. Neither at War nor at Peace: Martial Law and Policing in India**

1 Rain Liivoja, 'Military Justice', in Markus Dubber and Tatijana Horne (eds), *The Oxford Handbook of Criminal Law* (Oxford: Oxford University Press, 2014).

2 During the 1975-77 Emergency the Indian President, Fakhruddin Ali Ahmed, gave Prime Minister Indira Gandhi the power to rule by decree and suspended *habeas corpus,* a key protection against unlawful detention (following which thousands of Gandhi's opponents were placed in preventive detention). Such acts did not, however, constitute martial law, and the army was not involved in them.

3 Lisa Hajjar, *Courting Conflict: The Israeli Military Court System in the West Bank and Gaza* (Berkeley: University of California Press, 2005).

4 Mark Neocleous, 'From Martial Law to the War on Terror', *New Criminal Law Review: An International and Interdisciplinary Journal* 10, 4 (2007): 489-513; and Nasser Hussain, *The Jurisprudence of Emergency: Colonialism and the Rule of Law* (University of Michigan Press, Ann Arbor, 2003).

5 The Armed Forces (Special Powers) Act, 1958, available at https://www.mha.gov.in/sites/default/files/armed_forces_special_powers_act1958.pdf (last accessed 4 April 2024).

6 'The Armed Forces (Jammu and Kashmir) Special Powers Act, 1990', available at http://hrlibrary.umn.edu/research/af-specialpowersact1990.html; and 'The Armed Forces (Special Power) Act, 1958', Ministry of Home Affairs, available at https://www.mha.gov.in/en/commoncontent/armed-forces-special-power-act-1958 (both last accessed 4 July 2024).

7 AFSPA was modelled, notably, on the Armed Forces Special Powers Ordinance, enacted by the British in 1942 to repress the Quit India Movement, the aim of which was to end British rule in India.

8 KG Kannabiran, *The Wages of Impunity: Power, Justice and Human Rights* (Hyderabad: Orient Longman, 2004), p. 115

9 See, for e.g., Richard Clarke, *The Regulations of the Government of Fort William in Bengal in force at the end of 1853—to which are added, the Acts of the Government of India in force in that Presidency,* Vol. 1 (London: Cox, 1854), p. 754.

10 'Seizure and Trial of the Rebel Yemen Nair, the Principal Supporter of the Pyche Raja in Malabar', IOR F/4/268/5898, p. 9, British Library (BL).

11 Rivett Carnac, *The Presidential Armies of India* (London: Allen and Co., 1890); and Phillip Stern, 'Soldier and Citizen in the Seventeenth-Century English East India Company', *The Journal of Early Modern History*, 15, 11 (2011): 83-104. I thank Phillip Stern for emphasising the difference between martial law and military law in English legal thought.

12 John M Collins, *Martial Law and English Laws, c. 1500–c. 1700* (Cambridge University Press, 2016), p. 217.

13 Philip J Stern, *The Company-State: Corporate Sovereignty and the Early Modern Foundations of the British Empire in India* (New York: Oxford University Press, 2011).

14 Scott Kugle, 'Framed, Blamed and Renamed: The Recasting of Islamic Jurisprudence in Colonial South Asia', *Modern Asian Studies*, 35, 2 (2001): 259.

15 Collins, *Martial Law*, pp. 3-10; and Hussain, *The Jurisprudence of Emergency*, p. 101.

16 *Habeas Corpus* did not, notably, apply in East India Company territories in India until the establishment of Supreme Courts in Calcutta (1774), Madras (1800), and Bombay (1823), although its jurisdiction was restricted to such towns.

17 Collins, *Martial Law*, p. 164.

18 Ibid, p. 278.

19 Ibid, p. 209. The Kingdom of Great Britain was established in 1707, following the union of the Kingdom of England with the Kingdom of Scotland; the United Kingdom of Great Britain and Ireland was, in turn, formed in 1801 after the Kingdom of Ireland was added to this union.

20 Lauren Benton, *A Search for Sovereignty: Law and Geography in European Empires, 1400–1900* (Cambridge University Press, 2009).

21 Nasser Hussain, *The Jurisprudence of Emergency*, pp. 104-5.

22 Mark Neocleous, 'From Martial Law to the War on Terror'.

23 This was through Regulation 10 of 1804, which I will discuss in more detail below.

24 For an understanding of unequal treaties and how the Company used them in India see Robert Travers, 'A British Empire by Treaty

in Eighteenth-Century India', in Saliha Belmessous (ed.), *Empire by Treaty: Negotiating European Expansion, 1600-1900* (Oxford: Oxford University Press, 2015), pp. 132-160.

25 K Rajayyan, *South Indian Rebellion: The First War of Independence, 1800–1801* (Mysore: Rao and Raghavan, 1971). Some *palayakarar* were also, however, exiled or banished to the island of Penang, while those who conceded to the Company were restored as local landlords. A summary court-martial is the least formal type of court-martial, in which minor offences are tried by one officer. See Bryan Garner, *A Dictionary of Modern Legal Usage* (Oxford University Press, 2001), p. 298.

26 IOR/P/91/11, p. 10, BL.

27 Ibid.

28 IOR/F/4/168 2952, BL.

29 IOR/P/91/11, p. 11.

30 Ibid., p. 12.

31 Ibid., p. 10.

32 Ibid., p. 13.

33 Ibid.

34 Clarke, *The Regulations of the Government of Fort William*, p. 754.

35 39 George III, c. 11. See also Ronan Keane, '"The Will of the General": Martial Law in Ireland, 1535-1924', *Irish Jurist*, n.s., 25/27 (1990): 150–80; and Christopher M Roberts, 'From the State of Emergency to the Rule of Law: The Evolution of Repressive Legality in the Nineteenth Century British Empire', *Chicago Journal of International Law*, 20, 1 (2019): 1-61.

36 Marianne Elliott, *Wolfe Tone,* 2nd ed. (Liverpool: Liverpool University Press, 2012).

37 *Wolfe Tone* (1798) 27 St Tr 613; William Tone (ed.), *The Life of Theobald Wolfe Tone*, (London: Hunt and Clarke, 1828), p. 310; and William EH Lecky, *A History of Ireland in the Eighteenth Century*, Vol. 5 (London and Bombay: Longman, Green and Co., 1898), p. 78.

38 Thomas Frederick Simmons, *Remarks on the Constitution and Practice of Court Martial with a Summary of the Law of Evidence*

as *Connected with Such Courts* (London: F Pinkney, 1843 [1830]), pp. 631-5. See also Hussain, *The Jurisprudence of Emergency*, p. 104.

39 39 George III c. 11; and William EH Lecky, *A History of Ireland*, pp. 257-8.

40 Simmons, *Remarks on the Constitution,* p. 634; and Clarke, *The Regulations of the Government of Fort William*, p. 754.

41 IOR F/4/268/5898, p. 9. The traditional homeland of many Adivasi societies, Wayanad borders the uplands of Coorg and Mysore.

42 William Logan (ed.), *A Collection of Treaties: Engagements and Other Papers of Importance Relating to British Affairs in Malabar* (Madras: Superintendent Government Press, 1891 [1879]), pp. 237-8.

43 Logan, *Collection of Treaties*, p. 252.

44 IOR F/4/268/5898, p. 12.

45 Nayar had, in fact, already declared his support for the East India Company during its hostilities against Tipu Sultan and secured the Company's protection in 1799. See Logan, 'Certificate of Protection Granted to Pallur Eman Nayar', 19 May 1799, ii. cxc (190), p. 201.

46 IOR F/4/268/5898, pp. 48-49; IOR/F/4/279/6377; and IOR/E/4/905: 585-86, BL.

47 IOR F/4/268/5898, p. 43. The governor pronounced his annoyance with this outcome but accepted the sentence.

48 Richard Clarke, *The Regulations of the Government of Fort St. George* (London: J & H Cox, 1848), p. 156. In contrast to what happened to Nayar, however, the regulation required that individuals were required to be 'caught in open arms' to be tried via martial law.

## Chapter 3. Everyday Violence: Colonial Past to Post-colonial Present

1 'The India Cements Limited', *IndiaMart,* available at https://www.indiamart.com/theindia-cements-limited/aboutus.html (last accessed 12 March 2024).

2 The files still reside in the station's almirahs. I accessed them in 2013 as part of my PhD research.

3 GO 469 ms, Public Police, 26 September 1934; and GO 118 ms, Public Police, 27 February 1935, Tamil Nadu Archives.

4 For example, IR Jagadheesan, 'Tamil Nadu reels under caste clashes again', *India Today*, 19 October 1998, depicts caste as rooted in Tamil politics, while a weak police force attempts to put down violence. Available at https://www.indiatoday.in/magazine/states/story/19981019-tamil-nadu-reels-under-caste-clashes-again-827219-1999-10-18?onetap=true (last accessed 22 April 2024).

5 Rupa Viswanath, *The Pariah Problem: Caste, Religion, and the Social in Modern India* (New York: Columbia University Press, 2014).

6 This is especially true of the Nadar. See Robert Hardgrave Jr., *The Nadars of Tamilnad: The Political Culture of a Community in Change* (Berkeley: University of California Press, 1969).

7 VN Srinivasan, Superintendent, to Inspector, Tirunelveli, possibly June 1984, Manur station records.

8 Bernard S Cohn, 'The Census, Social Structure and Objectification in South Asia'", in *An Anthropologist Among the Historians and Other Essays* (Oxford University Press, 1987), pp. 224-254.

9 Manur Station, Melapillayarkulam Village, 1943.

10 Manur Station, Mavadi Village, 10 May 1943.

11 *Madras State Administration Report 1951-52* (Madras: Government Press, 1952).

12 *Madras State Administration Report 1964-65* (Madras: Government Press, 1965), para. 42.

13 Manur Station, Kurichikulam village, "Marava Sheet".

14 Edgar Thurston, assisted by K Rangachari, *Castes and Tribes of Southern India,* Vol. IV (Madras: Government Press, 1909).

15 Manur Station, Kurichikulam village, Station Crime History, 15 February 1952.

16 Ibid.

17 Manur Station, Therkukulam Station, Part IV Records, n.d., between 1933 and 1935.

18 I was allowed only a few hours at the station and scanned these in the pre-smartphone days with an old-fashioned scanner that blurred part of the text.

19 Manur Station, Therkukulam Station, Part IV Records, January 1947.

20 Manur Station, Therkukulam Station, Part IV Records, February 1952.

21 This view of caste society as a harmonious whole finds its way into many upper caste narratives, ranging from the writings of nineteenth-century Hindu reformers (Swami Vivekananda) and twentieth-century political leaders (Gandhi) to contemporary Hindutva websites.

22 Manur Station, Therkukulam Station, Part IV Records, December 1952.

23 Ranajit Guha, 'Prose of Counter-Insurgency', in *Subaltern Studies II*, ed. Guha (Delhi: Oxford University Press, 1983).

24 Thazhaiyoothu station, Chatram Kudiyiruppu records, 'Law and Order' files, 1938.

25 Ibid, October 1954.

26 Ibid, March 1959.

27 For more on this, see Susan Bayly, *Caste, Society and Politics in India from the Eighteenth Century to the Modern Age* (New York: Cambridge University Press, 1999).

28 Among others, see Mythily Sivaraman, *Haunted by Fire: Essays on Caste, Class, Exploitation and Emancipation* (New Delhi: LeftWord Books, 2013).

29 Anand Teltumbde, 'India's (Jati) Panchayati Raj', *Economic and Political Weekly,* 46, 3 (2011): 10-11; and C Aruna, 'Does Social Capital Make a Difference for Dalit Women Representatives in Local Self-Governance?', *Contemporary Voice of Dalit* 10, 1 (2018): 59-66.

30 A Vignesh, 'Talaiyuttu Kirusnaveni: cati veriyitam moti tanatu maranattai tottuppaartta oru talit pennin katai', 24 November 2020, *BBC News Tamil*, available at https://www.bbc.com/tamil/india-55040238 (last accessed 1 May 2023).

31 Bhanupriya Rao, 'Dalit Women Panchayat Leaders in Tamil Nadu have defied discrimination, even death', *Scroll*, 16 March 2017, available at https://scroll.in/article/831232/dalit-women-panchayat-leaders-in-tamil-nadu-have-defied-discrimination-and-even-death (last accessed 23 April 2024).

## Further Thoughts

1 Huri Islamoglu and Peter C Perdue (eds), *Shared Histories of Modernity: China, India and the Ottoman empire* (New Delhi: Routledge, 2020).

2 See Reinhard Koselleck, *Sediments of Time: On possible histories* (Stanford: Stanford University Press, 2007), on the concept of possible histories.

3 See, for example, Ashutosh Kumar and Kaushik Roy (eds), *Warfare and Society in British India, 1757–1947* (New Delhi: Routledge, 2022).

4 Cited in Douglas M Peers, 'Gunpowder Empires and the Garrison State: Modernity, Hybridity, and the Political Economy of Colonial India, circa 1750-1860', *Comparative Studies of South Asia, Africa and the Middle East* 27, 2 (2007): 245-258.

5 Farhana Ibrahim, *Settlers, Saints and Sovereigns: An ethnography of state formation in western India* (New Delhi: Routledge, 2020).

6 The concept of jurisdiction has emerged in recent years as important for understanding the image of law and governance of much greater relevance than its narrow function within legal technology would suggest, and yet famous legal judgements are cited to show the difficulties of giving it a precise definition. See Asha Kaushal, 'The politics of jurisdiction', *The Modern Law Review* 78, 5 (2015): 759-792; Justin B Richland, 'Jurisdiction: Grounding law in language', *Annual Review of Anthropology* 42, 1 (2013): 209-226; and Mariana Valverde, *Chronotopes of Law: Jurisdiction, Scale and Governance* (Abingdon: Routledge, 2015).

7 Michel Foucault, Michel, *'Society must be defended': Lectures at the Collège de France, 1975-1976* (London: Macmillan, 2003).

8 David Arnold, *Police Power and Colonial Rule: Madras, 1859–1947* (Delhi: Oxford University Press, 1986).

9 *Report of the Commissioners for the Investigation of Alleged Cases of Torture in the Madras Presidency* (Madras: Fort St. George Gazette Press, 1855).

10 See Achille Mbembe, 'The Power of the Archive and its Limits', in Carolyn Hamilton et al (eds), *Refiguring the Archive* (Dordrecht:

Springer, 2002), pp. 19-27; and Thomas Osborne, 'The ordinariness of the archive', *History of the Human Sciences* 12, 2 (1999): 51-64.

11 Fmile Benveniste, *Indo-European Language and Society* (London: Faber and Faber, 1973).

12 I have been influenced by the powerful writings of Boddhisattva Kar, Pooja Satyogi, Vaibhav Saria, Megha Sehdev on violence; and in parallel by Wittgenstein's distinction between mere error and superstition in philosophical thinking.

13 Achille Mbembe, 'Necropolitics', *Public Culture* 15, 1 (2003): 11–40.

14 Dirk HA Kolff, *Grass in their Mouths: The Upper Doab of India under the Company's Magna Charta, 1793-1830* (Leiden: Brill, 2010).

15 Dirk HA Kolff, *Naukar, Rajput, and Sepoy: The ethnohistory of the military labour market of Hindustan, 1450-1850* (Cambridge University Press, 2002).

16 Kolff, *Grass in their Mouths.*

17 Veena Das and Deborah Poole (eds), *Anthropology in the margins of the state: Comparative ethnographies* (Santa Fe: School of American Research, 2004).

18 Bodhisattva Kar, 'Nomadic Capital and Speculative Tribes: A culture of contracts in the Northeastern Frontier of British India', *The Indian Economic & Social History Review*, 53, 1 (2016): 41-67.

19 Ibid, p. 54.

20 Ibid.

21 The Italian philosopher Maurizio Ferraris conceives of documents in what he calls a narrow sense, as those which make objects: they function in his view as reification of social acts that may change over space and time. Maruizio Ferraris, *Documentality: Why it is necessary to leave traces* (New York: Fordham University Press, 2012).

22 In *Police Matters,* Kumar notes that 'Ultimately, what we find in routine police writing in colonial Madras is neither a mirror image of the caste order nor a statistical registry of well-defined criminal types, but an alternative, shrunken order of things: *kavalgar*, Notified Member, and Known Depredator, seemingly lacking classificatory

logic but in fact reflecting the conjunction between caste and police authority'. Radha Kumar, *Police Matters: The everyday state and caste politics in South India, 1900-1975* (Ithaca: Cornell University Press, 2021).

23 See Peter Becker and William Clark (eds), *Little Tools of Knowledge: Historical essays on academic and bureaucratic practices* (Ann Arbor: University of Michigan Press, 2021).

24 Frederick S Mullaly, *Notes on Criminal Classes of the Madras Presidency* (Madras: Superintendent, Government Press, 1892).

25 In the Preface the author also thanks various police officials for making available their notes and sketches to him for compiling his own book. It seems likely that these are the notes that did not make it to any official documents showing the importance of text that hovers around a document but is not part of it.

26 See also Veena Das, 'Documents: A critical reading', *Contributions to Indian Sociology,* 57, 3 (2023): 191-214.

27 See Michele Foucault, *Power/knowledge: Selected Interviews and Other Writings,1972-1977* ed. Colin Gordon (New York: Pantheon, 1980); Cornelia Vismann, *Files: Law and Media Technology,* tr. Geoffrey Winthrop-Young (Stanford: Stanford University Press, 2018); and Craig Roberson, *The Filing Cabinet: A vertical history of information* (Minneapolis: University of Minnesota Press, 2022).

28 See, for example, GJ Bryant, 'The East India Company and the British Army: The crisis at Madras in 1783', *Journal of the Society for Army Historical Research* 62, 249 (1984): 13-27; and Arka Chowdhury, 'Debating the Doctrine of "Minimum Force": Small wars in the North-West frontier of India and Afghanistan, 1860–1920', in Kumar and Roy (eds), *Warfare and Society in British India,* pp. 158-181.

29 As Reported on Untold Lives Blog, British Library, available at https://blogs.bl.uk/untoldlives/page/97/ (last accessed 26 December 2024).

30 Bryant, 'The East India Company and the British Army: The Crisis at Madras in 1783.' *Journal of the Society for Army Historical Research* 62, 249 (1984): 13-27.

31 Ibid.

32 Other theories of sovereignty from within the Indo-European universe, as that of Georges George Dumézil's reflections on the pair, Mitra-Varuna, as representations of sovereignty theorised war quite differently, casting it as the *outside* of established juridical norms and pact-making on the one hand (the Mitra aspect), and exercise of force within the law on the other hand (the Varuna aspect). In this rendering the warrior function represented by Indra is the rogue element of sovereignty, with its excess of cruelty and of generosity. See George Dumézil, *Mitra-Varuna: An essay on two Indo-European representations of sovereignty,* tr. Derek Coltman (Chicago: HAU Books, 2024). For further elaboration, see Giles Deleuze and Félix Guattari, *A Thousand Plateaus: Capitalism and schizophrenia*, tr. Brian Massumi (Minnesota: Minnesota University Press, 1987); and Das, *Slum Acts.*(London: Polity Press, 2022)

33 Charles W Gwynn, *Imperial Policing* (London: Macmillan & Co., 1934). See also Kaushik Roy, 'Logistics of small wars in British India: 1840s–1913', *Small Wars & Insurgencies*, 2022: 1-23; and Chowdhury, 'Debating the Doctrine of 'Minimum Force: Small Wars in the North-West Frontier of India and Afghanistan, 1860–1920, in Ashutosh Kumar and Kaushik Roy (eds), *Warfare and Society in British India, 1757–1947* (New Delhi: Routledge India, 2022) 158-181.

34 Carl von Clausewitz, *On war* (London: Penguin, 2003). See also Hew Strachan and Andreas Herberg-Rothe (eds), *Clausewitz in the Twenty-first Century* (Oxford: Oxford University Press, 2007).

## PART II: CUSTODIAL VIOLENCE, LAW, AND THE COURTS

### Chapter 4. Justice in Custody: Doctors as Semi-state Actors

1 Amy Goodman, and Nermeen Shaikh, 'Racism and Racial Terrorism Has Fueled Nationwide Anger', *Truthout*, 1 June 2020, available at https://truthout.org/video/racism-and-racial-terrorism-has-fueled-nationwide-anger/ (last accessed 11 July 2024).

2 I will be using the English spellings for the names of both father and son most commonly employed by the Indian police, although

alternate spellings in use include *Jayaraj, Bennix, Bennicks and Fenix.*

3 Jinee Lokaneeta, 'India's George Floyd Moment: Custodial Torture and Policing in a Democracy', *Jadaliyya* 16 July 16 2020, available at https://www.jadaliyya.com/Details/41432/India%E2%80%99s-George-Floyd-Moment-Custodial-Torture-and-Policing-in-a-Democracy-41432 (last accessed 4 June, 2024). See also Law Commission of India, 'One Hundred and Fifty Second Report on Custodial Crimes', 1994, available at chromeextension://efaidnbmnnnibpcajpcglclefindmkaj/https://cdnbbsr.s3waas.gov.in/s3ca0daec69b5adc880fb464895726dbdf/uploads/2022/08/2022080893-2.pdf; Asian Centre for Human Rights, 'Torture in India: A State of Denial', June 2008, available at chrome-extension://efaidnbmnnnibpcajpcglclefindmkaj/https://idsn.org/uploads/media/ACHR_tortureinIndia_2008_01.pdf; Human Rights Watch, '"Bound by Brotherhood": India's Failure to End Killings in Police Custody", December 2016, available at chrome-extension://efaidnbmnnnibpcajpcglclefindmkaj/https://www.hrw.org/sites/default/files/report_pdf/india1216_web_0.pdf; and Law Commission of India, 'Report No. 273: Implementation of "United Nations Convention against Torture and other Cruel, Inhuman and Degrading Treatment or Punishment' through Legislation', October 2017, available at chrome-extension://efaidnbmnnnibpcajpcglclefindmkaj/https://cdnbbsr.s3waas.gov.in/s3ca0daec69b5adc880fb464895726dbdf/uploads/2022/08/2022081620.pdf (all last accessed 11 July 2024).

4 See, for example, 'Watch: Scenes from protests against the custodial deaths of Jayaraj and Bennix in Tamil Nadu', *Scoll.in,* 27 June 2020, available at https://scroll.in/video/965857/watch-scenes-from-protests-against-the-custodial-deaths-of-jeyaraj-and-fenix-in-tamil-nadu; Anupama Subramanian, 'Celebrities demand justice for Jayaraj and Fenix' (sic), *Deccan Chronicle,* 28 June 2020, available at https://www.deccanchronicle.com/entertainment/kollywood/280620/celebrities-demand-justice-for-jayaraj-and-fenix.html?infinitescroll=1; Som Thomas, 'Every Custodial Death

a Reminder of Why India Must Ratify the Convention Against Torture', *The Wire,* 27 June 2020, available at https://thewire.in/rights/custodial-deaths-india-convention-against-torture; and Omkar Khandekar, 'Rethinking the angry cop in Indian cinema', *Mint Lounge,* 13 July 2020, available at https://lifestyle.livemint.com/how-to-lounge/movies-tv/rethinking-the-angry-young-cop-in-indian-cinema-111634476144273.html (all last accessed 11 July 2024).

5 For some notable exceptions see, for example, KP Saikiran, 'Kerala: Doctors in 3 hospitals…should've suspected custodial torture', *The Times of India*, 7 June 2021, available at https://timesofindia.indiatimes.com/city/thiruvananthapuram/kerala-doctors-in-3-hospitals-shouldve-suspected-custodial-torture/articleshow/83296329.cms; and Jatinder Kaur Tur, '"My torture would have been suppressed": Five medical reports before GMCH recorded no signs of custodial violence on Shiv Kumar', *The Caravan*, 20 March 2021, available at https://caravanmagazine.in/crime/five-medical-reports-before-gmch-recorded-no-signs-custodial-violence-shiv-kumar-interview (all last access 11 July 2024).

6 United Nations General Assembly Resolution 37/194, 'Principles of Medical Ethics Relevant to the Role of Health Personnel, particularly Physicians, in the Protection of Prisoners and Detainees Against Torture and Other Cruel, Inhuman or Degrading Treatment or Punishment', 1982. See also Amnesty International, 'Doctors and Torture', 2002, available at chrome-extension://efaidnbmnnnibpcajpcglclefindmkaj/https://www.amnesty.org/en/wp-content/uploads/2021/06/act750012002en.pdf. The Hippocratic Oath is a code of ethics to which medical doctors are required to subscribe. See Practo, 'The Hippocratic Oath: The Original and Revised Version', 10 March 2015, available at https://doctors.practo.com/the-hippocratic-oath-the-original-and-revised-version/. An Indian version, known as the IMA Pledge, is available at https://www.ima-india.org/ima/free-way-page.php?pid=18#:~:text=Even%20under%20threat%2C%20I%20will,my%20duty%20and%20my%20patient (all last accessed 12 July 2024).

7 'New Guidelines to Fight Covid 19', Ministry for Home Affairs, Press Release, 30 May, 2024, available at https://pib.gov.in/PressReleasePage.aspx?PRID=1627965#:~:text=Union%20Ministry%20of%20Home%20Affairs,will%20have%20an%20economic%20focus; and Prabhakar Tamilarasu, 'Sexual torture inflicted on father-son in TN police custody: Witnesses', *The Federal,* 24 June 2020, available at https://thefederal.com/states/south/tamil-nadu/sexual-torture-inflicted-on-father-son-duo-before-death-in-tn-eyewitnesses/ (both last accessed 10 April 2024).

8 All quotes are from the First Information Report, or chargesheet, filed in the case against the police officials by the CBI, which I have a copy of, which will henceforth be referred to as 'chargesheet'. A chargesheet documents the evidence the police have gathered during a criminal investigation and serves as a formal charge, or accusation, against an accused for a particular offence or offences.

9 Chargesheet, p. 18.

10 Ibid, pp. 18-19.

11 A head police constable, S Ravichandran, informed the CBI that the police essentially manufactured the documents pertaining to the case, including the arrest memo (which details the name of the accused, the time, date and place of their arrest, and their suspected offence) and case diary (which details all aspects of a police investigation). They sought to explain the injuries on the bodies of the accused, moreover, by claiming that these were result of a scuffle with the police.

12 Chargesheet, p. 16

13 The requirement for jail officials to fill out such a proforma was introduced by the National Human Rights Commission (NHRC) in 1999 and revised in 2010 to combat the spread of contagious diseases in Indian jails; a Special Rapporteur and Chief Co-ordinator of the Commission's Custodial Justice Programme was also appointed to monitor these efforts. However, in contravention of NHRC guidelines such examinations are not always conducted by doctors and they do not focus on capturing custodial violence. See National Human Rights Commission, 'NHRC directs all State Governments

and Prison Administrators on medical examination of Prison inmates' n.d., available at https://nhrc.nic.in/press-release/nhrc-directs-all-state-governments-and-prison-administrators-medical-examination; and 'Proforma for Health Screening of Prisoners on Admission to Jail', 17 May 2010, available at https://nhrc.nic.in/sites/default/files/Medical%20Examination%20of%20Prisoners%20on%20Admission%20to%20Jail.pdf (both last accessed 12 July 2024).

14 Chargesheet, p.19

15 Ibid.

16 *DK Basu* v *State of West Bengal* 1997 (1) SCC 416. A parallel provision already existed, however, in section 54 of the 1973 Criminal Procedure Code, which entitles an accused person to a medical examination, on request, at any time following their arrest.

17 In 2009, the DK Basu guidelines regarding medical exams were codified.

18 Manisha Sethi captures the lack of safeguards in terrorism cases in *Kafkaland: Prejudice, Law and Counterterrorism in India* (Gurgaon: Three Essays Collective, 2014), p. 24.

19 While twelve men were convicted of the crime in 2015, all maintain their innocence. See Abdul Wahid Shaikh, *Innocent Prisoners: Begunah Qaidi* (New Delhi: Pharos Media, 2021 [2018]).

20 Chargesheet, p.55. Also see Megha Kaeri, 'Justice for Jayaraj and Bennix: Timeline of two shocking custodial deaths in TN', *The News Minute*, 28 June 2020, available at https://www.thenewsminute.com/article/justice-jayaraj-fenix-bennix-timeline-two-shocking-custodial-deaths-tn-127424 (last accessed 15 April 2024). A report focusing on the first production and remand in Delhi Courts notes that the general practice of questioning an accused in front of the police who may have been involved in his or her torture is a flaw in the Indian criminal justice system. See Jinee Lokaneeta and Zeba Sikora, *Magistrates and Constitutional Protections: An ethnographic study of first production and remand in Delhi courts* (Delhi: Project 39A, National Law University, Delhi, 2024).

21 Jinee Lokaneeta, *The Truth Machines: Policing, Violence and*

*Scientific Interrogations in India* (Ann Arbor: The University of Michigan Press & Orient Blackswan, 2020).

22 For scholarship that examines the role of bureaucracy in erasing police violence see, for example, Beatrice Jauregui, *Provisional Authority: Police, Order, and Security in India* (Chicago: University of Chicago Press, 2016); Santana Khanikar, *State, Violence, and Legitimacy in India* (Delhi: Oxford University Press, 2018); and Mayur Suresh, *Terror Trials: Life and Law in Delhi's Courts* (New York: Fordham University Press, 2023).

23 Chargesheet, p. 20.

24 Jeyaraj's sister held on to one of the blood-stained shirts and later gave it to the examining magistrate to be used as evidence against the police.

25 Chargesheet, statements of wife, relatives, and other witnesses recorded under section 161 of the Criminal Procedure Code.

26 Ibid, p. 88.

27 Ibid, statement of Dr. Pon Essaky, p. 195.

28 Ibid, statement of Nurse Dernit, p. 86.

29 See *Guidelines for Medico-Legal Examination in Police Custody and Documenting Custodial Torture* (Mumbai: CEHAT, 2020), available at https://www.cehat.org/uploads/files/Guidelines%20for%20Medico%20legal%20examination%20in%20police%20custody%20and%20documenting%20custodial%20torture1.pdf (last accessed 15 April 2024).

30 Chargesheet, statement of Superintendent Shankar, p. 91.

31 Chargesheet, p. 94.

32 Ibid.

33 Maja Daruwala, 'There Isn't Anything 'Shocking' About Official Apathy In The Jayaraj-Bennicks Case', *The Wire*, 23 October 2020, available at https://thewire.in/rights/jayaraj-bennicks-torture-murder-apathy (last accessed 15 April 2024). For the role of medical professionals in custodial torture see Stephen Miles, *The Torture Doctors* (Georgetown University Press, 2020); Amar Jesani, 'Doctors and Police Interrogation of Detainees', *BioEthics Links*, 12, 1 (2016), available at https://siut.org/bioethics/cbec-newsletter-

bioethics-links2/ (last accessed 15 April 2024); Chiara Lepora and Joseph Millum, 'The Tortured Patient: A Medical Dilemma', *Hastings Center Report* 41, 3 (May-June 2011): 38-47; and Jinee Lokaneeta, *Transnational Torture: Law, Violence and State Power in the United States and India* (New York: New York University Press, 2011).

34 'Sathankulam doctor who issued medical fitness certificate for Jeyaraj-Beniks goes on leave', *The New Indian Express,* 30 June 30 2020, available at https://www.newindianexpress.com/states/tamil-nadu/2020/Jun/30/sathankulam-doctor-who-issued-medical-fitness-certificate-for-jeyaraj-beniks-goes-on-leave-2163597.html (last accessed 15 April 2024). According to another article, Dr Vinila stated that she only reported the injuries that the father-son duo told her about. See Priyanka Thirumurthy, 'Jayaraj-Bennix custodial deaths: Bloodstained blanket submitted as evidence', *The News Minute,* 1 July 2020, available at https://www.thenewsminute.com/article/jayaraj-bennix-custodial-deaths-bloodstained-blanket-submitted-evidence-127746 (last accessed 15 April 2024).

35 See Amar Jesani, 'Doctors and Police Interrogation of Detainees'; and *Guidelines for Medico-Legal Examination in Police Custody.*

36 Chargesheet, statement of Dr Pon Essaky, p. 195.

37 Sameena Mulla, *The Violence of Care: Rape Victims, Forensic Nurses, and Sexual Assault Intervention* (New York: New York University Press, 2014).

38 Ibid, p. 217.

39 Lokaneeta, *The Truth Machines*, pp. 14-15. See also Harris Solomon, *Lifelines: The Traffic of Trauma* (Durham, NC: Duke University Press, 2022).

40 This is paraphrased from an interview with a forensic psychologist, November 2013

41 *Istanbul Protocol Manual on the Effective Investigation and Documentation of Torture and Other Cruel, Inhuman or Degrading Treatment or Punishment* (New York and Geneva: United Nations, 2004), available at chrome-extension://efaidnbmnnnibpcajpcglclefindmkaj/https://www.ohchr.org/sites/default/files/Documents/

Publications/training8Rev1en.pdf (last accessed July 16 2024). See also Jesani, 'Doctors and Police Interrogation of Detainees'.

42 Ibid. See also Jesani, 'Doctors and Police Interrogation of Detainees'.

43 This is despite the fact that the role of doctors is different from that of forensic psychologists and forensic nurses, whose primary role is to secure evidence for use in criminal trials.

44 *Guidelines for Medico-Legal Examination in Police Custody*, p. 6

45 Ibid, p. 25.

46 Ibid, p. 11.

## Chapter 5. Confronting the Violence Within: Courts, Police Custody, and Criminal Investigations

1 I am grateful to the editors for their time and patience in helping me to develop this chapter. Many thanks also to Ms Nishtha Jindal for her valuable assistance.

2 See, for example, Jinee Lokaneeta, 'Defining an Absence: Torture "Debate" in India', *Economic and Political Weekly*, 49, 26-27, 28 June 2014: 71; *Police Practices: Obstruction to Poor People's Access to Justice* (New Delhi: Commonwealth Human Rights Initiative, 2003), p. 27, available at chrome-extension://efaidnbmnnnibpcajpcglclefindmkaj/https://humanrightsinitiative.org/publications/police/police_practices_obstruction_to_poor_people.pdf (last accessed 28 August 2024); Mayur R Suresh, *Terror Trials: Life and Law in Delhi's Courts* (New York: Fordham University Press, 2023), p. 66; and Jinee Lokaneeta and Amar Jesani, 'India', in Richard Carver and Lisa Handley (eds), *Does Torture Prevention Work?* (Liverpool: Liverpool University Press, 2016), pp. 501–47.

3 Jinee Lokaneeta, *The Truth Machines: Policing, Violence, and Scientific Interrogations in India* (Ann Arbor: University of Michigan Press, 2020), p. 36.

4 Act XXXXV of 1860; Act I of 1872; Act II of 1874, Act XXXXV of 2023; Act XXXXVII of 2023; and Act XXXXVI of 2023, respectively. See also Mahendar Singh Manral, 'India's 3 new criminal laws to come into force from July 1', *The Indian Express*, 25 February

2024, available at https://indianexpress.com/article/india/bharatiya-nyaya-sanhita-india-new-criminal-laws-july-1-9178612/ (last accessed 3 April 2024)

5 Sections 2(h) and 173, Act II of 1974.

6 See, for example, *Abhinandan Jha & Ors* v *Bihar*, 1968 AIR 117 (Supreme Court of India, Two Justices' Bench).

7 Sections 93, 91, 61, 41, 44, Act II of 1974.

8 Section 16, Act II of 1974.

9 Section 41, Act II of 1974.

10 Chapter V, Act II of 1974.

11 Section 438, Act II of 1974.

12 Sections 53, 53A, 311-A, Act II of 1974.

13 Section 25, Act I of 1872. The only limited exception to this rule is that such statements made to the police can be used to contradict what the person then proceeds to say in court during their trial.

14 Section 27, Act I of 1872 notes that, 'Provided that, when any fact is deposed to as discovered in consequence of information received from a person accused of any offence, in the custody of a police-officer, so much of such information, whether it amounts to a confession or not, as relates distinctly to the fact thereby discovered, may be proved'.

15 *Pulukuri Kotayya* v. *King-Emperor*, (1947) 74 IA 65.

16 KN Chandrasekharan Pillai, *RV Kelkar's Criminal Procedure* (Lucknow: Eastern Book Company, 2014), p. cxxvii; and sections 44, 56, 57, Act II of 1974.

17 Jinee Lokaneeta, 'Time is essential to ensuring justice in custodial death cases', *The Indian Express,* 23 June 2021, available at https://indianexpress.com/article/opinion/columns/time-is-essential-to-ensuring-justice-in-custodial-death-cases-7371096/ (accessed 4 April 2024).

18 See, for e.g., *Hidayat Ullah Khan* v *Crown*, AIR 1949 Lah 77 (FB) (Lahore High Court); *Amir Chand & Anr* v *Crown,* (1949) ILR II EP 515 (High Court for East Punjab); and *State* v *Mangilal Shankarlal Jaiswal & Anr*, AIR 1952 MB 161 (Madhya Bharat High Court, Indore Bench).

19 *Report No. 41* (Law Commission of India, 1969).

20 UP Act XVI of 1976 was, however, repealed in 2019 by UP Act IV of 2019. Question by Sh. DG Gawai for the Minister for Home Affairs, *Lok Sabha Debates* (Third Series), 14 December 1977, pp. 15-16. The Emergency, which was in effect from 25 June 1975 to 21 March 1977, gave Prime Minister Indira Gandhi the authority to rule India by decree, rather than by Parliament; during this period elections were also cancelled and civil liberties were suspended.

21 *Gurbaksh Singh Sibbia* v *State of Punjab*, ILR (1978) 1 P&H 108 (FB) (Punjab & Haryana High Court, Full Bench).

22 *Gurbaksh Singh Sibbia & Ors* v *State of Punjab*, (1980) 2 SCC 565 (Supreme Court of India, Five Justices' Bench).

23 See, for example, Act XXVIII of 1987; Act LXI of 1985; and Act XXXIII of 1989.

24 See, for example, *Pokar Ram* v *State of Rajasthan*, (1985) 2 SCC 597 [6] (Supreme Court of India, Three Justices' Bench); *Pankaj D Suthar* v *State of Gujarat*, (1992) 1 GLR 405 [5]; *E Joseph & Anr* v *the Assistant Collector of Customs*, 1982 CriLJ 559 (Madras) [9]; *Rama Swaroop* v *State*, 1985 SCC OnLine Del 359 [26]; and *Sambhu Das* v *State of Tripura*, 1986 SCC OnLine Gau 46 [4].

25 See *Vineet Narain & Ors* v *Union of India & Anr*, 1998 (1) SCC 226 (Supreme Court of India, Two Justices' Bench).

26 *CBI* v *Anil Sharma*, (1997) 7 SCC 187 (Supreme Court of India, Two Justices' Bench).

27 Ibid.

28 *Sushila Aggarwal* v *State of NCT of Delhi*, (2020) 5 SCC 1 (Supreme Court of India, Five Justices' Bench); and *Chidambaram* v *Directorate of Enforcement*, (2019) 9 SCC 24 (Supreme Court of India, Three Justices' Bench).

29 *Miranda* v *Arizona*, 384 US 436 (1966) (Supreme Court of the United States).

30 AIR 1961 SC 1808 (Supreme Court of India, Eleven Justices' Bench).

31 Other charges included carrying and operating an unlicensed firearm.

32 Judgement dated 16 October 1956 in Sessions Case No. 7 of 1955

of the Court of Sessions Judge, Gohilwad. See also Abhinav Sekhri, 'The Right Against Self-Incrimination in India: The Compelling Case of Kathi Kalu Oghad', *Indian Law Review*, 3, 3 (2019): 180-211.

33 As the court noted, 'the accused was remanded to police custody for ten days. It is quite possible that he believed that he was remanded to police custody to help the police in [their] investigation, and, though he could in theory have refused to give his specimen handwriting, he may have thought that he [could not] refuse. Thus the element of compulsion was implicit in his being at that time in police custody. The writing was obtained without the interposition of a Court or a Magistrate who [could] apprise him that the object of making him write was to use the writing as evidence against him and that it was open to him not to executive the writing if he did not want to do so…therefore, the procedure adopted by the police was in contravention of Article 20(3) of the Constitution'. As a result, evidence 'obtained by the police while the accused was in their custody should in principle be treated as a kind of compelled testimony'. *State of Bombay* v *Kathi Kalu Oghad*, AIR 1961 SC 1808 (Supreme Court of India, Eleven Justices' Bench), See also Sekhri, 'The Right Against Self-Incrimination in India".

34 *State of Bombay* v *Kathi Kalu Oghad*.

35 Ibid, Judgement dated 15 November 1956 in Criminal Jail Appeal No. 73 of 1956 before the High Court of Bombay at Rajkot.

36 *State of Bombay* v *Kathi Kalu Oghad*, AIR 1961 SC 1808 [11] (Supreme Court of India, Eleven Justices' Bench).

37 Ibid.

38 Ibid.

39 Ibid.

40 Ibid.

41 This view was critiqued at the time. See, for example, KR Dixit, 'Protection against Self-incrimination', *Journal of the Indian Law Institute*, 4, 1 (1962): 150; Indian Law Institute, *Self-Incrimination: Physical and Medical Examination of The Accused* (New Delhi: Indian Law Institute, 1963); and KK Nigam, 'Due Process of Law: A

Comparative Study of Procedural Guarantees Against Deprivation of Personal Liberty in the United States and India', *Journal of the Indian Law Institute* 4, 1 (1962): 126.

42 Vishnu Mitter, *The Police, Investigation and the Courts* (Allahabad: Law Book Co., 1965), pp. 126-128.

43 Ibid, pp. 76-77; see also pp. 132–37, 126.

44 Order dated 12.12.2019 in Writ Petition(s)(Criminal) No(s). 348/2019 (Supreme Court of India, Three Justices' Bench).

45 *V Senthil Balaji* v *State*, 2023 SCC OnLine SC 934 (Supreme Court of India, Two Justices' Bench).

**Chapter 6. Hate Crimes as the New 'Legitimate': Anti-CAA protests and Policing in Aligarh Muslim University and Jamia Millia Islamia, 2019**

1 See, for example, Sharjeel Usmani, 'Charting history of Indian Muslims and the police: From British era to AMU violence, a story of injustice', *FirstPost*, 27 April 2020, available at https://www.firstpost.com/india/charting-history-of-indian-muslims-and-the-police-from-british-era-to-amu-violence-a-story-of-injustice-8303531.html; and Jayshree Bajoria, 'India's Police Found Complicit in Anti-Muslim Mob Violence', *Human Rights Watch*, 17 July 2020, available at https://www.hrw.org/news/2020/07/17/indias-police-found-complicit-anti-muslim-mob-violence (both last accessed 14 June 2024).

2 Campaign Against Witch-hunt of Anti-CAA Activists, 'The Night of The Broken Glass: Testimonies From Jamia Millia Islamia', 2019, available at https://pdfcoffee.com/the-night-of-the-broken-glass-testimonies-from-jamia-millia-islamia-pdf-free.html; Karwan-e-Mohabbat, 'The Siege of Aligarh Muslim University: A Fact Finding Report', 2019, available at https://www.newsclick.in/Siege-Aligarh-Muslim-University-Fact-Finding-Report; and Citizens Against Hate, 'The Dismantling of Minority Education', 2020 (this is not available on-line, but for an overview see Niharika Ravi, 'Report: Police Violence in Jamia and AMU Violates International Conventions and Indian Court Judgements on Rights Protestors', *Janata*

*Weekly*, 27 December 2020, available at https://janataweekly.org/report-police-violence-in-jamia-and-amu-violates-international-conventions-and-indian-court-judgments-on-rights-of-protestors/ (all last accessed 14 June 2024).

3 For understandings of what constitutes 'reasonable' force and 'law and order' with respect to the right of the police to enter and search premises, and detain suspects, as well as maintain law and order, see, for e.g., the Model Police Act, 2006, available at https://www.mha.gov.in/sites/default/files/ModelAct06_30_Oct_0.pdf.

4 Christophe Jaffrelot, *Modi's India: Hindu Nationalism and the Rise of Ethnic Democracy*, trans. Cynthia Schoch (Princeton: Princeton University Press, 2021).

5 Article 30 of the Indian Constitution gives minorities the right to 'establish and administer educational institutions of their choice'. See also Faizan Mustafa, 'The Government Has a Duty to Protect the Minority Character of Aligarh Muslim University', *The Wire*, 17 January 2016, https://thewire.in/law/governments-view-on-minority-character-of-aligarh-muslim-university-is-unconstitutional; MM Special Correspondent, 'BJP led govt planning to strip Jamia Millia Islamia of its minority status', *Muslim Mirror*, 16 January 2016, available at https://muslimmirror.com/eng/bjp-led-govt-planning-to-strip-jamia-millia-islamia-of-its-minority-status/; Usmani, 'Charting history of Indian Muslims and the police'; and Ansab Amir, 'One year of anti-CAA movement; State targeting of Aligarh Muslim University was conspicuous', *Maktoob Media*, 15 Dec 2020, available at https://maktoobmedia.com/india/one-year-of-anti-caa-movement-state-targeting-of-aligarh-muslim-university-was-conspicuous/ (all last accessed 17 June 2024).

6 For examples of some of the important human rights interventions the NHRC has made see, for example, WP 129 of 2012, available at https://main.sci.gov.in/supremecourt/2012/29000/29000_2012_Judgement_14-Jul-2017.pdf, and https://nhrc.nic.in/press-release/some-important-interventions-nhrc (last accessed 14 June 2024).

7 Editorial, 'The Protests are Not Just Anti-CAA, But Pro-Constitution', *The Wire*, 31 Dec 2019, available at https://thewire.in/rights/india-

citizenship-protests-democracy-constitution-caa (last accessed 17 June 2024).

8 On the 2016 Jat protests, see Varinder Bhatia, 'Haryana Jat Agitation: On road to mayhem, alerts ignored, cops shackled', *The Indian Express,* 4 March 2016, available at https://indianexpress.com/article/explained/jat-reservation-stir-in-fact-on-road-to-mayhem-alerts-ignored-cops-shackled/. On the 2016 Dalit protests, see 'SC/ST Act: Dalits call for Bharat bandh on April 2, Centre to file review petition; everything you need to know', *The Indian Express,* 1 April 2018, available at https://indianexpress.com/article/india/sc-st-act-dalits-protest-bharat-bandh-centre-review-petition-supreme-court-5119765/ (both last accessed 17 June 2024).

9 Ranabir Samaddar, 'An Insurgent Constitutionalism is Driving Popular Politics in India Today', *The Wire*, 26 January 2020, available at https://thewire.in/politics/an-insurgent-constitutionalism-is-driving-popular-politics-in-india-today (last accessed 17 June 2024).

10 For a full list of these protests, see 'Citizenship Amendment Act Protests', *Wikipedia,* available at https://en.wikipedia.org/wiki/Citizenship_Amendment_Act_protests. Also see Mahtab Alam, 'CAA: The Peaceful Protests by Muslims That No One is Talking About', *The Wire,* 29 December 2019, available at https://thewire.in/rights/caa-peaceful-protests-muslims (both last accessed 21 February 2024).

11 See, for e.g., Maanvi, 'CAA Protests: Internet Suspended in UP, Assam and Karnataka', *The Quint,* 20 December 2019, available at https://www.thequint.com/news/india/airtel-mobile-services-twitter-internet-shutdown-delhi-ito-amid-anti-citizenship-amendment-act-protests; and 'Mobile internet shutdowns in Lucknow, Ghaziabad, Mangalore amid anti-CAA protests', *The Indian Express,* 20 December 2019, available at https://indianexpress.com/article/technology/tech-news-technology/anti-citizenship-act-protests-mobile-internet-shutdown-in-parts-of-delhi-confirm-airtel-and-vodafone-6174586/#:~:text=The%20Citizen%20(Amendment)%20Act%20protests,of%20South%2024%2DParganas%20districts (both last accessed 17 June 2024).

12 Swati Shikha, 'Delhi Burning: A Timeline of Anti-CAA Protests and Northeast Delhi Violence', *Outlook*, 4 February 2023, available at https://www.outlookindia.com/national/delhi-burning-a-timeline-of-caa-protests-and-northeast-delhi-violence-news-265077; Naresh Singaravelu, 'Data: How many people died during anti-CAA protests?', *The Hindu*, 6 January 2020, available at https://www.thehindu.com/data/data-how-many-people-died-during-anti-caa-protests/article30494183.ece; and PTI, '1026 persons arrested in 12 days for anti-CAA stir in Assam: CM', *Deccan Herald*, 20 December 2021 (all last accessed 21 February 2024).

13 Prabhash K Dutta, 'Anti-CAA Protests: Why political parties are hiding behind students', *India Today*, 20 December, 2019, available at https://www.indiatoday.in/news-analysis/story/anti-caa-protests-why-political-parties-are-hiding-behind-students-1630048-2019-12-20 (last accessed 15 February 2024).

14 'Unending Witch-Hunt of Muslims: Eminent Citizens Condemn Targeted Arrests', *The Wire*, 19 April 2020, available at https://thewire.in/communalism/muslims-witch-hunt-caa-protests (last accessed 17 June 2024).

15 Sobhana K Nair, 'CAA rules, police deployment attempt to provoke Muslims', *The Hindu*, 15 March 2024, available at https://www.thehindu.com/news/cities/Delhi/caa-rules-police-deployment-attempt-to-provoke-muslims/article67952307.ece (last accessed 17 June 2024).

16 See, for example, speech of Dr Zakir Husain, Vice Chancellor of AMU on the occasion of President Rajendra Prasad's visit to the university, 1951, in AG Noorani, 'A Blot on India's Secularism', *Frontline*, 7 June 2017, available at https://frontline.thehindu.com/the-nation/a-blot-on-indias-secularism/article23595824.ece (last accessed 21 February 2024).

17 L Gautier, 'A Laboratory for a Composite India? Jamia Millia Islamia around the time of partition', *Modern Asian Studies*, 54, 1 (2020): 199-249.

18 Dev NC, 'India Needs to Understand Why the North-East is Protesting', *The Wire*, 5 January 2020, available at https://thewire.

in/rights/caa-protest-northeast-indigenous (last accessed 18 June 2024).

19 'Citizenship Act protests: FIR against AMU students for defying prohibitory orders', *Indian Express,* 12 December 2019, available at https://scroll.in/latest/946590/citizenship-act-protests-fir-against-amu-students-for-defying-prohibitory-orders (last accessed 18 December 2024)

20 'Aligarh Muslim University in Hindutva Regime', *Maktoob Media*, 2 February 2020, available at https://maktoobmedia.com/opinion/aligarh-muslim-university-in-hindutva-regime/; and Fazal Abdali, 'Social Protest and Police Brutality', *Human Rights Law Network*, 20 June 2020, available at https://www.slic.org.in/uploads/2020/06-June/23-Tue/Report%20AMU%20(15-6-2020).pdf (both last accessed 18 June 2024).

21 Anuja Jaiswal, 'Citizenship Amendment Act: Aligarh administration thwarts attempt of AMU Students to take out mega march against the CAB', *Times of India*, 13 December 2019, available at https://timesofindia.indiatimes.com/city/agra/citizenship-amendment-act-aligarh-administration-thwarts-attempt-of-amu-students-to-take-out-mega-march-against-the-cab/articleshow/72545948.cms (last accessed 18 June 2024).

22 'Citizenship Amendment Act protests live updates: Jamia students call off university "lockdown"', *Times of India*, 14 December 2019, available at https://timesofindia.indiatimes.com/city/guwahati/cab-assam-protests-live-updates-curfew-in-guwahati-pm-modi-urges-calm/liveblog/72500044.cms (last accessed 18 June 2024).

23 This incident has been referred to as 'the night of the broken glass' and compared to the pogrom against Jews by Nazi paramilitary forces on November 9-10, 1938. See Campaign Against Witch-hunt of Anti-CAA Activists, 'The Night of The Broken Glass'.

24 Geeta Pandey, 'Jai Shri Ram: The Hindu chant that became a murder cry', *BBC*, 10 July 2019, available at https://www.bbc.com/news/world-asia-india-48882053 (last accessed 18 June 2024).

25 Indian law provides custodial safeguards such as the right to access a lawyer, the right to family members when arrested, the right to

medical help, the right to be produced before a magistrate within 24 hours of being arrested, and the right to evoke habeas corpus against unlawful detention, in pursuance of the individual's rights to liberty, security, and a fair trial. These have long been established through the guidelines on police custody laid out by the Supreme Court in the 1997 DK Basu and 1994 Joginder Kumar cases. See LawBhoomi, 'Case Briefs: DK Basu v. State of West Bengal', 21 October 2023, available at https://lawbhoomi.com/dk-basu-vs-state-of-west-bengal/ (last accessed 19 February 2023) and *Joginder Kumar* v *State of Uttar Pradesh*, JT (1994) 3 SC 423 (430).

26 '50 students, detained during protests in Jamia, released: Police', *Economic Times,* 16 December 2019, available at https://economictimes.indiatimes.com/news/politics-and-nation/50-students-detained-during-protests-at-jamia-released-police/articleshow/72723604.cms?from=mdr (last accessed 18 June 2024).

27 Such critique came from politicians, lawyers, filmmakers, activists, and student unions. See, for example, 'Protests erupt across India over CAA, police action against Jamia students', *The Economic Times,* 16 December 2019, available at https://economictimes.indiatimes.com/news/politics-and-nation/from-lucknow-to-hyderabad-protests-across-campuses-against-police-crackdown-in-jamia/articleshow/72743549.cms?from=mdr; Karan Tripathi, 'Jamia Violence: "Purpose of Police Attack Was to Threaten Students to Never Participate in Anti-CAA Protests", Submits Sr Adv Gonsalves in Delhi HC', 4 August 2020, available at https://www.livelaw.in/top-stories/jamia-violence-purpose-of-police-attack-threaten-students-in-anti-caa-protests-gonslaves-delhi-hc-160936; 'CAA uproar: Swara Bhasker, Vir Das slam Delhi Police for Jamia violence; Chetan Bhagat questions decision-making', *The Economic Times,* 16 December 2019, available at https://economictimes.indiatimes.com/magazines/panache/caa-uproar-swara-bhasker-vir-das-slam-delhi-police-for-jamia-violence-chetan-bhagat-questions-decision-making/articleshow/72748979.cms?from=mdr; and 'Over 400 students, alumni from US campuses join student groups in India protesting police action', *Scroll.in,* 17 December 2019,

available at https://scroll.in/latest/947067/citizenship-act-protests-student-groups-denounce-police-action-say-it-violates-human-rights (all last accessed 18 June 2024).

28 'Delhi Police Admits To Firing During Crackdown On Violent Anti-CAA Protest On December 15: Reports', *India.com*, 5 January 2020, available at https://www.india.com/news/india/delhi-police-admits-to-firing-during-crackdown-on-violent-anti-caa-protest-on-december-15-reports-3899803/. See also Maja Daruwala, GP Joshi, and Mandeep Tiwana, 'Police Act, 1861: Why we need to replace it?', *Commonwealth Human Rights Initiative*, July 2005, available at https://www.humanrightsinitiative.org/programs/aj/police/papers/advocacy_paper_police_act_1861.pdf (both last accessed 19 February 2024).

29 See, for e.g., *Francis Coralie Mullin* v. *Administrator, UT of Delhi*, AIR 1981 SC 608; and *Nilabati Behera* v *State of Orissa*, AIR 1993 SC 1960. There is also a rich jurisprudence on the responsibility of the Indian state to award compensation for acts committed by its agents.

30 *Education and National Development: Report of the Education Commission 1964-66* (also called, Kothari Commission Report), Chapter XIII, pp. 644-645, available at https://dtf-du.org/wp-content/uploads/2013/02/kc_v3.pdf. See also *Vijaykumar* v *State of Kerala* 2004 (2) KLT 627, para 9.

31 CrPC ss. 165, 166 and s.48. See also LCI 177th Report on Law Relating to Arrests (2001) and SNM College *v* SI of Police, 15 December 2006, 2007 (1) KLT 282.

32 For example, courts have directed the police to establish permanent police units outside campuses to 'maintain law and order'. Some courts have also allowed police interventions into university matters to ensure such institutions maintain 'disciplined operation(s)' in the face of 'miscreants' on campuses, on the ground that freedoms associated with Article 19 of the Constitution—in this case, the freedom of association—are not absolute. See *President Mahavidyalaya* v *State of Bihar & Ors*; Suo Motu Proceedings initiated based on a representation submitted by Sri

N Ramachandran IPS regarding the efforts to be undertaken to curb the increasing menace of drug abuse, 3 November 2021, Kerala HC, available at https://indiankanoon.org/doc/120791222/ (last accessed 18 December 2024); *State of Rajasthan* v *Sarita Choudhary*, 2006, 3 February 2006, RLW 2006 (3) Raj 2507; and *Ram Kishore Singh* v *State of UP*.

33 *See State of Rajasthan* v *Sarita Choudhary*, 3 February 2006, RLW 2006 (3) Raj 2507; *Ram Kishore Singh* v *State of UP*, 20 March 2015, available at https://www.casemine.com/judgement/in/56b49302607dba348f003bd4; and Against the Judgement in WP (C) 1624/2014 of the High Court of Kerala dated 18 July 2014, available at https://indiankanoon.org/doc/172603020/) (last accessed 18 December 2024)

34 *Asha Sahay* v *Bhimrao Ambedkar Bihar University*, Civil Writ Jurisdiction Case No. 18581 of 2015 along with IA No. 3284 of 2018, paras 9-10, available at https://indiankanoon.org/doc/132979889/; and *President Mahavidyalaya* v *State of Bihar*, AIR 1995 Pat 7, decided 17 May 1994, available at https://indiankanoon.org/doc/618887/ (both last accessed 18 December 2024).

35 See *Dr Ram Manohar Lohia* vs *State Of Bihar And Others* on 7 September, 1965, 1966 AIR 740.

36 *Vijay Kumar Goal* v *University of Delhi*, CWP No. 1737179, decided on 16 April 1980(2); *State of Rajasthan* v *Sarita Choudhary*, 3 February 2006, available at https://www.casemine.com/judgement/

## Further Thoughts

1 Press release, Ministry of Home Affairs, 11 August 2023, available at https://pib.gov.in/PressReleaseIframePage.aspx?PRID=1947941. For the texts of all three bills, and their predecessors, see https://prsindia.org/files/bills_acts/bills_parliament/2023/Bharatiya_Nyay_(Second)_Sanhita_2023.pdf; https://prsindia.org/billtrack/the-bharatiya-nagarik-suraksha-second-sanhita-2023; https://prsindia.org/billtrack/the-bharatiya-sakshya-second-bill-2023; chrome-extension://efaidnbmnnnibpcajpcglclefindmkaj/https://www.indiacode.nic.in/bitstream/123456789/4219/1/THE-

INDIAN-PENAL-CODE-1860.pdf; https://www.indiacode.nic.in/bitstream/123456789/15272/1/the_code_of_criminal_procedure%2C_1973.pdf; and https://www.indiacode.nic.in/bitstream/123456789/6819/1/indian_evidence_act_1872.pdf (all last accessed 28 September 2024).

2 The Indian government has, however, made repeated commitments to ratify CAT, including before the UN Human Rights Council (HRC). See United National General Assembly (UNGA), 'Annex to the note verbale dated 16 February 2011 from the Permanent Mission of India to the United Nations and addressed to the President of the General Assembly: Voluntary pledges and commitments by India', available at https://documents.un.org/doc/undoc/gen/n11/244/93/pdf/n1124493.pdf; UNGA, 'Annex to the note verbale dated 16 October 2014 from the Permanent Mission of India to the United Nations and addressed to the President of the General Assembly: Candidature of India to the Human Rights Council, 2015-2017: Voluntary pledges and commitments pursuant to General Assembly resolution 60/251', available at https://documents.un.org/doc/undoc/gen/n14/579/72/pdf/n1457972.pdf; and UNGA, 'Annex to the note verbale dated 29 August 2018 from the Permanent Mission of India to the United Nations and addressed to the President of the General Assembly: Candidature of India to the Human Rights Council, 2019–2021: Voluntary pledges and commitments pursuant to General Assembly resolution 60/251', available at https://documents.un.org/doc/undoc/gen/n18/306/97/pdf/n1830697.pdf (all last accessed 28 September 2024).

3 Law Commission of India, Report No. 273, 'Implementation of 'United Nations Convention against Torture and other Cruel, Inhuman and Degrading Treatment or Punishment' through Legislation', October 2017, available at chrome extension://efaidnbmnnnibpcajpcglclefindmkaj/https://cdnbbsr.s3waas.gov.in/s3ca0daec69b5adc880fb464895726dbdf/uploads/2022/08/2022081620.pdf (last accessed 1 October 2024).

4 *DK Basu* v *State of West Bengal*, 1997 (1) SCC 416.

5 *Guidelines for Medico-Legal Examination in Police Custody and*

*Documenting Custodial Torture* (Mumbai: Centre for Enquiry into Health and Allied Themes, 2020), available at https://www.cehat.org/uploads/files/Guidelines%20for%20Medico%20legal%20examination%20in%20police%20custody%20and%20documenting%20custodial%20torture1.pdf (last accessed 15 April 2024).

6 See, for example, Divya Shukla, 'An analytical study of decreasing rate of conviction in India', *International Journal of Law,* 4, 2 (2018), 91-94, available at chrome-extension://efaidnbmnnnibpcajpcglclefindmkaj/https://www.lawjournals.org/assets/archives/2018/vol4issue2/4-2-54-365.pdf; and Bidisha Mandal, 'Differences in conviction rates across violent crimes in India', *World Development Perspectives,* 14, 2 (2019), https://doi.org/10.1016/j.wdp.2019.02.011 (both last accessed 7 October 2024).

7 For an overview of this attack see 'Parliament attack: when it was more than smoke 22 years ago', *India Today,* 13 December 2023, available at https://www.indiatoday.in/india/story/indian-parliament-terrorist-attack-2001-lashkar-e-taiba-jaish-2475579-2023-12-13 (last accessed 1 October 2024). For an insightful analysis of this incident and its aftermath, see Arundhati Roy, *The Hanging of Afzal Guru and the Strange Case of the Attack on the Indian Parliament* (New Delhi: Penguin, 2013).

8 See Soni Sori: India's fearless tribal activist', *BBC News,* 22 March 2016, available at https://www.bbc.co.uk/news/world-asia-india-35811608 (last accessed 26 August 2024). On the Naxalite movement see Sumanta Banerjee, *India's Simmering Revolution: The Naxalite Uprising* (London: Zed Books, 1984).

9 See Arghya Sengupta, 'Anti-corruption litigation in the Supreme Court of India', Open Society Foundations, March 2016, available at https://www.justiceinitiative.org/publications/anti-corruption-litigation-supreme-court-india#:~:text=The%20Indian%20Supreme%20Court%20has,a%20strongly%20counter%2Dmajoritarian%20Court; and Ramanath Jha, 'Crime in India: A Critical Review of Data Collection and Analysis', Observer Research Foundation, 16 May 2024, available at https://www.

orfonline.org/research/crime-in-india-a-critical-review-of-data-collection-and-analysis (both last accessed 5 October 2024).

10 See Jinee Lokaneeta, *The Truth Machines: Policing, Violence and Scientific Interrogations in India* (Ann Arbor: University of Michigan Press, 2020).

11 *Status of Policing in India Report, 2018: A Study of Performance and Perceptions* (New Delhi: Common Cause & Lokniti—Centre for the Study Developing Societies, 2018).

12 Ibid, p. 71.

13 Ibid.

14 Ibid.

15 *Zulfikar Nasir* v *State of UP*, 2018 SCC OnLine Del 12153, para. 101.

16 Ibid.

17 Ibid, para. 102.

18 Ibid, paras. 102, 104.

19 *Kismatun* v *State of NCT of Delhi through Home Department & Ors*, 2024 SCC OnLine Del 4996, para. 28, available at https://indiankanoon.org/doc/158204709/ (last accessed 7 October 2024).

20 Ibid. See also AIR 2018 SUPREME COURT 3354, (2018), available at https://indiankanoon.org/doc/71965246/ (both last accessed 7 October 2024).

## PART III: COMPLICATING UNDERSTANDINGS OF POLICE VIOLENCE

### Chapter 7. Perceiving Threats and Policing Concerns: The Annual Conferences of the Director and Inspector Generals of Police in India

1 GC Singhvi, 'National Planning and Police;, *Indian Journal of Public Administration*, 17, 4 (1971): 745-753. Modelled on the system of development planning first implemented by Vladimir Lenin in the Soviet Union in 1928, the post-colonial Indian state has, until 2017, sought to address colonial underdevelopment, poverty, and inequality through a series of five-year plans, which were implemented, after 1951, by a Planning Commission (and, after

2015, by the NITI Aayog). See MM Sury, *Five Year Plans of India*, 3 vols. (New Delhi: New Century Publications, 2013).

2 Ibid, pp. 746-752

3 Safi Ahsan Rizvi (ed.), *Golden Jubilee: DGsP/IGsP Conference Since 1950* (New Delhi: Intelligence Bureau, 2015), 'Editor's Note', p. 6, available at https://www.police.gov.in/sites/default/files/ebooks/ebooks.pdf (last accessed on 22 April 2024). Since the book contains no references, it is not always clear who gave the speeches included in it. I have, therefore, only indicated individual speakers where this information is available.

4 These conferences became annual from 1983.

5 *Golden Jubilee*, p. 8

6 Ibid, p. 9.

7 Ibid.

8 Ibid.

9 Ibid. Founded in 1925, although remaining largely an underground movement in the colonial era, the CPI is the oldest communist party in India.

10 Ibid.

11 China had expansionist ambitions in Tibet, which were viewed as endangering India's external security, as noted in the welcome remarks at the conference made by the Director, IB, TG Sanjevi Pillai. *Golden Jubilee*, p. 11.

12 Javeed Alam, 'State and the Making of Communist Politics in India', *Economic and Political Weekly*, 25, 45 (1991): 2575.

13 Rahul De, 'The Drive to Industrialize under Nehru's Leadership: 1950-66', in *A History of Economic Policy in India: Crisis, Coalitions, and Contingency* (Cambridge: Cambridge University Press, 2023), p. 48.

14 Ibid.

15 Tarlochan Singh, 'Reminiscing on the Dramatic Moment When Pundit Nehru Was Shouted Down', SikhNet, 16 September 2022, available at https://www.sikhnet.com/news/reminising-dramatic-moment-when-pundit-nehru-was-shouted-down (last accessed 12 June 2024).

16 JS Grewal, *Master Tara Singh in Indian History* (Oxford University Press, 2018); and Singh, 'Reminiscing on the Dramatic Moment'.
17 *Golden Jubilee,* p. 19.
18 Ramchandra Guha, *India After Gandhi: A History* (London: Macmillan, 2007), Part Two. For an overview of the Naxalbari uprising, see the interview with Shalini Gera in this volume. See also Sumanta Banerjee, *India's Simmering Revolution: The Naxalite Uprising* (London: Zed Books, 1984).
19 *Golden Jubilee* p. 26.
20 Ibid.
21 See Asghar Ali Engineer, 'Communal conflict after 1950: a perspective', *Economic and Political Weekly,* 27, 34 (1992): 1782-1785.
22 *Golden Jubilee,* p. 26.
23 See, for e.g., Paul R Brass, *The Production of Hindu-Muslim Violence in Contemporary India* (Seattle: University of Washington Press, 2011).
24 *Golden Jubilee,* p. 36.
25 Ibid, p. 42.
26 Ibid.
27 Ibid, p. 36.
28 Ibid, p. 49.
29 Rakesh Ankit, 'Janata Party (1974-77): Creation of an All-India Opposition', *History and Sociology of South Asia,* 11, 1 (2017): 39-54.
30 *Golden Jubilee,* p. 57.
31 Ibid.
32 Ibid, pp. 57-58.
33 Ibid.
34 De, 'The Drive to Industrialize under Nehru's Leadership', p. 97.
35 Ibid
36 Atul Kohli, 'Politics of Economic Growth in India, 1980-2005: Part I: The 1980s', *Economic and Political Weekly,* 41, 13 (April 1-7, 2006): 1251-1259.
37 Ibid, p. 98.

38 *Golden Jubilee*, pp. 58-59.

39 'Anand Marga: Tantric terrorists', *India Today*, 9 September 2014 (updated 3 April, 2015), available at https://www.indiatoday.in/magazine/special-report/story/19820531-ananda-marga-spiritual-saviours-or-tantrik-terrorists-771819-2013-09-20 (last accessed 2 March 2024).

40 *Golden Jubilee*, pp. 62 and 79. See also Thomas Blom Hansen, *The Saffron Wave: Democracy and Hindu Nationalism in Modern India* (Princeton: Princeton University Press, 1999).

41 See, for e.g., C Christine Fair and Sumit Ganguly (eds), *Policing Insurgencies: Cops as Counterinsurgents* (Delhi: Oxford University Press, 2014).

42 Ibid, pp. 75 and 87.

43 See, for e.g., Brass, *The Production of Hindu-Muslim Violence in Contemporary India*.

44 *Golden Jubilee*, p. 59. See also Pratiksha Baxi, 'Impunity of law and custom: Stripping and parading of women in India', in Uma Chakravarti (ed.), *Faultlines of History: The India Papers II* (Delhi: Zubaan, 2018) pp. 291–334.

45 *Golden Jubilee*, p. 59. See also *Khatri and Others* v *State of Bihar and Others* ((1981) 1 SCC 627); and Dhruba Jyoti Purkait, 'Blind rage and helplessness in Bhagalpur', letter to the editor, *Hindustan Times ST (Jaipur)*, 12 October 2015, available at https://www.pressreader.com/india/hindustan-times-st-jaipur/20151012/281908771977619 (last accessed 28 August 2024).

46 *Golden Jubilee*, p. 59.

47 Ibid, p. 65.

48 See Matthew McCartney, *Political Economy, Growth and Liberalisation in India, 1991-2008* (London: Routledge, 2009); Tanika Sarkar and T Basu (eds), *Khaki Shorts and Saffron Flags: Critique of the Hindu Right* (Hyderabad: Orient Longman, 1993); AG Noorani, *The Destruction of the Babri Masjid—A National Dishonour* (New Delhi: Tulika, 2014); and *Reservation for Backward Classes: Mandal Commission Report of the Backward Classes Commission, 1980* (New Delhi: Akalank Publications, 1991), available at https://archive.

org/details/dli.jZY9lup2kZl6TuXGlZQdjZI8k0Uy (last accessed 18 December 2024).

49 *Golden Jubilee*, p. 100.

50 On the development and evolution of human rights in India see A Gudavarthy, 'Human Rights Movements in India: State, civil society and beyond', *Contributions to Indian Sociology* 42, 1 (2008): 29-57.

51 *Golden Jubilee*, p. 98

52 Ibid, p. 125

53 Peter R Lavoy (ed.), *Asymmetric Warfare in South Asia: The Causes and Consequences of the Kargil Conflict* (Cambridge: Cambridge University Press, 2009).

54 *Golden Jubilee*, p. 127

55 Anil Divan Foundation, 'Jain Hawala Diaries"', Parts, 1-3, 'Friend of the Court', podcast, available at https://www.anildivanfoundation.org/friend-of-the-court. See also Gene Tausk, 'White Collar Crime and Fraud', podcast, available at https://podcasters.spotify.com/pod/show/gene-tausk/episodes/Season-2-Episode-3---Hawala---An-ancient-form-of-money-transfer-e1f0gpl/a-a77j0c7 (both last accessed 9 March 2024).

56 *Golden Jubilee*, p. 128.

57 See, for example, Bulent Gokay and RBJ Walker, *11 September 2001: War, Terror and Judgment* (London: Frank Cass, 2003); and Judith Butler, *Precarious Life: The Powers of Mourning and Violence* (London: Verso, 2004).

58 Rahul Roy-Chaudhury, 'India's anti-terrorism and security policy in the first UPA government', in Lawrence Saez and Gurpal Singh (eds), *New Dimensions of Politics in India: The United Progressive Alliance in Power* (London: Routledge, 2012).

59 *Golden Jubilee*, pp. 147, 149; and Alpa Shah and Judith Pettigrew, 'Windows into a Revolution: Ethnographies of Maoism in South Asia', *Dialectical Anthropology*, 33, 3/4 (2009-12): 225-251.

60 Krittivas Mukherjee, 'Indian PM says fight against Maoists is failing, *Reliefweb*,15 September 2009, https://reliefweb.int/report/india/indian-pm-says-fight-against-maoists-failing; Aroon Purie, Editorial, *India Today*, 26 October 2009, https://www.indiatoday.

in/magazine/editors-note/story/20091026-from-the-editor-in-chief-741034-2009-10-14; and Special Correspondent, 'Naxalism is the greatest threat, says Manmohan', *The Hindu*, 22 October 2010, https://www.thehindu.com/news/Naxalism-is-the-greatest-threat-says-Manmohan/article15788298.ece (all last accessed 10 March 2024).

61 DH Web Desk, 'How the term Urban Naxal came into being', *Deccan Herald*, 11 October 2022, available at https://www.deccanherald.com/india/how-the-term-urban-naxal-came-to-being-1152587.html; and Shaurya Karabir Gurung, 'Urban Naxals: How the term came about', *The Economic Times*, 20 August 2018, https://economictimes.indiatimes.com/news/defence/urban-naxals-its-not-such-a-new-thing/articleshow/65598483.cms?from=mdr (both last accessed 18 May 2024).

62 Rahul V Pisharody, 'Civil society, the new frontier of war, can be manipulated to hurt a nation's interest: Ajit Doval', *Indian Express*, 12 November 2021, available at https://indianexpress.com/article/cities/hyderabad/ajit-doval-nsa-warfare-civil-society-7619555/#; and MK Venu and Maya Mirchandani, 'Locating Pegasus in Doval's Civil Society as New Frontier of War', *The Wire*, 29 November 2021, available https://thewire.in/government/locating-pegasus-in-dovals-civil-society-as-new-frontier-of-war (both last accessed 10 March 2024).

63 Rhys Machold, *After 26/11: India, Palestine/Israel, and the Fabrication of Homeland Security* (New Delhi: Navayana, 2024).

64 Vijaita Singh and Dinakar Peri, 'India has lost access to 26 out of 65 Patrolling Points in eastern Ladakh, says research paper', *The Hindu*, 24 January 2023, available at https://www.thehindu.com/news/national/india-has-lost-access-to-26-out-of-65-patrolling-points-in-eastern-ladakh-says-research-paper/article66428193.ece#:~:text=Photo%20Credit%3A%20PTI-,India%20has%20lost%20access%20to%2026%20out%20of%2065%20Patrolling,Delhi%2C%20accessed%20by%20The%20Hindu (last accessed 18 May 2024).

65 Deeptiman Tiwary, 'At DGP meet, officers flag Islamist, Hindutva

outfits in radicalisation', *Indian Express,* 27 January 2023, available at https://indianexpress.com/article/india/at-dgp-meet-officers-flag-islamist-hindutva-outfits-in-radicalisation-8406869/?utm_source=substack&utm_medium=email (last accessed 15 March 2024).

## Chapter 8. Distrusted Force: The Police in India's Counterinsurgency in Kashmir

1 On India's occupation of Jammu and Kashmir since 1947 see Yousaf Junaid, 'Occupied Jammu and Kashmir: A human rights black hole', *Daily Sabah,* 5 August 2023, available at https://www.dailysabah.com/opinion/op-ed/occupied-jammu-and-kashmir-a-human-rights-black-hole. See also Suhrith Parthasarathy, 'An Exercise of Executive Whim: Negation of Article 370 In J&K Doesn't Stand Up to Constitutional Test, Strikes at Federalism', Blog, *Times of India,* 7 August 2019, available at https://timesofindia.indiatimes.com/blogs/toi-edit-page/a-plainly-illegal-order-why-the-overturning-of-article-370-in-jk-doesnt-stand-up-to-constitutional-test/ (both last accessed 18 June 2024). I will henceforth refer to Jammu and Kashmir simply as 'Kashmir'.

2 Yola Verbruggen, 'Rule of law: tensions high in Jammu and Kashmir as elections approach', *International Bar Association*, 30 March 2023, available at https://www.ibanet.org/rule-of-law-tensions-high-jammu-kashmir (last accessed 18 June 2024).

3 Balu G Nair, 'Abrogation of Article 370: Can the President Act Without the Recommendation of the Constituent Assembly?', *Indian Law Review* 3, 3 (2019), p. 254. See also Akshay Deshmane, 'Kashmir: Scrapping Article 370 "Unconstitutional", "Deceitful," Says Legal Expert AG Noorani', *Huffpost,* 5 August 2019, available at https://www.huffpost.com/archive/in/entry/kashmir-article-370-scrapping-constitutional-expert-reacts-noorani_in_5d47e58de4b0aca341206135 (last accessed 18 June 2024). As specified in Article 1(1) of the Indian Constitution (and elaborated in Parts V and VI), India, like the United States, is a 'union of states'.

4 Goldie Osuri, 'Kashmiris Are Living a Long Nightmare of Indian Colonialism', *The Conversation*, 21 August 2019, available at https://theconversation.com/kashmiris-are-living-a-long-nightmare-of-indian-colonialism-121925; Jeffrey Gettleman, 'In Kashmir, Growing Anger and Misery', *New York Times,* 30 September 2019, available at https://www.nytimes.com/2019/09/30/world/asia/Kashmir-lockdown-photos.html; 'Full Text: Womens Voice; Fact-Finding Report on Kashmir', *Maktoob*, 24 September 2024, available at https://maktoobmedia.com/2019/09/24/full-text-womens-voice-fact-finding-report-on-kashmir/; and Kashmir Law and Justice Project, '*They Should Be Beaten and Skinned Alive*': *The Final Phase of India's War on Kashmiri Civil Society (October 2020-2022)*, March 2024, available at https://www.kljp.org/articles/they-should-be-beaten-and-skinned-alive-the-final-phase-of-indias-war-on-kashmiri-civil-society-october-2020-2022 (all last accessed 19 June 2024).

5 Gregory Stanton, 'Genocide Alert for Kashmir, India', *Genocide Watch,* 15 August 2019, available at https://www.genocidewatch.com/single-post/2019/08/15/Genocide-Alert-for-Kashmir-India (last accessed 19 June 2024).

6 MAS, Personal Communication, 12 January 2022; and Medha, 'The Revocation of Kashmir's Autonomy: High-Risk Hindutva Politics at Play', *GIGA Focus Asia*, 5 (2019), available at https://www.giga-hamburg.de/en/publications/giga-focus/the-revocation-of-kashmir-s-autonomy-high-risk-hindutva-politics-at-play (last accessed 18 June 2024).

7 Ananya Bharadwaj, 'J&K cops can't please anyone—Kashmiris call them traitors, central forces mistrust them', *The Print*, available at https://theprint.in/india/jk-cops-cant-please-anyone-kashmiris-call-them-traitors-central-forces-mistrust-them/294180/; and Abishek Bhalla, 'J&K: Weapons of over 250 SPOs seized over fear of them joining terror groups', *India Today*, 17 August 2019, available at https://www.indiatoday.in/india/story/jammu-and-kashmir-abrogation-article-370-weapons-of-over-250-spos-seized-terror-groups-1581829-2019-08-17 (both last accessed 24 June 2024).

8 Aijaz Hussain, 'Indian Order Leaves Kashmir Police Dispirited, Even Disarmed: Kashmiri Police Officers Have Been Sidelined', 27 August 2019, available at https://thediplomat.com/2019/08/indian-order-leaves-kashmir-police-dispirited-even-disarmed/ (last accessed 19 June 2024).

9 Sandhu Kamaljit Kaur, 'Jammu and Kashmir: Cops turn mentors for stone pelters', 7 April 2017, available at https://www.indiatoday.in/mail-today/story/jammu-and-kashmir-cops-counselling-stone-pelters-969968-2017-04-07 (last accessed 24 June 2024).

10 Umer Maqbool, '"Trojan Horse": Opposition Questions Union Govt's "Takeover" of J&K Police Budget', *The Wire,* 8 August 2024, available at https://thewire.in/government/trojan-horse-opposition-questions-union-govts-takeover-of-jk-police-budget (last accessed 12 August 2024).

11 Gowhar Fazili, 'Police Subjectivity in Occupied Kashmir: Reflections on an Account of a Police Officer', in H Duschinski, M Bhan, A Zia and C Mahmood (eds), *Resisting Occupation in Kashmir* (Philadelphia: University of Pennsylvania Press, 2018).

12 Fareed Rifat, 'Why Kashmir's local policemen have become rebels' new targets', *Al Jazeera,* 22 September 2018, https://www.aljazeera.com/features/2018/9/22/why-kashmirs-local-policemen-have-become-rebels-new-targets (last accessed 19 June 2024).

13 Andrew Whitehead, *A Mission in Kashmir* (New Delhi: Penguin Viking, 2008), pp. 26-27.

14 H Duschinski, and S Ghosh, 'Constituting the Occupation: Preventive Detention and Permanent Emergency in Kashmir', *Journal of Legal Pluralism and Unofficial Law* 49, 3 (2017): 314.

15 Mushtaq A Geelani, 'Kashmir: A History Littered With Rigged Elections', *Media Monitors Network,* 25 June 2001, available at https://web.archive.org/web/20160304051443/http://www.mediamonitors.net/jeelani4.html (last accessed 20 June 2024).

16 Sanjib Baruah, 'AFSPA: legacy of colonial constitutionalism', *Seminar,* n.d., available at https://www.india-seminar.com/2010/615/615_sanjib_baruah.htm; Office of the High Commissioner for Human Rights, *Report on the Situation of Human*

*Rights in Kashmir: Developments in the Indian State of Jammu and Kashmir from June 2016 to April 2018, and General Human Rights Concerns in Azad Jammu and Kashmir and Gilgit-Baltistan*, 14 June 2018, available at https://www.ohchr.org/en/documents/reports/report-situation-human-rights-kashmir-developments-indian-state-jammu-and-kashmir; and Amnesty International, *India: 'If they are dead, tell us': 'Disappearances' in Jammu and Kashmir*, 1999, available at http://www.amnesty.org/en/library/info/ASA20/002/ (all last accessed 24 June 2024).

17 '"Everyone Lives in Fear": Patterns of Impunity in Jammu and Kashmir', *Human Rights Watch*, 18, 11 (2006): 1-152, available at https://www.hrw.org/sites/default/files/reports/india0906web.pdf (last accessed 24 June 2024). While India is a signatory to important international conventions for the protection of human rights, such as the 1948 Universal Declaration of Human Rights and the 1949 Geneva Conventions, it has not ratified the 1977 Additional Protocols to the latter, under which guerilla warfare and state counterinsurgency operations are, to some extent, brought within the remit of international humanitarian law. As a number of contributions to this book note, India has also not ratified the 1987 Convention Against Torture and Other Cruel, Inhuman or Degrading Treatment or Punishment. See Srinivas Burra, 'Why India Should Consider Signing the Additional Protocols of the Geneva Conventions', *The Wire*, 8 June 2017, available at https://thewire.in/diplomacy/india-humanitarian-law-additional-protocols#:~:text=The%20four%20Geneva%20Conventions%20attained,Protocols%20of%201977%2C%20including%20India (last accessed 24 June 2024).

18 Haley Duschinski, 'Reproducing Regimes of Impunity: Fake Encounters and the Informalization of Everyday Violence in Kashmir Valley', *Cultural Studies* 24, 1 (2010): 110–132; Haley Duschinski, Mona Bhan, Ather Zia, and Cynthia Mahmood (eds), *Resisting Occupation in Kashmir* (Philadelphia: University of Pennsylvania Press, 2018); Ather Zia, *Resisting Disappearance: Women's Activism and Military Occupation in Kashmir* (Seattle:

Washington University Press, 2020); and Hafza Kanjwal, *Colonizing Kashmir: State-building Under Indian Occupation* (Stanford: Stanford University Press, 2023).

19 Amnesty International, *'Denied': Failures in accountability for human rights violations by security force personnel in Jammu and Kashmir*, 21 July 2015, ASA 20/1874/2015, available at https://www.amnesty.org/en/documents/asa20/1874/2015/en/; Kashmir Law and Justice Project, *'They Should Be Beaten and Skinned Alive'*; and Venkatesh Nayak, 'MoD, Army "Don't Have Files" on Rejected Pleas to Prosecute Security Personnel', 30 April 2018, available at https://thewire.in/security/defence-ministry-army-jammu-and-kashmir-security-forces-afspa-rti (all last accessed 24 June 2024).

20 Basharat Masood, 'J-K admin paves way to notify 'strategic areas' for armed forces', *Indian Express*, 18 July 2020, available at https://indianexpress.com/article/india/j-k-admin-paves-way-to-notify-strategic-areas-for-armed-forces-6511300/; Duschinski et al, *Resisting Occupation in Kashmir;* 'Top 10 Countries with Highest Military Spending: India among top 5; where do China, Russia, US stand? Check List', *Times of India,* 16 May 2024, available at https://timesofindia.indiatimes.com/business/india-business/top-10-countries-with-highest-military-spending-india-among-top-5-where-do-china-russia-us-stand-check-list/photostory/110186237.cms; and 'Center Spent over Rs 9000 crore on Security in J&K', *Times Now*, updated 30 April 2022, available at https://www.timesnownews.com/india/centre-spent-over-rs-9000-crore-on-security-in-jammu-and-kashmir-till-2021-since-article-370-abrogation-article-91208203 (all last accessed 24 June 2024). With 1.1 million soldiers, India also has the third largest army in the world, as well as one of the largest defence budgets.

21 'QuickFacts: Dallas City, Texas', US Census Bureau, 1 July 2023, available at https://www.census.gov/quickfacts/fact/table/dallascitytexas/PST045217. See also Mohammed Hanief, 'India Annexes Kashmir and Brings Us Back to Partition', *The New York Times,* 7 August 2019, available at https://www.nytimes.com/2019/08/07/opinion/kashmir-india.html (both last accessed 24 June 2024).

22 Aquib Javeed, 'Inside The Shadowy, Deadly World Of Kashmir's Teenage "Hybrid Militants"', *Article 14*, 6 October 2022, available at https://article-14.com/post/inside-the-shadowy-deadly-world-of-kashmir-s-teenage-hybrid-militants--633e3b285e987 (last accessed 24 June 2024).

23 '"Breaking people's will": In Kashmir, gunfights leave a trail of destroyed homes and rising anger', *Scroll.in*, 20 September 2018, available at https://scroll.in/article/894739/breaking-peoples-will-in-kashmir-gunfights-leave-a-trail-of-destroyed-homes-and-rising-anger#:~:text=According%20to%20official%20data%20accessed,-shortly%20after%20tracking%20down%20militants; and JKCCS, 'Bi-annual HR Review: 229 killings, 107 CASO's, 55 internet shutdowns, 48 properties destroyed', January-June 2020, available at https://jkccs.info/bi-annual-hr-review-229-killings-107-casos-55-internet-shutdowns-48-properties-destroyed/ (both last accessed 24 June 2024).

24 JKCCS, 'Bi-annual HR Review'; and Peoples Dispatch, 'Family of 65-year-old Kashmiri civilian says he was killed by security forces', 3 July 2020, available at https://peoplesdispatch.org/2020/07/03/family-of-65-year-old-kashmiri-civilian-says-he-was-killed-by-security-forces/ (last accessed 24 June 2024).

25 Prem Mahadevan, *The Politics of Counterterrorism in India: Strategic Intelligence and National Security in South Asia* (London and New York: IB Tauris, 2011); Yateendra Singh Jafa, 'Defeating Terrorism: A Study of Operational Strategy and Tactics of Police Forces in Jammu & Kashmir (India)', *Police Practice and Research*, 6, 2 (2005): 141-164; *and 'Raising the Stakes in Jammu and Kashmir', The Crisis Group, 5 August 2020, available at* https://www.crisisgroup.org/asia/south-asia/kashmir/310-raising-stakes-jammu-and-kashmir (all *last accessed* 20 June 2024).

26 Paul Staniland, 'Kashmir since 2003', *Asian Survey*, 53, 5 (2013): 931-957; and 'J&K Police: The Enemy Within?', *NDTV News*, 23 January 2020, available at https://www.ndtv.com/video/j-k-police-the-enemy-within-538633 (last accessed 20 June 2024).

27 Fayaz Wani, 'Eight cops including officer beaten by army men in

Kashmir, police files case', *The New Indian Express*, 22 July 2017, available at https://www.newindianexpress.com/nation/2017/Jul/22/eight-cops-including-officer-beaten-by-army-men-in-kashmir-police-files-case-1632173.html (last accessed 24 June 2024).

28 Bharadwaj, 'J&K cops can't please anyone'.

29 Sanjoy Hazarika, 'Indian Army Troops Crush Revolt by Police in Kashmir', *The New York Times*, 29 April 1993, available at https://www.nytimes.com/1993/04/29/world/indian-army-troops-crush-revolt-by-police-in-kashmir.html (last accessed 21 June 2024).

30 For the origins, and history, of UNMOGIP, see 'UNMOGIP Fact Sheet', United Nations Peacekeeping, available at https://peacekeeping.un.org/en/mission/unmogip (last accessed 21 June 2024).

31 Harinder Baweja, 'Police revolt shows glaring flaws in Centre's plan to restore normalcy in Kashmir', *India Today*, 15 May 1993, available at https://www.indiatoday.in/magazine/special-report/story/19930515-police-revolt-shows-glaring-flaws-in-centre-plan-to-restore-normalcy-in-kashmir-811088-1993-05-14 (last accessed 21 June 2024).

32 Ibid.

33 Sanjoy Hazarika, 'Indian Army Troops Crush Revolt by Police in Kashmir'.

34 Ibid.

35 'Authorities fire 79 police for fomenting rebellion', *UPI Archives*, 5 May 51993, available at https://www.upi.com/Archives/1993/05/05/Authorities-fire-79-police-for-fomenting-rebellion/9352736574400/ (last accessed 21 June 2024).

36 Aijaz Hussain, 'Despite anti-India protests, Kashmiris seek police jobs', *Go Erie*, n.d., available at https://eu.goerie.com/story/news/nation-world/2016/10/09/despite-anti-india-protests-kashmiris/24543241007/#:~:text=A%20top%20police%20officer%20speaking,our%20belly%2C%22%20Mir%20said (last accessed 21 June 2024).

37 Hilal Mir, 'SPOs: The dark underbelly of India's security system in Kashmir', *TRT World*, 2018, available at https://www.trtworld.com/

magazine/spos-the-dark-underbelly-of-india-s-security-system-in-kashmir-20918 (last accessed 21 June 2024).

38 'Population of Jammu and Kashmir', *Statistics Times,* available at https://statisticstimes.com/demographics/india/jammu-and-kashmir-population.php (last accessed 18 December 2024).

39 'J&K Police Recruitment 2019 last date: Apply for 2700 posts before Oct 22', *The Business Standard*, 20 November 2019, available at https://www.business-standard.com/article/jobs/j-k-police-recruitment-2019-last-date-on-oct-22-apply-for-2700-posts-now-119102100162_1.html (last accessed 21June 2024).

40 Mir, 'SPOs: The dark underbelly of India's security system in Kashmir'; Fareed, 'Why Kashmir's local policemen have become rebels' new targets'; and Irfan Mehraj and Freny Manecksha, 'The Life and Death of a Pro-Government Militant in Kashmir', *The Wire,* 5 May 2017, available at https://thewire.in/politics/rashid-billa-kashmir-ikhwan (all last accessed 22 June 2024).

41 Snehesh Alex Philip, 'Jammu & Kashmir's elite anti-terror unit gets full-time head after a gap of 5 months', *The Print,* 10 October 2021, available at https://theprint.in/defence/jammu-kashmirs-elite-anti-terror-unit-gets-full-time-head-after-a-gap-of-5-months/748515/ (last accessed 22 June 2024).

42 Ashiq Peerzada, 'Armed village defence groups to be re-established in Jammu: BJP', *The Hindu*, 4 March 2022, available at https://www.thehindu.com/news/national/other-states/armed-village-defence-groups-to-be-re-established-in-jammu-bjp/article65186964.ece (last accessed 22 June 2024).

43 Rana Ayub, 'Behind The Facade Of Modi's "New Kashmir"', *Noēma,* 5 June 2024, available at https://www.noemamag.com/behind-the-facade-of-modis-new-kashmir/; 'In Kashmir, Indian bulldozers are now carrying out settler-colonial policy', *Middle East Eye*, 12 March 2023, available at https://www.middleeasteye.net/opinion/india-kashmir-settler-colonial-policy-bulldozers-carrying-out; and 'India: Government Policies, Actions Target Minorities: Year After Delhi Violence, Bias Against Muslims Taints Investigation', *Human Rights Watch*, 19 February 2021, available at https://www.hrw.

org/news/2021/02/19/india-government-policies-actions-target-minorities (all last accessed 22 June 2024).

44 'At Least 1700 Police Personnel Including 508 PSOs Killed Since 1990', *The Kashmiriyat,* 15 December 2020, available at https://thekashmiriyat.co.uk/at-least-1700-police-personnel-including-508-psos-killed-since-1990/ (last accessed 22 June 2024).

45 Fayaz Bukhari, 'Police officer's son among 2 LeT militants killed', *The Daily Excelsior,* 16 May 2014, available at https://www.dailyexcelsior.com/police-officers-son-among-2-let-militants-killed/; and KL News Network, 'Cop Father Slain Within 26 Months of His Son's Killing', *Kashmir Life,* 13 July 2022, available at https://kashmirlife.net/cop-father-slain-within-26-months-of-his-sons-killing-296493/ (both last accessed 22 June 2024).

46 M Saleem Pandit, 'Mob lynches DSP outside J&K mosque', *The Times of India,* 24 June 2017, available at https://timesofindia.indiatimes.com/india/mob-lynches-dsp-outside-jk-mosque/articleshow/59293121.cms (last accessed 22 June 2024).

47 Bharadwaj, 'J&K cops can't please anyone'; and Betwa Sharma, 'In Times of Unrest, a Kashmiri Cop Lives Between a Rock and a Hard Place', *HuffPost,* 12 July 2016, available at https://www.huffpost.com/archive/in/entry/in-times-of-unrest-a-kashmiri-cop-lives-between-a-rock-and-a-ha_in_5c10b234e4b09dcd67fb483d (last accessed 24 June 2024).

48 Even when they are in uniform, however, JKP members may be stopped by Indian troops and made to show their identity cards and other supporting documents.

49 Fareed, 'Why Kashmir's local policemen have become rebels' new targets'.

50 Ibid. SPOs are ill-paid and ill-trained intelligence-generation counterinsurgency officers within the JKP that are culled from surrendered militants, small-time criminals, and people desperate for jobs. While they are, on the one hand, notorious for their enactment of extortion and extra-judicial killings, many of them have also deserted the force to join (or re-join) the militant ranks. Mir, 'SPOs: The dark underbelly of India's security system in

Kashmir'; and 'Special Police Officials (SPO)', *Kashmir Life,* 13 December 2020, available at https://kashmirlife.net/special-police-officials-spo-1086/ (last accessed 22 June 2024).

51 Mona Bhan, *Counterinsurgency, Democracy, and the Politics of Identity in India: From Warfare to Welfare?* (London and New York: Routledge, 2013).

52 In my book *Resisting Disappearance,* I have analysed, in depth, the nature of 'military humanitarianism' in Kashmir. See also Hannah Gurman (ed.), *Hearts and Minds: A People's History of Counterinsurgency* (New York: The New Press, 2013).

53 Zia, *Resisting Disappearance.* See also, for e.g., Colonel Sandeep Kapoor, 'A Relook at Operation Sadbhavana in J&K', *Journal of the United Service Institution of India,* CXLV, 600 (2015), available at https://www.usiofindia.org/publication-journal/a-relook-at-operation-sadbhavana-in-jk.html (last accessed 24 June 2024).

54 'Civic Programmes', Jammu & Kashmir Police, available at https://www.jkpolice.gov.in/Civic-Progammes (last accessed 24 June 2024).

55 See, for e.g., 'JKP organising national level cycle race in Srinagar', *DailyExcelsior.com,* 16 May 2015, available at https://www.dailyexcelsior.com/jkp-organising-national-level-cycle-race-in-srinagar/; 'JKP on forefront to provide platform to youth to showcase their skills: DGP', *Kashmir Reader,* 23 October 2020, available at https://kashmirreader.com/2020/10/23/jkp-on-forefront-to-provide-platform-to-youth-to-showcase-their-skills-dgp/; Idrees Lone, 'To help the local talent, Jammu and Kashmir police organises musical competition', *WION,* 12 March 2022, available at https://www.wionews.com/india-news/to-help-the-local-talent-jammu-and-kashmir-police-organises-musical-competition-461715; and 'Press Release', Jammu & Kashmir Police, 28 February 2023, available at https://www.jkpnewsportal.in/newsdet.aspx?q=6821 (all last accessed 24 June 2024).

56 'Governor witnesses Exhibition match between JKP Team, Real Kashmir Football Club', *Daily Excelsior,* 24 January 2019, available at https://www.dailyexcelsior.com/governor-witnesses-exhibition-match-between-jkp-team-real-kashmir-football-club/ (last accessed 24 June 2024).

57 Safwat Zargar, 'De-radicalisation? India's Kashmir policy pushed stone pelters to become militants, say families', *Scroll.in,* 29 January 2020, available at https://scroll.in/article/951098/de-radicalisation-india-s-kashmir-policy-pushed-stone-pelters-to-become-militants-say-families (last accessed 24 June 2024).

58 Bashir *Assad, 'Lead Role of JK Police, Synergy in Anti-Terrorist Operations', VIF India, 25 July 2019, available at* https://www.vifindia.org/article/2019/july/25/lead-role-of-jk-police-synergy-in-anti-terrorist-operations *(last accessed 24 June 2024).*

59 'Right-wing commentator calls for 'Israel-like' solution in Kashmir', *The Kashmiriyat,* 12 June 2024, available athttps://thekashmiriyat.co.uk/right-wing-commentator-calls-for-israel-like-solution-in-kashmir/#google_vignette *(last accessed 24 June 2024).*

## Chapter 9. Policing and Intimacy: Narratives from Terrorism Trials in Delhi

1 Human Rights Watch, *The 'Anti-Nationals': Arbitrary Detention and Torture of Terrorism Suspects in India* (2019), available at https://www.hrw.org/sites/default/files/reports/india0211W.pdf (last accessed June 10, 2024); Gautam Navlakha, 'POTA: Freedom to Terrorise', *Economic and Political Weekly,* 38, 29 (2003): 3038–40; and Jayant Krishnan, 'India's Patriot Act: POTA and the Impact on Civil Liberties in the World's Largest Democracy', *Law and Inequality,* 22, 2 (2004): 265–300. See also *State* v *Saquib Rahman,* available at https://indiankanoon.org/doc/93854339/ (all last accessed 18 December 2024). According to a 1994 report by the National Human Rights Commission, of 76,036 individuals arrested for committing acts of terrorism in India, twenty-five per cent were never charged and only thirty-five per cent went to trial—and of these, only 1.5 per cent ended in a conviction. This means that out of a total number of 76,036 arrests, only roughly 400 people were ever convicted. Only two per cent of those arrested under the 1967 Unlawful Activities (Prevention) Act between 2015 and 2019, furthermore, were eventually convicted. See Ministry of Home Affairs, Government of India, Memorandum

to the full Commission of National Human Rights Commission Annexure 1, 19 December 1994, cited in Ram Narayan Kumar et al., *Reduced to Ashes: The Insurgency and Human Rights in Punjab* (Kathmandu: South Asia Forum for Human Rights, 2003); and Rahul Tripathi, 'Below 2% of Those Arrested under UAPA Convicted in 2015–19: NCRB', *Economic Times*, 18 June 2023, available at https://economictimes.indiatimes.com/news/politics-and-nation/below-2-of-those-arrested-under-uapa-convicted-in-2015-19-ncrb/articleshow/83624754.cms?from=mdr (all last accessed 6 May 2024).

2 Jody Greene, 'Hostis Humani Generis', *Critical Inquiry*, 34, 4 (2008): 683–705.

3 All conversations recorded in this chapter are taken from the fieldnotes I took during the course of the ethnographic research discussed above.

4 Beatrice Jauregui, 'Intimacy: Personal Policing, Ethnographic Kinship, and Critical Empathy', in Didier Fassin (ed.), *Writing the World of Policing: The Difference Ethnography Makes* (Chicago: University of Chicago Press, 2017), p. 74.

5 See Mayur Suresh, *Terror Trials: Life and Law in Delhi's Courts* (New York: Fordham University Press, 2023). For other ways in which the role of the police has been conceptualised through the framework of intimacy, see also Jinee Lokaneeta, *The Truth Machines: Policing, Violence and Scientific Interrogations in India* (Ann Arbor: University of Michigan Press, 2020); Beatrice Jauregui, *Provisional Authority: Police, Order and Security in India* (Chicago: University of Chicago Press, 2016); and Santana Khanikar, *State, Violence and Legitimacy in India* (New Delhi: Oxford University Press, 2018).

6 As such a suggestion demonstrates, understanding police violence is complex. For insights in regard to such complexities see, for example, Walter Benjamin, 'Critique of Violence', in Peter Demetz (ed.), *Reflections: Essays, Aphorisms, Autobiographical Writings* (New York: Harcourt Brace Jovanovich, 1978); David Arnold, *Police Power and Colonial Rule: Madras 1859–1947* (Delhi:

Oxford University Press, 1986); Didier Fassin, *Enforcing Order: An Ethnography of Urban Policing* (Cambridge: Polity Press, 2013); Julia Eckert, 'The Trimurti of the State: State Violence and the Promises of Order and Destruction', *Max Planck Institute for Social Anthropology Working Papers*, no. 80, 2005, available at https://www.eth.mpg.de/cms/en/publications/working_papers/wp0080 (last accessed 17 April 2024); Jean Comaroff and John Comaroff, 'Criminal Obsessions, after Foucault: Postcoloniality, Policing and the Metaphysics of Disorder', in Comaroff and Comaroff (eds), *Law and Disorder in the Postcolony* (Chicago: University of Chicago Press, 2006), pp. 273-98; and Veena Das, 'The Signature of the State: The Paradox of Illegibility', in Veena Das and Deborah Poole (eds), *Anthropology in the Margins of the State* (New Mexico: School of American Research Press, 2004), pp. 225-52.

7 Michael Taussig, *Shamanism, Colonialism and the Wild Man: A Study in Terror and Healing* (Chicago: University of Chicago Press, 1987).

8 All names referred to in this chapter have been anonymised.

9 Naxals are communists who adhere to Maoist political ideology. The term *Naxal* comes from the village of Naxalbari, in West Bengal, where the Communist Party of India (Marxist) fomented an uprising in 1967. While this was brutally repressed, the Naxals went on to wage what has been referred to as the world's longest running 'people's war'. See, for example, Prakash Singh, *The Naxalite Movement in India* (New Delhi: Rupa & CO., 1999); Ranabir Sammadar (ed.), *From Popular Movements to Rebellion: The Naxalite Decade* (London: Routledge, 2018); Bernard d'Mello, *India After Naxalbari: Unfinished History* (New York: Monthly Revie Press, 2018); Alpa Shah, *Nightmarch: Among India's Revolutionary Guerillas* (London: Hurst, 2018); and Shivaji Mukherjee, *Colonial Institutions and Civil War: Indirect Rule and Maoist Insurgency in India* (Cambridge: Cambridge University Press, 2021).

10 I will refrain from citing such cases in order to preserve Bhandari's anonymity.

11 During the period between their arrest and the filing of charges against them, the suspects were produced before a magistrate once

a week. Most of the hearings were very perfunctory—the suspects would be produced, the prosecutor would request an extension of their period of detention, and the magistrate would grant it (bail is, notably, virtually impossible to obtain under the Unlawful Activities (Prevention) Act, India's current anti-terrorism law).

12 In addition to providing a narrative of the alleged criminal acts committed by an accused, a chargesheet outlines the specific laws under which he or she is charged with an offence (or offences).

## Further Thoughts

1 K Balagopal, 'Deaths in Police Custody: Whom and Why Do the Police Kill', *Economic and Political Weekly,* 21, 42 (22 November 1986): 2028-2029.

# PART IV: INTERVIEWS AND REFLECTIONS ON POLICE VIOLENCE AND MEANS OF REDRESS

## Policing and Democracy

1 *Bulldozer policing* refers to the implementation, by the police, of local government orders to demolish houses, which are predominantly inhabited by Muslims (some of whom have protested against or critiqued the BJP government). This is done, in places like Uttar Pradesh (UP) with little notice or due process, on the grounds that their dwellings are illegal. See Geeta Pandey, 'How bulldozers became a vehicle of injustice in India', *BBC News,* 19 June 2022, available at https://www.bbc.com/news/world-asia-india-61837134 (last accessed 17 June 2024).

2 *Report of the Indian Police Commission, 1902-03* (Simla: Printed at the Government Central Printing Office, 1903), available at https://archive.org/details/dli.csl.887 (last accessed 26 August 2024).

3 The eight reports produced by the National Police Commission are available via the Hindu Centre for Politics and Public Policy at https://www.thehinducentre.com/resources/reports-of-the-national-police-commission-1979-1981/article67792347.ece (last accessed 26 August 2024).

4 *Prakash Singh & Ors* v *Union of India & Ors*, Supreme Court of India, 22 September 2006, available at https://indiankanoon.org/doc/1090328/ (last accessed 26 July 2024).

5 See chapter one in this volume.

**Better Training, Representation, and Capacity Building as Keys to Addressing Police Violence in India**

1 For more on the living conditions of the police, see chapter seven.

2 See Sushant Kulkarni, 'Indian Police foundation Data: 900 Covid deaths among police forces, CAPFs; "number sounds note of caution for festive season"', *The Indian Express*, 29 October 2020, available at https://indianexpress.com/article/india/indian-police-foundation-data-900-covid-deaths-among-police-forces-capfs-number-sounds-note-of-caution-for-festive-season/ (last accessed 8 August 2024).

3 Following a decades-long socio-political dispute about whether the mosque had been built on the birthplace of the Hindu deity Rama, it was destroyed on December 6, 1992, by activists mobilised by right-wing Hindu organisations including the Vishva Hindu Parishad and the Bharatiya Janata Party. See 'Ayodhya: Temple to open at India's religious fault-line', *BBC News*, 21 January 2024, available at https://www.bbc.co.uk/news/world-asia-india-68030712 (last accessed 8 August 2024); and Tanika Sarkar and T Basu (eds), *Khaki Shorts and Saffron Flags: Critique of the Hindu Right* (Hyderabad: Orient Longman, 1993)

4 For more information on this case, see chapter four in this volume.

5 See Johanna Deeksha, 'The Tamil Nadu police's brutal violence against the state's weakest citizens', *Scroll.in*, 8 July 2024, available at https://scroll.in/article/1068691/the-tamil-nadu-polices-brutal-violence-against-the-states-weakest-citizens; and People's Watch reports, available at https://www.peopleswatch.org/reports (both last accessed 8 August 2024).

6 See Manash Pratim Gohain, '81% of northeast women harassed in Delhi: Survey', *The Times of India*, 24 January 2014, available at https://timesofindia.indiatimes.com/city/delhi/81-of-northeast-

women-harassed-in-delhi-survey/articleshow/29270244.cms (last accessed 8 August 2024). The National Commission for Women is a statutory body of the Government of India which advises it on policy matters affecting women.

7 'Barriers in Accessing Justice: The experiences of 14 rape survivors in Uttar Pradesh, India', Commonwealth Human Rights Initiative, 2020, available at chrome-extension://efaidnbmnnnibpcajpcglclefindmkaj/https://www.humanrightsinitiative.org/download/CHRI%20and%20AALI%20Barriers%20in%20accessing%20justice%20English.pdf (last accessed 8 August 2024).

8 See 'Meerut riots of May 1987: PUCL report', People's Union for Civil Liberties, 1987, available at https://web.archive.org/web/20120817150551/http://www.pucl.org/Topics/Human-rights/2006/meerut-riots.html (last accessed 8 August 2024).

9 See '"Tamasha bana diya hai": Patna HC slams police for illegally bulldozing petitioner's house', *Deccan Herald,* 4 December 2022, available at https://www.deccanherald.com/india/tamasha-bana-diya-hai-patna-hc-slams-police-for-illegally-bulldozing-petitioners-house-1168299.html (last accessed 8 August 2024).

10 See, for example, Ishan Marvel, 'In the Name of the Mother: How the state nurtures the gau rakshaks of Haryana', *The Caravan,* 1 September 2016, available at https://caravanmagazine.in/reportage/in-the-name-of-the-mother (last accessed 8 August 2024).

11 See Soutik Biswas and Umang Poddar, 'Umar Khalid: Indian activist languishes in jail without bail or trial', *BBC News,* available at https://www.bbc.co.uk/news/world-asia-india-67980484 (last accessed 8 August 2024). On the CAA protests, see also chapter six in this volume.

12 See 'Govt approves Rs 25,000-crore mega internal security scheme', *Business Standard,* 27 September 2017, available at https://www.business-standard.com/article/pti-stories/govt-approves-rs-25000-crore-mega-internal-security-scheme-117092700853_1.html (last accessed 8 August 2024).

13 Bharti Jain, 'Women's representation in Indian police falls short of 33% target: Home Ministry report', *The Times of India,* 5 December 2023, available at https://timesofindia.indiatimes.com/india/

womens-representation-in-indian-police-falls-short-of-33-target-home-ministry-report/articleshow/105762632.cms#:~:text=The%20percentage%20of%20women%20in,the%20majority%20serving%20as%20constables (last accessed 8 August 2024).

14 See 'The List of Do's and Don'ts under Armed Forces (Special Powers) Act, 1958, as cited in the judgement of the Supreme Court of India in the matter of Naga People's Movement of Human Rights and Ors Vs. Union of India (AIR 1998 SC 465)', Humanrightsinitiative.org, available at chrome-extension://efaidnbmnnnibpcajpcglclefindmkaj/https://www.humanrightsinitiative.org/download/AFSPA%20Do's&Don'ts-Comparative%20Table-ChitrangdaS&VenkatN-Jun2012.pdf (last accessed 8 August 2024). For more on AFSPA see the chapters by Bhavani Raman and Ather Zia in this volume.

**The Impunity of Police Encounters in Uttar Pradesh**

1 See '183 Criminals Killed in Uttar Pradesh Police Encounters Since 2017', NDTV, 14 April 2023, available at https://www.ndtv.com/india-news/183-criminals-killed-in-uttar-pradesh-police-encounters-since-2017-3948169 (last accessed 5 August 2024). The report, *Extinguishing Law and Life: Police Killings and Cover-up in the State of Uttar Pradesh*, is available at chrome-extension://efaidnbmnnnibpcajpcglclefindmkaj/https://yhrd.in/documents/wp-content/uploads/2021/10/up-final-export.pdf (last accessed 18 December 2024).

2 See Tanima Biswas, 'Calling It Hindu Exodus A Mistake By My Team: BJP MP On Kairana', *NDTV*, 14 June 2016, available at https://www.ndtv.com/india-news/on-kairana-bjp-lawmakers-u-turn-its-not-a-hindu-muslim-issue-1418763 (last accessed 26 August 2024).

3 See Arvind Ojha and Samarth Srivastava, 'Gangster Mukim Kala, Mukhtar Ansari's aide dead in shootout at Chitrakoot jail', *India Today*, 14 May 2021, available at https://www.indiatoday.in/india/story/gangster-mukim-kala-mukhtar-ansari-aide-dead-shootout-clash-chitrakoot-jail-1802547-2021-05-14 (last accessed 26 August 2024).

4 On the rise in hate crimes against Muslims, including lynchings by Hindu mobs, since the BJP came to power in India in 2014, see 'Muslims In India Still Under Threat As Mob Attacks, Lynchings Continue', *Outlook*, 26 June 2024, available at https://www.outlookindia.com/national/muslims-in-india-still-under-threat-as-mob-attacks-lynchings-continue (last accessed 5 August 2024).

5 Information on Balagopal's many writings is available at https://balagopal.org/. Kannabiran's writings include *The Wages of Impunity: Power, Justice and Human Rights* (Himayatnagar, Hyderabad: Orient Longman, 2004) and *The Speaking Constitution: A Sisyphean Life in Law*, trans. Kalpana Kannabiran (Gurugram: HarperCollins India, 2022), first published in Telugu in 2009.

6 See Sumati Sharma, 'Law On Police Encounters: Supreme Court Guidelines', *The Law Advice*, 14 April 2023, available at https://www.thelawadvice.com/articles/what-is-the-law-on-police-encounters (last accessed 5 August 2024).

7 See Prachi Bhardwaj, 'CBI to probe into the Manipur Extra Judicial killings by AFSPA', *SCC Online*, 14 July 2017, available at https://www.scconline.com/blog/post/2017/07/14/cbi-directed-to-probe-into-the-manipur-extra-judicial-killings-by-afspa/; and *Extra-judicial Execution Victim Families Association* v *Union of India*, (2016) 14 SCC 536, para 253, 254, Supreme Court of India, available at https://indiankanoon.org/doc/51378140/ (both last accessed 26 August 2024).

8 See Geeta Pandey, 'Hyderabad case: Why Indians are celebrating the killings', *BBC News*, 6 December 2019, available at https://www.bbc.co.uk/news/world-asia-india-50683615 (last accessed 7 July 2024).

9 See 'UP Police uses statistics to prove to Mayawati that they don't need to learn about encounters from Telangana police', *OpIndia*, 6 December 2019, available at https://www.opindia.com/2019/12/hyderabad-rape-encounters-up-police-we-better-mayawati/ (last accessed 7 July 2024).

10 See 'HC for special laws to deal with gangster culture in Punjab, Haryana', *Hindustan Times (Chandigarh)*, 14 May 2019, available

at https://www.pressreader.com/india/hindustan-times-chandigarh/20190514/281719796031478 (last accessed 7 July 2024).

**The War Against Adivasis in Chhattisgarh**

1 For an explanation of the term *Naxalites,* see chapter nine.

2 See 'Burkapal Naxal Attack: Court Acquits 121 Tribal Persons for Lack of Evidence', *The Wire,* 17 July 2022, available at https://thewire.in/law/burkapal-naxal-attack-121-tribal-persons-acquitted#:~:text=New%20Delhi%3A%20A%20court%20in,lack%20of%20evidence%20against%20them (last accessed 26 July 2024).

3 See *Citizens' Report on Security and Insecurity, Bastar Division, Chhattisgarh*, Asia Indigenous Peoples Pact, 12 August 2024, available at aipnet.org/citizens-report-on-security-and-insecurity/ (last accessed 24 August 2024).

4 See Vijaita Singh, 'BSF got tip-off on Maoist group presence in Chhattisgarh: official', *The Hindu*, 17 April 2024, available at https://www.thehindu.com/news/national/modi-government-will-eliminate-naxals-in-very-short-period-of-time-home-minister-amit-shah/article68075517.ece (last accessed 26 August 2024).

5 See *Citizens' Report on Security and Insecurity*.

6 See Deepika Joshi, '4 Killed in Police Firing in Chhattisgarh's Silger, Thousands Oppose Security Camp', Land Conflict Watch, 24 March 2022, available at https://www.landconflictwatch.org/conflicts/4-killed-in-police-firing-in-chhattisgarh-s-silger-thousands-oppose-security-camp (last accessed 24 August 2024).

7 See Ejaz Kaiser, 'Sukma SP orders surveillance of Christian missionaries' activities in tribal areas', *The New Indian Express,* 13 July 2021, available at https://www.newindianexpress.com/nation/2021/Jul/13/sukma-sp-orders-surveillance-of-christian-missionaries-activities-in-tribal-areas-2329667.html (last accessed 26 August 2024).

8 The RSS, founded in 1925, is a right-wing Hindu nationalist paramilitary organisation.

9 See 'Chhattisgarh Police Intimidates Jagdalpur Legal Aid Group

and Journalist Malini Subramaniam', *The Caravan*, 18 February 2016, available at https://caravanmagazine.in/vantage/chhattisgarh-police-intimidate-jagdalpur-legal-aid-group-malini-subramaniam (last accessed 26 August 2024).

10 See Ritesh Mishra, '2019 Yearender: Lowest Maoist violence in last five years in Chhattisgarh', *Hindustan Times*, 26 December 2019, available at https://www.hindustantimes.com/india-news/2019-yearender-lowest-maoist-violence-in-last-five-years-in-chhattisgarh/story-Ww4eg03lbvKFcNMN7EjZkI.html (last accessed 26 August 2024).

11 See 'Soni Sori: India's fearless tribal activist', *BBC News*, 22 March 2016, available at https://www.bbc.co.uk/news/world-asia-india-35811608 (last accessed 26 August 2024).

12 See Mimi P Thomas, 'Jailed, raped, tortured', *The Week*, 3 July 2016, available at https://www.theweek.in/theweek/cover/tribal-woman-naxalism.html (last accessed 26 August 2024).

13 See Ejas Kaiser, 'Chhattisgarh cops make hardcore Maoists' info public, seek their "Ghar Wapsi"', *The New Indian Express*, 13 June 2020, available at https://www.newindianexpress.com/nation/2020/Jun/13/chhattisgarh-cops-make-hardcore-maoists-info-public-seek-their-ghar-wapsi-2156209.html (last accessed 26 August 2024).

14 See Ritesh Mishra, 'Chattisgarh: Allegations cloud alleged suicide of surrendered woman "Maoist"', *Hindustan Times*, 25 February 2021, available at https://www.hindustantimes.com/india-news/chhattisgarh-allegations-cloud-alleged-suicide-of-surrendered-woman-maoist-101614240338633.html (last accessed 26 August 2024).

15 See Dhananjay Mahapatra, 'Anti-Naxal Salwa Judum faces axe over rights abuse', 20 September 2008, available at https://timesofindia.indiatimes.com/india/anti-naxal-salwa-judum-faces-axe-over-rights-abuse/articleshow/3504703.cms (last accessed 26 August 2024).

16 See '*India Today* investigation: Police, Samajik Ekta Manch force activists to leave Bastar', *India Today*, 15 April 2016, available at https://www.indiatoday.in/india/story/

ground-report-police-vigilante-nexus-exposed-in-maoist-hit-chhattisgarh-318083-2016-04-14 (last accessed 26 August 2024).

17 See Krishn Kaushik, 'The Police in Chhattisgarh may be Intimidating Journalists Through a New Vigilante Organisation', 17 February 2016, available at https://caravanmagazine.in/vantage/kalluri-chhattisgarh-samajik-ekta-manch-vigilante-media-freedom; and Raksha Kumar, 'Is Salwa Judum back in Bastar in the form of the Samajik Ekta Manch? ', *Scroll.in,* 8 April 2016, available at https://scroll.in/article/806080/is-salwa-judum-back-in-bastar-in-the-form-of-the-samajik-ekta-manch (both last accessed 26 August 2024).

18 See 'Chhattisgarh Police Intimidates Jagdalpur Legal Aid Group'.

19 See Supriya Sharma, 'How the Chhattisgarh police succeeded in hounding out those who questioned it', *Scroll.in,* 19 February 2016, available at https://scroll.in/article/803821/how-the-chhattisgarh-police-succeeded-in-hounding-out-those-who-questioned-it (last accessed 26 August 2024).

20 See Vineet Khare, 'Why a top Indian activist is facing threats to her life', *BBC News,* 20 February 2017, available at https://www.bbc.co.uk/news/world-asia-india-38903571 (last accessed 26 August 2024). See also Bela Bhatia, *India's Forgotten Country: A View from the Margins* (Gurgaon: Viking India, 2024).

21 See Divya Trivedi, 'A fake encounter in Chhattisgarh', *Frontline,* 20 December 2019, available at https://frontline.thehindu.com/the-nation/article30336712.ece (last accessed 26 August 2024).

22 See '81 CRPF Personnel Awarded Gallantry Medals on Valour Day', Ministry of Home Affairs, 9 April 2016, available at chrome-extension://efaidnbmnnnibpcajpcglclefindmkaj/https://crpf.gov.in/writereaddata/images/Press_Release/Press_Release-Valour_Day-2016.pdf (both last accessed 26 August 2024).

23 See Aman Sethi, 'Activists shocked at gallantry award for Chhattisgarh cop', *The Hindu,* 17 November 2021, available at https://www.thehindu.com/news/national/activists-shocked-at-gallantry-award-for-chhattisgarh-cop/article2834675.ece; and Raksha Kumar, 'As Bastar's top police officer exits amid charges of excesses, activists

cheer but with caution', *Scroll.in,* 3 February 2017, available at https://scroll.in/article/828395/as-bastars-top-police-officer-exits-amid-charges-of-excesses-activists-cheer-but-with-caution (both last accessed 26 August 2024).

24 See Joseph John, 'No toilets at camps, cops are easy target in Naxal hotbed', *The Indian Express,* 15 July 2009, available at https://indianexpress.com/article/news-archive/web/no-toilets-at-camps-cops-are-easy-target-in-naxal-hotbed/ (last accessed 26 August 2024).

25 See, for example, 'Command responsibility and failure to act', International Committee of the Red Cross, available at chrome-extension://efaidnbmnnnibpcajpcglclefindmkaj/https://www.icrc.org/sites/default/files/document/file_list/command-responsibility-icrc-eng.pdf (last accessed 26 August 2024).

26 See *AP Civil Liberties Committee (APCLC)* v *Govt. of AP,* Andhra Pradesh High Court, 6 February 2009, available at https://www.casemine.com/judgement/in/56ea70ae607dba369a6ee67a (last accessed 26 August 2024).

27 See *Andhra Pradesh Police Officers' Association* v *AP Civil Liberties Committee,* Supreme Court of India, 18 July 2019, available at https://www.casemine.com/judgement/in/5e04ae238ef152127cab74da (last accessed 26 August 2024).

28 See *People's Union for Civil Liberties* v *State of Maharashtra,* Supreme Court of India, 23 September 2014, available at https://indiankanoon.org/doc/25812914/ (last accessed 26 August 2024).

29 See also the interviews with Vikash Narain Rai and Mangla Verma and Vipul Kumar in this volume.

30 Prakash Singh v. Union of India, (2006) 8 SCC.

## A Reflection on Living with Violence in India's Northeast

1 Sanjib Baruah, *In the Name of the Nation: India and Its Northeast* (Stanford: Stanford University Press, 2020).

2 Quoted in AG Noorani, 'AFSPA: License to Kill', *Frontline,* 17 April 2015, p.106.

3 'Punish Guilty Personnel Protected under AFSPA', *People's Union for Democratic Rights,* 1 April 2022, available at https://www.pudr.

org/press-statements/punish-guilty-personnel-protected-under-afspa/ (last accessed 22 July 2024).

4 Ibid.

5 Santana Khanikar, *State, Violence and Legitimacy in India* (Delhi: Oxford University Press, 2018).

6 Jin Haritaworn, Adi Kuntsman and Silvia Prosocco, 'Introduction', in Haritaworn, Kuntsman and Prosocco (eds), *Queer Necropolitics* (London: Routledge, 2014), p. 3.

7 Dolly Kikon, 'Fifty Years of Justice: The Predicament of the Armed Forces Special Powers Act in India', *Contemporary South Asia*, 17, 3 (2009): 271-282.

8 Protections are enshrined in the Indian Constitution for communities deemed Scheduled Tribes (STs). Since getting ST status carries benefits in regard to political representation and reserved seats in schools and government jobs, it is highly sought after. Since 1960, the number of STs has, as a result, risen from 225 to over 700 today—which has fostered, in turn, resistance to such a status.

9 Baruah, *In the Name of the Nation*, p. 5.

## What Makes Police Violence Possible in India

1 See Mahesh Langa, 'Public flogging of Muslim men: Gujarat HC sentences four policemen to 14 days' imprisonment', *The Hindu*, 19 October 2023, available at https://www.thehindu.com/news/national/other-states/public-flogging-of-muslim-men-gujarat-hc-sentences-four-policemen-to-14-days-imprisonment/article67439340.ece (last accessed 7 August 2024).

2 For more on Shaikh's experience with the Indian criminal justice system see his book *Innocent Prisoners: Begunah Qaidi* (New Delhi, Pharos Media & Publishing Pvt Ltd, 2021 [2018]).

3 Satish Jha, '2004 Ishrat Jahan encounter case disposed of without trial as case against last two IBS officers dropped', *Deccan Herald*, 20 April 2021, available at https://www.deccanherald.com/india/2004-ishrat-jahan-encounter-case-disposed-of-without-trial-as-case-against-last-two-ib-officers-dropped-976396.html (last accessed 7 July 2024).

4 *Ramanand Nandlal Bharti* v *State of Uttar Pradesh* (2022) 5 SCR 162.

5 '*Status of Policing in India Report 2019: Police Adequacy and Working Conditions, Common Cause and Lokniti-Centre for the Study of Developing Societies*', 2019, available at https://www.csds.in/uploads/custom_files/1566973059_Status_of_Policing_in_India_Report_2019_by_Common_Cause_and_CSDS.pdf (last accessed 7 July 2024).

6 See https://www.youtube.com/channel/UC_UiB3lsftPB-bAyxMneOhA. Shaikh also chronicles, on his channel, the lost lives of Muslim men falsely charged and incarcerated on terrorism-related offences.

7 For an analysis of the problems with section 43(D) see Abhinav Sekhri, 'How The UAPA Is Perverting The Idea Of Justice', *Article 14*, 16 July 2020, available at https://article-14.com/post/how-the-uapa-is-perverting-india-s-justice-system (last accessed 8 July 2024).

8 See the 2021 Amnesty International report, *JCB Off Track: Evading responsibility for human rights violations committed with JCB machines in the Occupied Palestinian Territories*,on Israel's use of the company JCB's machines to perpetrate human rights abuses in the Palestinian territories, available at https://www.amnesty.org/en/documents/mde15/4985/2021/en/; and Al Jazeera, 'People "buried alive" outside Gaza hospital during Israeli raid', 18 December 2023, available at https://www.aljazeera.com/program/newsfeed/2023/12/18/people-buried-alive-during-israeli-raid-on-gaza-hospital (both last accessed 8 July 2024). For the use of bulldozers to target minorities in India see Geeta Pandey, 'How bulldozers became a vehicle of injustice in India', *BBC News*, 20 June 2022, available at https://www.bbc.co.uk/news/world-asia-india-61837134 (last accessed 8 June 2024), and the interview with Vikash Narain Rai in this volume.

9 See *DK Basu* v *State of West Bengal* (1997) (1) SCC 416; Shaikh, *Innocent Prisoners*; and chapter four in this volume.

10 See chapter four.

11 For more on Shaikh's experience with the Indian criminal justice system, see *Innocent Prisoners*.

12 For more on the legal backlog in India see Sameer Yasir, '"A Lifelong Nightmare": Seeking Justice in India's Overwhelmed Courts', *The New York Times*, 13 January 2024, available at https://www.nytimes.com/2024/01/13/world/asia/india-judicial-backlog.html?login=smartlock&auth=login-smartlock (last accessed 8 July 2024).

13 See MP Nathaniel, 'Why policemen kill themselves', *The Hindu*, 3 July 2019, available at https://www.thehindu.com/opinion/op-ed/why-policemen-kill-themselves/article28263242.ece (last accessed 7 July 2024).

14 See'Sanjay Raut's Arrest by ED "Illegal", a "Witch Hunt" Says Court While Granting Bail', November 9, 2022. https://thewire.in/law/sanjay-raut-uddhav-thackerays-close-aide-gets-bail-in-pmla-case (last accessed June 18, 2024).

15 See chapter six for more on these protests.

16 For Raut's case see 'Sanjay Raut's Arrest by ED "Illegal"'.For the cases of Nawab Malik and Jitendra Awahd see Rebecca Samervel and Vijay V Singh, 'NCP leader Nawab Malik goes home from hospital after bail', *Times of India*, 15 August 2023, available at https://timesofindia.indiatimes.com/city/mumbai/nawab-malik-goes-home-from-hospital-after-bail/articleshow/102735758.cms; and Nishikant Karlikar, 'Thane: Jitendra Awhad, 11 others released on bail in film assault case', *Times of India*, 13 November 2022, available at https://timesofindia.indiatimes.com/city/thane/thane-jitendra-awhad-11-others-released-on-bail-in-film-assault-case/articleshow/95480197.cms (both last accessed 8 July 2024).

## How the Dehumanisation of the Police and Dehumanisation they Enact Work in Tandem

1 Jason Burke, 'Delhi rape: how India's other half lives', *The Guardian*, 10 September 2013, available at https://www.theguardian.com/world/2013/sep/10/delhi-gang-rape-india-women; Editorial, 'Impunity in Hathras', *The Indian Express*, 1 October 2020, available at https://indianexpress.com/article/opinion/editorials/hathras-dalit-woman-gangrape-6654041/; and Bismee Taskin, 'Politics of

showing Dalits their place—Hathras victim's family slams acquittals of 3 Thakur men', *The Print,* 2 March 2023, available at https://theprint.in/india/politics-of-showing-dalits-their-place-hathras-victims-family-slams-acquittals-of-3-thakur-men/1412127/ (all last accessed 8 August 2024).

2 See, for example, Sofia Amaral, Sonia Bhalotra, and Nishith Prakash, 'Gender, Crime and Punishment: Evidence from Women Police Stations in India', IZA DP No. 14250, April 2021, available at chrome-extension://efaidnbmnnnibpcajpcglclefindmkaj/https://repec.iza.org/dp14250.pdf; Uttar Pradesh Police Mahia Samman Prakoshth, available at https://uppolice.gov.in/article/en-about-us-mahila-samman-prakostha; and Nishtha Anushree, 'Uttar Pradesh to Have Two Women Police Stations in Every District, Will Operate Under CM Yogi Adityanath', *Swarajya,* 26 September 2023, available at https://swarajyamag.com/news-headlines/uttar-pradesh-to-have-two-women-police-stations-in-every-district-will-operate-under-cm-yogi-adityanath (all last accessed 8 August 2024).

3 UP has set up what it refers to as a 'Women Power Line', that women can call to report harassment and other issues to. See Uttar Pradesh Police, https://uppolice.gov.in/article/en/women-power-line (last accessed 8 August 2024).

4 See 'UP to get 79 women police chowkis; all-female PAC battalions also in offing', *The Hindustan Times,* 28 February 2023, available at https://www.hindustantimes.com/cities/others/up-to-get-79-women-police-chowkis-all-female-pac-battalions-also-in-offing-101677524229931.html (last accessed 8 August 2023).

5 See Miriam Cruz, 'Violence, Masculinity, and Policeman with a capital "P": Toxic masculinity in Brazilian Law enforcement', *FiLia*, 23 October 2021, available at https://www.filia.org.uk/latest-news/2021/10/23/violence-masculinity-and-policeman-with-a-capital-p-toxic-masculinity-in-brazilian-law-enforcement (last accessed 8 August 2024); and Sarah Hautzinger, 'Criminalising Male Violence in Brazil's Women's Police Stations: From Flawed Essentialism to Imagined Communities', *Journal of Gender Studies* 11, 3 (2002): 243-251.

6 See Sam Levin, 'The movement to defund police has won historic victories across the US. What's next?', *The Guardian,* 15 August 2020, available at https://www.theguardian.com/us-news/2020/aug/15/defund-police-movement-us-victories-what-next; Jennifer Fleetwood, 'Defunding the police in the UK: Critical questions and practical suggestions', *The Howard Journal of Crime and Justice,* 61, 2 (June 2022): 167-184, available at https://onlinelibrary.wiley.com/doi/full/10.1111/hojo.12468; and Mike Cummings, 'Resistance to "defund" or "abolish" the police rooted in policy proposals', *YaleNews,* 4 February 2022, available at https://news.yale.edu/2022/02/04/resistance-defund-or-abolish-police-rooted-policy-proposals (all last accessed 8 August 2024).

7 In the case of the US, for example, see Steven Greenhouse, 'How Police Unions Enable and Conceal Abuses of Power', *The New Yorker,* 18 June 2020, available at https://www.newyorker.com/news/news-desk/how-police-union-power-helped-increase-abuses (last accessed 8 August 2024).

8 See Beatrice Jauregui, 'Police Work and the Politics of Expendability in India', *Security Dialogue,* 2024, available at https://journals.sagepub.com/doi/full/10.1177/09670106241230431 (last accessed 13 August 2024).

9 See *The Indian Police Journal,* special issue on *Occupational Stress and Mental Health Issues Among Uniformed Personnel,* 66, 3 (July-September 2019), available at chrome-extension://efaidnbmnnnibpcajpcglclefindmkaj/https://bprd.nic.in/uploads/pdf/201910220443407520366JULYSEPTEMBER20192.pdf (last accessed 8 August 2024).

10 Sushant Kulkarni, 'Indian Police Foundation data: 900 Covid deaths among police forces, CAPFs; "number sounds note of caution for festive season"', *The Indian Express,* 29 October 2020, available at https://indianexpress.com/article/india/indian-police-foundation-data-900-covid-deaths-among-police-forces-capfs-number-sounds-note-of-caution-for-festive-season/ (last accessed 8 August 2024).

11 'Death Toll is 40 in Indian State As Revolt by Police Continues', *The New York Times,* 24 May 1973, available at https://

www.nytimes.com/1973/05/24/archives/death-toll-is-40-in-indian-state-as-revolt-by-police-continues.html?auth=login-google1tap&login=google1tap (last accessed 8 August 2024).

12 See chrome-extension://efaidnbmnnnibpcajpcglclefindmkaj/https://www.mca.gov.in/Ministry/actsbills/pdf/Societies_Registration_Act_1860.pdf (last accessed 8 August 2024).

13 Other Backward Class is a term used by the Government of India to classify communities that are deemed in need of educational or social uplift.

14 See Iqbal Siddiqui, 'Uttar Pradesh Police Association', blog, available at https://uppoliceassociation.blogspot.com/2015/01/blog-post_55.html; 'Cop in Soup for Anna Show', *The Times of India,* 28 August 2011, available at https://timesofindia.indiatimes.com/city/lucknow/Cop-in-soup-for-Anna-show/articleshow/9765016.cms; and 'UP Police Association President Subodh Yadav Arrested', *Amar Ujala Mainpuri,* 23 October 2018, available at https://www.amarujala.com/uttar-pradesh/agra/uttar-pradesh-police-association-president-subodh-yadav-arrested-from-safai (all last accessed 13 August 2024).

15 The Party's Facebook page is available here: https://www.facebook.com/RJMPARTY1/ (last accessed 13 August 2024).

16 See Hamilton Nolan, 'It's time to kick police unions out of the labor movement. They aren't allies', *The Guardian,* 13 June 2020, available at https://www.theguardian.com/commentisfree/2020/jun/13/police-unions-afl-cio-labor-movement; and Ryan Hayes, 'It's time to talk about police in our unions', *Briarpatch,* 20 June 2020, available at ttps://briarpatchmagazine.com/articles/view/its-time-to-talk-about-police-in-our-unions (both last accessed 13 August 2024).

17 The most notable of these is the Indian Police Commission, set up in 1979, which published eight reports between 1979 and 1981. Most of its recommendations remain unimplemented. Other commissions include the Robeiro Committee, which published reports in 1998 and 1999; the Padmanabhaiah Committee which, in its report in 2000, made over 240 recommendations for police

reform; and the Malimath Committee, which submitted its report in 2003.

18 The guidelines issued by the Supreme Court in 2006 on reforms to curb police violence, in *Prakash Singh & Ors* v *Union of India*, were codified in the Model Police Act that same year. See chrome-extension://efaidnbmnnnibpcajpcglclefindmkaj/https://www.mha.gov.in/sites/default/files/ModelAct06_30_Oct_0.pdf (last accessed 8 August 2024).

19 A *laathi* is a heavy stick, often made with bamboo and bound with iron, which the Indian police use as a weapon.